Web of Faith

GOD BLESS
PRAY FOR US

Fr. Ken Brighenti and Fr. John Trigilio

Web of Faith
A Curious Catholic's Answers
to Theological Questions

EWTN PUBLISHING, INC.

Irondale, Alabama

Nihil obstat: Reverend John G. Hillier, Ph.D., *Censor Librorum*
Imprimatur: Most Reverend James F. Checchio, JCD, MBA
Diocese of Metuchen, NJ
November 23, 2020

The *nihil obstat* and the *imprimatur* are official declarations that a book or pamphlet is free of doctrinal or moral error. No implication is contained therein that those who granted the *nihil obstat* and the *imprimatur* agree with the contents, opinions, or statements expressed.

EWTN Publishing, Inc.
5817 Old Leeds Road, Irondale, AL 35210

Distributed by Sophia Institute Press, Box 5284, Manchester, NH 03108.

paperback ISBN 978-1-68278-060-2

ebook ISBN 978-1-68278-061-9

Library of Congress Control Number: 2021932842

First printing

Contents

Introduction

Recently I attended an excellent presentation on evangelization by a dedicated Catholic layman. During the animated question-and-answer period, he was asked, "Why are we Catholics so reluctant to talk to others about our Faith?" His response caught me off guard. He said, "Most often we are afraid of the 'second question.'" Like me, the audience was clueless until he explained. When someone asks us if we are Catholic—which is the first question—what happens next often goes something like this: "Okay, so if you are a Catholic, why does the Church teach ... or forbid ... or make you ...?" That's the second question, and because Catholics often feel unable to give a convincing response, we keep quiet to avoid that question.

The book you are holding is an excellent resource to help dispel any fear of the second, third, or fourth question. Drawing from the rich archives of their EWTN presentations, Fr. Brighenti and Fr. Trigilio present their latest work, *Web of Faith*, which, as we have come to expect, is written in clear, understandable language and in complete fidelity to the Church's Magisterium. While many good sources of accurate information about what we Catholics believe and why we believe it are available, not all are so readable or written in such a conversational style. This work invites the reader to eavesdrop on a lively conversation between two good friends who love Christ and His Church and who want others to know the truth more fully in order to love the truth more intensely.

Nor do the authors mistakenly think that such a serious task requires relentless solemnity. Rather, their deliberately light touch and regular doses of humor give abundant evidence that these priests believe that joy must be the most distinguishing characteristic of the disciple of Christ.

By whichever means you found this book and whatever induced you to open it, you are in for a delightful journey with enriching information, insight, and inspiration. Take and read.

—Most Reverend Ronald W. Gainer
Bishop of Harrisburg

Web of Faith

Chapter 1

Doctrine

1. Crucifixes and Crosses

Is there a reason as to why Catholics wear a cross with the Corpus of Jesus Christ on it and non-Catholic Christians typically do not?

Fr. Brighenti: The idea of only wearing a plain cross really came about during the Protestant Reformation, and Catholics may wear plain crosses as well. There's no standing rule on this. But normally, you would not see Protestants wearing a crucifix, either on a ring or as a pendant around their necks, nor do they have them in their churches, unless they're High Anglicans or of similar denominations. Following Martin Luther's revolt from the Catholic Church, Protestant reformers such as Zwingli and his fellow cohorts committed a serious mistranslation, identifying Christian icons as a form of idol worship as seen in the Old Testament (such as the stipulation about the golden calf and other blasphemies of that nature). The Orthodox and Byzantines had to overcome this error in the nineteenth century as well, under what they called the "Triumph of Iconoclasm." There was a whole scenario in that era where the Orthodox, or the Eastern Church, were getting rid of religious icons because of this same mistranslation. There's now a feast day on the Byzantine calendar called the "Triumph of Orthodoxy," in which the use of icons was restored in the Orthodox Church.

Fr. Trigilio: It was a brutal battle at times.

Fr. Brighenti: Likewise, these various reformers in the Protestant Reformation era were mistranslating that quote. As Catholics, we don't worship an image, a statue, or a holy card. We say that an image or a stained-glass window represents and reminds us of a particular saint in Heaven, and that these images point us to Christ. Furthermore, Catholic worship is very Incarnational. It involves the senses. One of our senses is sight, so we employ art. One of the clarifications that the Second Vatican Council offered was that art in churches should be the worthiest art that you can afford to employ, so Styrofoam doesn't really cut it.

Fr. Trigilio: Or papier-mâché.

Fr. Brighenti: That's why Catholics wear the crucifix, because the Corpus of Jesus Christ reminds us of the price of our salvation. We certainly have a great feast on September 14 called the Triumph of the Cross, which reminds us of the victory that Christ has won for us on Good Friday. That is the sacrifice which is perpetuated and brought to us in the Holy Sacrifice of the Mass. It's the same sacrifice at Calvary. Therefore, we both *need* and *want* to be reminded of that.

Fr. Trigilio: Exactly. I think this is what made such an impression on me as a young person. For my family, putting up a crucifix didn't take a second thought. You had a crucifix, not just in your bedroom, but in the main living room, too. You saw it when you came in and out of the house. That crucifix was a constant reminder that there's going to be some suffering in your life, but also that you can identify with Jesus since He suffered for you. Seeing Him in His Passion is a means of encouragement. It's not a means to intimidate or scare you, but it's a loving reminder that Jesus did this *for* you. Alternatively, if you just saw the cross without the Corpus, you could very easily miss the point; that's why when the film *The Passion of the Christ*[1] came out, many Christians who didn't have the crucifix or the Stations of the Cross like we do were overwhelmed with tears when they saw the movie, because they had never pondered and meditated on the Passion of Our Lord as we do quite frequently as Catholics.

Fr. Brighenti: We went through a little burp of that ourselves in the late sixties and early seventies, maybe even up into the nineties when crucifixes were being replaced with the Risen Christ. I'll always remember Fr. William Heidt, our liturgy professor. He said, "You have to have the sacrifice first before you can have the Easter Resurrection." The crucifix doesn't take away from the Risen Christ, and certainly not during Eastertide. When I was pastor of an Italian parish, I put the statue of the Risen Christ out, and I know that many of the Eastern European churches do as well, but we still keep the crucifix, because we want to be reminded of what Christ went through for us and the price of our sins that were nailed with Him on the Cross.

Fr. Trigilio: And we have the new rubrics for the Mass, with particular thanks to Pope Benedict, who wants a crucifix on every altar so that the priest and the people will be reminded that the Sacrifice of the Mass is the same sacrifice at Calvary, but in an unbloody manner. The crucifix is important both for the priest and the people to see during the Sacred Liturgy.

[1] Directed by Mel Gibson (Icon Productions, 2004).

Fr. Brighenti: I love the EWTN chapel here because they have the Corpus on both sides, which is very nice. When I was pastor, I had the crucifix in the center of the altar, and it always faced me. But behind me, over the Tabernacle, was a large and beautiful crucifix for the people to gaze upon as well.

2. Original Sin

What was the Original Sin? It seems to me that in the beginning of human history, Adam and Eve didn't know anything about life — including right and wrong — so how could they have been held accountable?

Fr. Trigilio: Original Sin is the sin of Adam and Eve, and it was a direct act of disobedience. Even though Adam and Eve, we might say, were not as sophisticated as you and I, at the same time they did not suffer from the crippling effects of Original Sin when they were created, as they were formed in a state of innocence. Because of Original Sin, we now have a darkened intellect, a weakened will, and a disorder of the lower passions. We call this "concupiscence." Adam and Eve did not yet experience those consequences of sin, so they had more culpability. They knew what they were getting into, and they knew it was wrong, even though they didn't know about iPads or astrophysics or relativity. God said, "Don't do this. If you eat of the tree of life or eat from the forbidden tree, there will be consequences." Adam and Eve knew that they were to do good and avoid evil, as that's the first moral principle; anyone with an intellect and reason knows this. So, they are responsible for the initial act of disobedience. It was a very heinous act, not because they ate a piece of fruit, but because they disobeyed God, and they had been given a command, "Don't do this." Their will was opposed to God's will, and sin entered the world, the ramifications having distorted the whole cosmos. Not only did they break a law of God, but now there's disharmony, death and suffering, pain and toil. Now there's a need for redemption, because a serious wound was made to human nature. Adam and Eve knew what they were doing.

Fr. Brighenti: There are two points to be made here. First of all, the root of all sin is pride, and therefore, in redemption Adam and Eve signify the vice of pride. Then the New Adam and the New Eve—of course, the New Eve being Mary, the Mother of God, and the New Adam, Christ, Our Blessed Savior—symbolize humility and obedience, which stand in direct opposition to this vice, and this is precisely what was needed to rectify the sin of pride. Secondly, our Lord wanted to involve us in His will, and this is why in the whole plan of salvation, He took on human flesh, to help us with this process in our sacred humanity. So, when humanity was nailed to the Cross, under that Divine Person of Jesus Christ, we were also brought into our redemption, and we participated in that redemption. It helped us in a very special way. Not only did we receive the graces of redemption through sanctifying grace, but it was accomplished in a way wherein we could participate through our sacred humanity.

Fr. Trigilio: Those are two excellent points, that this was more than just a juridical effect. Sometimes people see sin as merely, "Well, I broke the law." But it's not just a legal system, because sin wounded human nature itself. God could have simply said by decree, "Okay, you're forgiven. You're redeemed. You're saved." But He wanted to heal that wound. So, you have the humanity of Jesus hypostatically united to His divinity. You have, hanging on the Cross, the Man-God Who died for us. The submission of His human will to the divine will not only affects forgiveness and salvation, but also restores the grace and heals humanity's wound.

3. Rapture

In the rapture, when the dead in Christ will be raised, will this include the saints from the Old Testament? If not, when will they be raised?

Fr. Trigilio: Well, first of all, the concept of rapture is relatively new. If you were to drop the word "rapture" in front of Martin Luther, John Calvin, Zwingli, Hus, or any other of the Protestant reformers at the time, they wouldn't know what you were talking about. It's more of a nineteenth or later twentieth-century term among certain Protestant theologians. Because of the popularity of the *Left Behind* books[2] and film series that have come out, belief in rapture has become more and more ingrained among Evangelicals, and it is this idea that people are going to disappear one day into thin air. There's a scene in the first movie where people on a plane suddenly disappear, and all that's left behind are their clothes; the plane is crashing, and there's all these people left on earth. The implication is that the people who vanished were taken up to Heaven, while the ones who were left behind are going to be left to their own devices at the end of the world. But in actuality, when you look at the scriptural texts, particularly Luke 17:34, Jesus says, "I tell you, in that night there will be two men in one bed; one will be taken and the other left." Well, the text doesn't tell us where the one that was taken has been taken to, and that doesn't necessarily mean that he's been taken to Heaven. When you die, a particular judgment takes place, and you're judged on what you did or didn't do in terms of sins of omission. But your position for eternity isn't determined by *when* you're taken or *where* you're taken from

---

[2] Tim LaHaye and Jerry B. Jenkins, *Left Behind* (Wheaton, IL: Tyndale House, 2005).

in terms of the location upon when you die. It's the life you live—that's what's important. People are so obsessed with these little details. Obviously, if I'm on a plane, I don't want the pilot to be taken away, because otherwise we're in big trouble. But if you're on that plane, you make a sincere Act of Contrition, and the plane crashes, guess what? You'll go to Heaven. You're in a state of grace. The pilot is only there for the physical well-being of your body. Your soul is in your control, whether you're living a life of grace or not.

Fr. Brighenti: An Act of Contrition would be just in time in this scenario, and that's an example of when general absolution is valid, when your plane is going down or the Titanic's sinking, and you don't have a priest on board to absolve your sins. But if you do survive, you should still go to Confession afterward. Yes, there is an obsession with the end times, a panic that the end is near, and we saw a lot of that at the turn of the millennium. I remember being in a parish as an associate when it was 1999, and of course New Year's Eve was going to take us into the year 2000. The computers were supposedly going to stop working, electricity was going to be cut off, and people were storing up food and water.

Fr. Trigilio: Dogs and cats were going to be living together.

Fr. Brighenti: Because we had a Midnight Mass on New Year's Eve, the pastor said to the sacristan, "Shut off all the lights," and everybody gasped! And then the lights came back on, and he said, "See, you're putting too much trust into all this speculation. Keep your trust in Christ, in His teachings and the Church, and do not listen to all these soothsayers." Like you've said before, and as we've said many times: when you die, that is your end, and that's when you're going to be judged. So live a good and upright moral life.

4. Piety

What is piety, in the true sense of the word? I have heard Christians say that they have a deep faith, but they shy away from anything that sounds pious. When I asked a friend if she wanted to become a saint, she said, "Yeah, right!" This comes from someone who is a professed, born-again Christian. Why does there seem to be a disconnect between holiness and faith?

Fr. Brighenti: Well, there should not be any distinction between holiness and your faith, and in fact, piety is one of the seven gifts of the Holy Spirit. Piety doesn't mean being saccharine or superficial, but a pious soul is instead one that's striving toward holiness. Hopefully, the more we receive the graces of the sacraments and the more God refines us, the holier we become in our lives and in our Lord. I think everybody should know that we are all called to be saints through Baptism. I tell the children that in the Sacrament of Baptism, we're all saints in the making. We now have to be refined, and we have to be molded in the Lord through the gifts of grace in the sacraments. That's what our final destination is: to be a saint, and to be a saint is to be in Heaven with God for all eternity. That's really the beauty of All Saints' Day. It's for all of those who are not officially recognized in the canonization of saints but nevertheless are experiencing the Beatific Vision.

Fr. Trigilio: If you think of the word "piety," it begins with a P, and so does the word "personal." Piety is my personal expression of my faith, whereas religion is my public practice of the faith. So, if I go to Mass, that's an act of religion. Whereas if I'm praying the Rosary by myself, if I'm wearing a crucifix, if I'm wearing my scapular, or if I'm doing my personal devotions, those are all acts of piety. We need to do both. Even in Protestantism, there's been a tradition, particularly in the Methodist Church founded by John Wesley, which really promotes the sense of piety that you do things by yourself to cultivate your faith. There's also public worship, whether it's hearing a preacher in the Protestant Church or going to Mass at the Catholic Church. We must have both personal and public ways of expressing our faith and cultivating it.

Fr. Brighenti: Pope Benedict has said many times that it's not *either-or*; it's *both-and*. Our private prayer life nourishes our public worship. Our public worship of the Lord then nourishes us during the day and throughout the week in our private devotions. There's no competition here. Each of these help us grow closer to God.

Fr. Trigilio: I think that one of the other important things His Holiness has reminded the people of, since we've recently had the fiftieth anniversary of the opening of the Second Vatican Council, is that Vatican II did not get rid of piety. It kept piety where it belongs, and this is something that needs to be done. Piety is something that's both personal and private, and it does not need to be in competition with public worship. Neither should it replace or disorient or dethrone the preeminence of public worship, which is predominately the Sacred Liturgy and the practice of the sacraments. I remember my grandmother reading her Polish prayer book, and it took her the whole morning to get through the entire thing. That was her personal act of piety. I remember my Italian grandmother praying the Rosary, or her statues of St. Anthony, St. Francis, St. Rita, and all the rest of the saints on her windowsill. These are examples of her personal act of piety: to pray and to focus her attention on the statues and images of saints throughout the house.

Fr. Brighenti: But it didn't replace the Mass. It didn't replace the Eucharist. Rather, they're not in competition. Your private prayer life disposes you to be more receptive in the public Liturgy and the sacraments, to be in an act of participation.

Fr. Trigilio: Churches will even have little niches where they've set up shrines to honor specific saints, and they all complement one another.

5. The Church Militant

Could you define, in terms of today's Catechism, the various aspects of the "Church Militant" and how this applies in practical ways to the laity today?

Fr. Brighenti: This is an excellent question, and we've dealt with some of the aspects of this question in several of our discussions before. We like to remind people that the Church is broader than just those of us down here on earth. There are the saints and angels in Heaven around the throne of God, and we call them the Church Triumphant. There is the Church Suffering, which consists of the holy souls in Purgatory waiting to enter Heaven. They died as friends of God, but due either to some attachment to the world that they may have had, or a need for further cleansing from their sins, or penances that they didn't complete here on earth for which they must still make amends, they recognize that they are not ready to enter Heaven but will do so eventually. Consider the Church Suffering as sitting on a porch, a vestibule to Heaven. There is then the Church Militant, which is a term that we use for those of us who are still here on earth. We are in spiritual warfare, not a warfare against other religions, but rather a warfare against the devil, and we, the baptized and the confirmed, are soldiers of Christ.

We try to keep up the fight of good against evil. Because all three Churches are very much present, and especially at the Eucharist, we also help the souls in Purgatory, as do the saints in Heaven interceding for them. Adding to the treasury of merits, we offer our own prayers, penances, and sufferings up for the holy souls in Purgatory so that their time of cleansing will be shortened, and it requires that we keep our guard up, keep ourselves spiritually fit in the Lord, and certainly keep ourselves in the state of grace.

Fr. Trigilio: A crucial point you brought up, Fr. Brighenti, is that we're not at war with non-Catholics or non-Christians, but we're at war with the devil. The Church Militant is not the Christian version of Jihad. This fight is against sin and against error, and for those people who get involved, we're trying to help them and pray for them, as opposed to conquering them. St. Peter says it so well in his epistle, "Be sober, be watchful. Your adversary the devil prowls around like a roaring lion, seeking some one to devour" (1 Peter 5:8). Our adversary and enemy is the devil. The devil is the author of all lies, the son of perdition, the embodiment of all that is evil, and that's who we are fighting against. That's with whom we're waging spiritual warfare, and we're trying to win souls for Christ, which results in stealing soldiers away from the devil. I remember when we were kids, there was a big push to be politically correct, and they didn't want us to say Church Militant or refer to ourselves as Soldiers of Christ anymore. There has been an agenda to pacify us into an entity of peaceniks.

Fr. Brighenti: They want us to appear as weak as water.

Fr. Trigilio: That's because this is a war, but it's a war against evil. The evil that the Nazis performed in the Holocaust is just despicable, and we must fight and oppose that kind of evil. We have to fight the evil that is being done, as well as the people who are committing this evil, but you have to try to convert them and win them over to Christ as opposed to trying to kill them or annihilate them, because our opponent is not them, it's the one that they follow, or the one by whom they're being misled.

Fr. Brighenti: Following the deaths of so many of the early Roman martyrs, their persecutors were converted. Even in the concentration camps during World War II, Nazis were converted because of the holy examples that saints were living out as they were being persecuted. Saints, like Maximilian Kolbe, were always kind and charitable, and they prayed for their persecutors. It's a work of peace and justice rather than that of a soldier with a gun or a knife. The saints' undying love for Christ shined forth in their lives and their actions in the midst of such terrible persecution.

Fr. Trigilio: I'm reminded of that beautiful movie about Monsignor O'Flaherty, where he's played by Gregory Peck, *The Scarlet and the Black*.[3] It was a real story about a priest who worked in the Vatican and saved over six thousand Jews and Allied soldiers during the Second World War, and Colonel Kappler was a German Nazi soldier who was in charge of the city of Rome just before the Allies won the war. Kappler tried to have O'Flaherty assassinated, but later he asked him to save his wife and children from vengeful partisans. At the end of the movie, it says that Kappler converted to the Catholic Faith and was baptized by O'Flaherty himself, who had visited him every month in prison. It was by Monsignor O'Flaherty's persistence, his love, and his

---

[3]   Directed by Jerry London (Rome: PBS, 1983).

mercy, that he was able to convince this nasty Nazi to repent. Colonel Kappler didn't get out of jail, as he had to pay for his crimes, but he was at least able to let go of all that evil.

6. Living by Faith

What exactly is required to surrender completely to Jesus Christ and live by faith?

Fr. Brighenti: Well, to surrender one hundred percent to Christ means that you are seeking to do God's will. Your disposition would be critical in how you're open to surrendering your will over to Christ. First of all, you would pray for it. This is why Adoration before the Blessed Sacrament is so important. Adoration is a two-way street, meaning you are giving adoration while talking to the Lord, but you're also remaining quiet so that the Lord can talk back to you. We're all usually pretty good at the first part of Adoration, as we often have a long list of things that we want to ask the Lord, but we're not very good at being quiet and letting the Lord speak back to us. There is a wonderful method that can help you in this meditative form of prayer, called *Lectio Divina*, which is a beautiful word that means "Divine Reading." You start by taking a Scripture or Gospel reading, perhaps from Mass, and you dwell on what's going on in that passage. You can either be an observer of that scene, or you can read a commentary that explains the meaning behind that passage, followed by a formal prayer, and then you remain silent for some time, maybe five or ten minutes. This is the part where we tend to get restless and can easily be distracted. When this happens, just bring yourself back to the center. I suggest to always do this in church, and it's even greater to do this before the Blessed Sacrament, but you can do this in the corner of your room as well. In this way, you're asking for God's will for you, and you're being very specific about it. God will reveal His will to you, and when He does, you will receive a sense of serenity, peace, and calm about the decision you have to make. You will always be most happy when you do God's will. You will never be bored either, because He is most creative, and you will be better off for it.

Fr. Trigilio: People need to be reminded that when you turn yourself over to God and put your trust in Him completely, it's not to be taken too literally in the sense that you empty your bank account and give everything away, as there was only one follower in the Gospels who was told, "sell what you possess and give to the poor" (Matthew 19:21). It's important to note that this man in particular was attached to his many earthly possessions. While Zacchaeus, another Bible character, said, "if I have defrauded any one of anything, I restore it fourfold" (Luke 19:8), yet he still kept a portion for himself. There were other wealthy people who weren't even challenged, because they were already being generous. It's not about the things you have but how you use them.

Fr. Brighenti: It's about your relationship to material things.

Fr. Trigilio: That's right. The things that I own cannot own me, and my possessions should not possess me. Unless God's calling you to live a contemplative life, like that of a cloistered monk or nun where you spend your whole life in prayer, it's perfectly normal to own things, but even then the religious are not in the chapel all day long; they've got to go out into the fields and do some work. Surrendering to Christ is not spending twenty-four hours a day on your knees, and it's not giving away everything that you own, but it's the priority. God comes first.

Fr. Brighenti: This is the reason why Pope John Paul the Great canonized so many laypeople, to show that sanctity can happen even in the workplace. St. Gianna was a famous doctor in Naples in the 1950s whom Pope John Paul later canonized. There are a multitude of saintly role models for people in the workplace or at home to look to and be reminded that they can become saints, too. But in order for these role models to become saints, they had to give themselves over to the Lord. Instead of putting themselves, people, places, or things in the center of their hearts, Jesus was in the center of their hearts, and everything else became a relationship to Jesus.

Fr. Trigilio: Exactly. I think one of the problems with our modern religious society at large is that people say, "Well, I give so much to God. I give ten percent to God," and they compartmentalize their faith. Well, God wants everything. He wants all of you. It's not that He wants all of your time, that you spend it all in church on your knees praying, or that He wants all your money, but instead it is that He wants you to depend on Him and relate to Him as your first and foremost. Everything else is secondary.

7. The Nicene Creed

What is the Creed, and why is it recited at every Mass?

Fr. Trigilio: The word *creed* in English comes from the Latin word *credo*, which basically means, "I believe." The Creed that we recite on Sundays and on Holy Days of Obligation is technically called the Nicene Creed, because it goes back to the Council of Nicaea in A.D. 325. It's an elaboration of the Apostles' Creed. At baptisms, confirmations, the Easter Vigil, or the Easter Mass the following day, people renew their baptismal promises and take the Creed, dividing it into three sections where the priest asks the following questions, "Do you believe in God, the Father Almighty, Creator of Heaven and earth? Do you believe in Jesus Christ, His only Son, our Lord, Who was born of the Virgin Mary, suffered death and was buried, rose again from the dead and is seated at the right hand of the Father? Do you believe in the Holy Spirit, the holy Catholic Church, the communion of saints, the forgiveness of sins, the resurrection of the body, and life everlasting?"

The people respond to each of those with "I do." Normally on Sundays and holy days, everyone says it together, and this goes back to apostolic times, because that's how they taught the faith back then, by memorizing this formula. They taught it to their children, and their children taught it to their children and so on, and our religion is explained through the faith. It was a catechetical tool that was made easy to memorize. It summarizes what the Church believes and teaches. When you look at the *Catechism*, at the four pillars of faith, the first pillar is the Creed. It includes both the Apostles' Creed and the Nicene Creed and elaborates further on what it is that we believe. A good analogy for this would be the United States' Constitution and Declaration of Independence both rolled into one.

Fr. Brighenti: The Creed we profess on Sunday is the Nicene-Constantinople Creed, which is a longer and fuller rendition, and there's also the Apostles' Creed upon which the Nicene Creed is based, but it's a bit shorter and easier to recite. It's also the one that we use when we begin praying the Rosary. When I was growing up in the Church, I had to learn the Creed by heart for Confirmation class. It was Sr. Mary Bonfilia, who I think was ninety years old at the time, and she would see to it that each one of us knew our Creed individually. I thank her for that, because to this day I have no problems in leading the Rosary since I know the Creed inside and out. It does become like the Constitution. The Creed is our "Declaration" of what we believe. It's been revealed to us in divine revelations.

Fr. Trigilio: And we share this Creed with other Christians. It's not just a Catholic thing. Every Christian religion says the same Creed or at least accepts the Creed. Protestant, Catholic, and Eastern Orthodox—they may not recite it every week like we do, but they still accept what it says. It's part of the Christian faith.

Fr. Brighenti: I think it's interesting that if you go back to the Latin, the word *credo* means "I believe," instead of "We believe." Yes, we're all reciting it together, but it's a personal statement. It's a personal conviction.

Fr. Trigilio: You're professing your belief, and we tweaked it a little bit, as people now say that Jesus is "Consubstantial with the Father," as opposed to "one in being." It means the same thing, but it's more precise now because the Latin word *consubstantialem* is the proper translation from the Greek word *Homoousios*. Jesus, in His divinity, shares the same substance with the Father. This Creed is something that Pope Benedict is encouraging all of us to say during the Year of Faith, not just on Sundays and holy days, but we are welcomed to recite it every single day as part of the renewal of our faith. We can then meditate on the different parts of the Creed and see how beautifully it explains the *Catechism*: Who is God the Father, Who is God the Son, Who is God the Holy Spirit? What do we mean by the Holy Catholic Church, one, holy, catholic, and apostolic? What do we mean by communion of saints? It's all in there. It's like the formula for the recipe for God's revealed truth. It's based on

Scripture; it's based on Sacred Tradition. It's a wonderful gift that we have here.

8. The Date of Jesus' Birth

Was Jesus really born on December 25, and what benefit, if any, is gained from celebrating it on that specific day?

Fr. Trigilio: Simply put, we do not know on what day Jesus was born. Regardless, the Church needed to pick a day since people wanted to celebrate this event, the coming of the Savior into the world. It's obvious to calculate that nine months before December 25 takes us to March 25, which is when we celebrate the Annunciation. Did the birth of Christ actually take place on December 25? Probably not, but I wouldn't rule it out completely. But why that particular day? Well, there's been some speculation that since there was a Roman pagan festival that took place on that day, the early Christians wanted to celebrate the birth of Christ at the same time to avoid drawing too much attention to themselves. Furthermore, St. Augustine said that the Church is wise and that it takes things that already exist rather than reinvent the wheel. So, the early Christians took an old pagan temple and converted it into a church. They took the convenience of a pagan holiday and conformed it to the Faith. They chose this particular season because that's when we have the shortest day of the year, followed by when the amount of light begins to increase. St. John the Baptist said, "He must increase, but I must decrease" (John 3:30). Jesus said, "I am the light of the world" (John 8:12). Light begins to increase immediately after the winter solstice, which takes place on December 21. The twenty-fifth is a spectacular day to celebrate Jesus' birthday, yet it just so happened to be a Roman pagan holiday as well.

Fr. Brighenti: December 25 was a Roman pagan festival day for the sun god.

Fr. Trigilio: S-U-N, and not the S-O-N.

Fr. Brighenti: Pagan Rome believed that because of the sun god, light would increase in the Northern Hemisphere from that day on. There were also plenty of pagan customs in the Roman times that predated Christianity, such as bringing evergreens into the home, evergreen being symbolic of the new spring; and people would burn the Yule log for twelve days, the log being a symbol for light, celebrating the coming restoration in nature. Then Christianity came along, and as St. Augustine had put it so well, it took the elements of these pagan customs, baptized the ones that weren't evil or wrong but could be good or neutral, and then gave them a new meaning. That was the whole success of our missionaries who had gone into foreign lands, be it with the Incas or to China or Japan. The missionaries would retain certain elements that were good in these societies and build upon them to introduce Christianity to the pagans. Likewise, in the Roman times, the sun god became the Son Who is the Light of the World, and it fits in so perfectly. The evergreen, too, then becomes a symbol of everlasting life, and the Yule log then becomes the fire which we celebrate on the Easter Vigil, the blessing of the new flames of purification, and the heat which is the cleansing that comes from the grace of the sacraments. It all has new meaning and distinction now.

Fr. Trigilio: I think when people watch some of these kooky television programs that come on during the holidays, whether it's Christmas or Easter, there are so many false claims that Christianity stole things from paganism. As we've discussed,

St. Augustine had spoken about appropriating pagan elements, such as transforming a temple into a church. But there are then claims that Christians took, for instance, the Egyptian goddess Isis and turned it into a Marian devotion. This never happened, but slanderous rumors like this are unfortunately circulated in books like *The Da Vinci Code* and other crazy historical fiction novels. What Christianity did was take benign pagan elements and gave them a religious twist, like the Roman vesture of a typical Roman citizen becoming the priestly vestments in the Catholic Mass. Vestments are a benign element. Worship of Isis, on the other hand, is idolatry, and there's no way you're going to transform that into *hyperdulia* of the Blessed Mother. Putting the transformation of vestments and temples next to worshipping a pagan goddess would be comparing apples to oranges.

9. Explaining the Trinity, Part 1

I have a Jewish friend who asked me to explain the Holy Trinity to her because her rabbi called Christianity a polytheistic religion. I tried to make sense of this mystery by using St. Patrick's metaphor of the shamrock and stated that Christians believe in one God in three Persons: The Father, Son, and Holy Spirit, but I don't think I explained this to my friend's satisfaction. Can you please help me better explain the Trinity?

Fr. Brighenti: For those people who don't know, a shamrock is a three-leafed clover, and because it consists of three leaves as one plant, St. Patrick used it as a means to explain the concept of the Trinity to the pagans. The Blessed Trinity, like a lot of our doctrines, is a mystery, and that means it is a sacred truth. We can't fully explain it, because we're finite and, of course, God is infinite. We can only do so analogously as St. Patrick did. There were other theologians who tried to explain it, but they fell into heresy, as there was no shortage of heresies in the first five centuries of the Catholic Church. There were Docetism, Arianism, and Montanism, and there were various councils, such as the Councils of Nicaea and Constantinople, that had to provide the correct, orthodox teaching of the Faith. A great example would be the Council of Ephesus in the fourth century, which began defining the Marian doctrines. When the Church officially defined the maternity of Mary, it said that the Second Person of the Trinity took flesh and became incarnate, and this meant that Mary is the Mother of God. In perfect harmony with the core teachings of the Faith, Marian doctrine became significant in defending the Christocentric beliefs relating to Jesus Christ. The Father, Son, and Holy Spirit are not three separate Gods, but they are rather three Persons—yet three personalities. These are three Persons but One divine essence, One divine God Who has a divine intellect and a divine will. The Father loves the Son, the Son loves the Father, and what aspirates out of this love is the Holy Spirit. It's a constant Communion. When we love in the correct sense, according to the way God designed it, our love is expressed like that of a mother and a father who then bring forth a child.

Fr. Trigilio: It's important for us to remember that this truly is a mystery and trying to explain it would be like teaching astrophysics to a kid who just learned the alphabet. It's so far beyond our limited comprehension, yet it's still true, and the truth of the Trinity is something you can never completely understand, because it's so far above us, and we can only scratch the surface. As we see in St. Thomas Aquinas's *Summa Theologica*, as well as the *Catechism*, the relationship between the terms are critical to better understanding and explaining this complex doctrine. In the Trinity, we start with the Father. Well, a father is a parent, and you're not a parent unless you have a child. So, the word *father* already implies that there's a son, and a son has a relationship with his father. The terminology that's used, "Father and Son," already implies that there's an inner personal relationship between the two Persons. As you stated, the mutual love of Father and Son is personified in the Holy Spirit. Now, St. Patrick applied the shamrock as an analogy for the pagans in Ireland, but it may not be as convincing for a person of the Jewish faith.

Fr. Brighenti: Even Aristotle, who was not a Christian, came to the conclusion that there was only one God, but the doctrine of the Trinity would have to be revealed to us in divine revelation. As early as in Genesis, God referred to Himself as "We." He was already preparing people for Who He is—the Father, Son, and Holy Spirit—and it took countless generations in order to teach this truth, the fullness of it coming through Our Blessed Savior, Jesus Christ.

Fr. Trigilio: The Blessed Trinity is unique to Christianity, because we are monotheistic, believing in one God like they do in Judaism as well as Islam. We don't believe in multiple gods. We believe in one God in three Persons, and it certainly is a mystery. In our human experience, when you've got one person, that's a separate entity all by itself. God is also one Supreme Being, yet He's also three Persons. These are not three manifestations or modalities, but three Persons. It's a concept that you can show as being both reasonable and rational as you begin to explain certain aspects of it, but you're not going to convince someone by argumentation alone to accept the doctrine of the Trinity. It has to be accepted by faith.

10. Papal Infallibility

I continue to inch closer and closer toward the Catholic Church, but one thing that stands in my way is the doctrine of papal infallibility and historical continuity in faith and practice. I'm afraid that once I become Catholic, I'll stumble upon evidence which will reveal popes having made attempts to bind the Church to erroneous, heretical teaching. Hypothetically, if I find such evidence, this would undermine claims to papal infallibility. Has this caused you any concern in the past or present?

Fr. Brighenti: First of all, welcome! We're so very happy that you're exploring the Catholic Church and its rich two-thousand-year history. Remember, the Catholic Church was instituted by Jesus Christ Himself and has existed now for over two millennia, and it will go on until the very end of time, as Our Blessed Savior says, "the powers of death shall not prevail against it" (Matthew 16:18). I think where some confusion regarding the doctrine of papal infallibility could lie is within the very role of the pope. The pope is not only the Head of the Church, but he's also in charge of the sovereign Vatican state. On several occasions, the pope will issue political commentaries around the world regarding social and economic systems that are not necessarily papal statements, and he himself will even say that these statements are not to be considered infallible. However, we give due credence to these statements, and we take the time to learn from and listen to them because of his prominent stature in the Church. But what the question is referring to is the gift from the Holy Spirit to the Church of papal infallibility. There is a very specific requisite in this area; papal infallibility is given only in the matters of faith and morals, and there are two occasions for this. There is Extraordinary Magisterium, which would be *ex* *cathedra*, or statements that are made from the chair of St. Peter, the latest having been in the twentieth century when Pope Pius XII defined the Assumption of Mary as dogma.[4] There is also the Ordinary Magisterium, where the pope is *ordinarily* teaching on matters of faith and morals. In both forms of Magisterium, he would be exercising the role of papal infallibility. That being said, the Holy Spirit does not grant the pope impeccability. The pope has to go to Confession just like the rest of us do. We also know from Church history that some of the popes were not saints and did not live the most moral lives, and there is no attempt to hide any of that. But the miraculous thing is that when they taught in matters of faith and morals, they were never in error, in spite of their personal lives.

Fr. Trigilio: Exactly. We've had some examples of bad popes in Church history, and we're not denying it. But when you consider there have been two hundred and sixty-six popes, you'll see that the percentage of bad ones is incredibly small, and even still, they never taught a heretical teaching in regard to matters of faith and morals as binding in the conscience of all believers, and we believe that the Holy Spirit would prevent that from happening. There were also some popes who may have not made good judgments; perhaps they could have said something more clearly or addressed a certain issue at hand. We need to keep in mind that papal infallibility is *not* the same as inspiration. Inspiration is when God motivates someone of His choosing to write down exactly what He wants and in the exact way He wants to say it. While papal infallibility is far more limited, it's

---

4   Pope Pius XII, apostolic constitution *Munificentissimus Deus* (November 1, 1950).

a guarantee that the Holy Spirit would intervene and prevent the pope from imposing a false teaching on all the faithful. For instance, if a particular pope—no matter how nice and pious he may be—wanted to say from the throne of St. Peter one day, "You know what? We're going to get rid of one of the Ten Commandments," we believe that the Holy Spirit would intervene and stop him. Either he would get a blood clot, an aneurysm, drop dead, or he would simply forget what he was going to decree, but something would happen that would prevent him from corrupting Church teaching. That's papal infallibility. It would stop him from imposing a heretical teaching. That certainly doesn't mean that there weren't popes who may have personally been heretical at some point in their lives, but they never imposed that heretical teaching from the chair of Peter. You never have to worry about accepting orthodox teaching and later on finding out that a certain pope believed in something to the contrary. Even if he personally believed a heresy, he never imposed that heresy as teaching upon the faithful. That's the key.

Fr. Brighenti: There is also a distinction between matters of faith and morals and Church discipline. Church discipline, of course, is what governs the Church, like the Code of Canon Law for example. Before 1969, the Mass was celebrated exclusively in Latin in what today we call the Extraordinary Form. After 1969, the standard offering of the Mass became what we know today as the "Novus Ordo," or the Ordinary Form. This change was allowed. It didn't contradict any preexisting teaching, but it was changed because it's part of Church discipline, not matters of faith and morals. It does not fall under papal infallibility.

Fr. Trigilio: Whenever we cover this topic, I always like to point out that there's a group of so-called Catholics who refer to themselves as sedevacantists, which is derived from the Latin phrase *sede vacante*, meaning "the seat being vacant." In the sedevacantist mindset, papal infallibility means that the Holy Spirit would prevent a pope from even ascribing to some heretical notion, and because of this, many of these kinds of Catholics believe there hasn't been a legitimate pontiff since Pope Pius XII. Unfortunately, this has led to a group of Catholics who've decided the present pope isn't authentically the head of the Church, simply because they don't like his prudential judgments, and while you don't have to like all of them, he still has supreme authority. Even if I don't like something he decrees, I still have to obey, just like I didn't always agree with my dad, but he was still my father, and I had to listen. Just as the father is head of the household, the pope is head of the Church.

Fr. Brighenti: Also, in a positive way, if the Church is a vehicle of the message of salvation, the truth of the message has to be available for every generation until the end of time. When I taught religious grammar school, we did a simple exercise. I whispered a little two-line sentence into the ear of one of my students, and he passed it on to the next one and on to the next one and all the way to the last student. I would then ask the last student, "What was handed on to you?" The answer the last student would give was always totally different from the statement that was originally given to the first. There's the need for papal infallibility because, throughout the generations, the message can be lost or lose its meaning unless there is this gift of the Holy Spirit in matters of faith and morals, a way to preserve the essentials for our way to salvation.

Fr. Trigilio: It's important to note that although it was the First Vatican Council which defined the dogma of papal infallibility, the popes have been anointed with this charism down from St. Peter. Jesus said in Matthew's Gospel, "And I tell you, you are Peter, and on this rock I will build my church, and the powers of death shall not prevail against it. I will give you the keys of the kingdom of heaven, and whatever you bind on earth shall be bound in heaven, and whatever you loose on earth shall be loosed in heaven" (16:18-19). It's more than just a jurisdictional authority; it's a doctrinal authority. For instance, when Pope John Paul II declared in the *Ordinatio Sacerdotalis* that we don't have the authority to ordain women, Cardinal Ratzinger—later Pope Benedict XVI—made it clear that what John Paul II had stated was an infallible teaching. It wasn't *ex cathedra*, but it was part of the Ordinary Magisterium that has been taught by every pope before John Paul II and was undoubtedly an infallible teaching in that document.

11. Explaining the Trinity, Part 2

I am married to a Jewish man who is so eager to learn about our beautiful faith. My husband asked me to explain the Holy Spirit to him. I'm so ashamed to say that I didn't know how to explain this mystery to my Jewish husband. Hopefully, you can help me explain it better.

Fr. Trigilio: Christianity is a monotheistic and Trinitarian religion, and we believe in One God in three Persons. That means that the Holy Spirit is as much God as the Father and as much God as the Son. The Holy Spirit shares the one and same divine intellect and divine will as the other two Divine Persons. The Holy Spirit is called the Advocate or Paraclete in the Bible. He is the author of Divine Inspiration, that is, the Holy Spirit inspired the sacred authors to write what they wrote when they put the Word of God onto paper (or, rather, parchment).

Fr. Brighenti: And at the Baptism of Jesus at the River Jordan, all three Divine Persons are present; the Holy Spirit is represented by the dove, the Father is present in His voice from Heaven, and of course, Our Blessed Lord is there, being baptized by His cousin, St. John. The Holy Spirit existed from all time and before time. He, like the Father and the Son, has no beginning and no end. He is eternal. All three are eternal. We often refer to the Holy Spirit as the Sanctifier, just as we refer to the Father as the Creator and the Son as the Redeemer. Yet, all three are One God. Remember, too, it was by the power of the Holy Spirit that the Virgin Mary conceived in her womb Our Lord, Jesus Christ. So, we can rightly call her the Spouse of the Holy Spirit.

Fr. Trigilio: And we say in the Creed on Sundays that the Holy Spirit proceeds from the Father and the Son. The Church is considered the Mystical Body of Christ and the Holy Spirit is the soul of that same Mystical Body. We can say that because it was the Holy Spirit Who came upon the apostles and the Virgin Mary at Pentecost (fifty days after Easter) in the Upper Room. Once filled with the Holy Spirit, the apostles were able to speak in foreign tongues. Ten days after His Ascension, Christ sent the Holy Spirit to fulfill His promise that the Advocate, the Paraclete, would come.

12. The Conversion of the Apostles

Jesus and the apostles were all Jewish. When did they convert to the Catholic Faith?

Fr. Trigilio: Jesus didn't convert to the Catholic Faith; He's the One Who founded it. You can't say that God in the Old Testament converted to Judaism, as He started religion, and the whole human race as well. There is no point of conversion with Christ, as with Paul on the road to Damascus. Jesus is the Groom, and the Church is His Spotless Bride. In Matthew 16:18, Jesus said to Peter, "And I tell you, you are Peter, and on this rock I will build my church, and the powers of death shall not prevail against it." Jesus is the Origin. He built the Church. He didn't convert to it; He's converting it to Him. Even though He was raised in the Jewish faith, He's the prophesied Messiah who unlocked the door to Christianity, and His Baptism in the Jordan wasn't a conversion moment but rather an example for the rest of us.

Fr. Brighenti: Jesus is the High Priest. He reveals all the truths necessary for our salvation and the tenants of our faith. As the Head of the Church, He governs us. The pope, who is the Visible Head of Christ on earth, used to wear what they call a papal tiara, which looked like three crowns stacked on top of one another, and it was worn to symbolize that it was the Head of the Church—the High Priest, Prophet, and King Jesus Christ—Who bestowed this authority upon the pope when He said, "On this rock I will build my church." We are united as one by Christ Himself.

Fr. Trigilio: It's interesting to note that other than St. Paul, there are no recorded instances of the apostles converting from Judaism into Christianity, which was a part of Judaism in the very beginning. It wasn't until the Temple of Jerusalem was destroyed in A.D. 70 that the Christians were sort of expelled from Judaism and became a religion unto themselves, so you really can't apply the concept of conversion to Jesus or any of the twelve apostles. *Conversion* is a wonderful term, and the word in the Greek is *metanoia,* which means to turn oneself back to God. Since Jesus is God, there is simply no room for conversion, while the rest of us are constantly in the process of conversion.

13. "Abba"

I have seen people on Facebook refer to God as "Abba." Where did this name come from? I don't remember seeing this anywhere in the Bible.

Fr. Trigilio: The word *Abba* is a very similar term to what we would call "Father." Some people say it's another word for "Daddy," but I feel like that's a rather diminutive interpretation. "Dad" would be more akin to it. In the Old Testament, *Abba* was not used in reference to God but for father figures among the people, such as Father Abraham. It's a Hebrew word, and in the Aramaic it also denotes a father relationship. Now in Mark's Gospel in the New Testament, Jesus uses this word before His Crucifixion when He says, "Abba, Father, all things are possible to thee; remove this cup from me; yet not what I will, but what thou wilt" (14:36). However, Jesus is the Son of God, and His relationship to the Father is unique. That's why in the Gospel of John, He said, "I am ascending to my Father and your Father" (20:17). His relationship to the Father is severely different than ours. He can say "Abba" with that fullness because He is the Son, while we don't have that same relationship. That's why we're hesitant to use this term indiscriminately. When Jesus taught His disciples how to pray, He Himself instructed them to say, "Our Father, Who art in Heaven."

Fr. Brighenti: The Our Father is a beautiful way of familiarizing the Lord with us, too. It's respectful, but the "Our" part makes it familiar. The Divine Praises are another beautiful way of not only praising the Father, but the Son and the Holy Spirit as well, all Three in a wonderful prayer that we should be using more often.

14. Why Did the Incarnation Happen Two Thousand Years Ago?

Why did the Incarnation take place when it did? Why didn't it take place, for example, one thousand years later? What effect, if any, did the Incarnation have on the souls of those who had died before it took place?

Fr. Brighenti: I've been working at the seminary for six years now, and my rector always says to never ask "why" questions. The reason *why* is because we don't know the answer to these kinds of questions besides that they were the will of God. We're human, and we have a limited understanding of divine things. God, however, in His infinite plan for our salvation, knew when it was exactly the right time for the Incarnation to take place. It's also important to consider that God doesn't exist in time. Time is a human concept, and while you and I exist in time, living and working our way through it, God is in an infinite *now* and always present. It's only safe to say that when the Incarnation took place, God willed it, and it was the perfect time for this pivotal moment in the history of our salvation.

Fr. Trigilio: Other "why" questions we could ask are: why did God wait so long for Moses to rescue the Hebrews from slavery in Egypt? Why didn't it happen sooner? Why didn't it happen later? You're asking a question where there may not be an answer that we can even begin to comprehend. In his book *Arise From Darkness*, Fr. Benedict Groeschel said that there are a lot of questions that may not have an answer. Faith doesn't give you all the answers, but it does give you the ability to live with unanswered questions. Consider Mother Teresa, who said that instead of asking why something did or didn't happen, ask, Who's the one

Person Who can make sense of this? Who's the one Person I can go to Who will give me guidance and strength? It's Jesus, and only Jesus. The question *why* becomes irrelevant. I had a brother who was killed by a drunk driver. There's no *why* in there.

Fr. Brighenti: When you look at the Old Testament, God was revealing hidden truths about the Trinity very slowly, because He knew that the people at the time wouldn't understand them. They were coming out of a culture of multiple pagan gods, and now there's one God, and later in Christianity there's one God in three Persons. It was so much to grasp, that salvation history took a while for God to prepare His people for the Incarnation, and that's another thing that we need to consider; the Incarnation occurred at just the right moment, as Our Lord said that the people were now ready for the Savior of the world to appear, following all the prophets and teachings that had led up to His advent.

Fr. Trigilio: Something that Fr. George Rutler had mentioned at one of our Opus Dei retreats is that unlike stories and fairy tales that start with, "Once upon a time," the Book of Genesis opens with, "In the beginning," and the Gospel of St. John with, "In the beginning was the Word." So many critical events throughout human history took place at a particular time and place, like Jesus' birth, death, and Resurrection, but asking *why* something took place on a particular day is not only an irrelevant question, but the answer is simply that it was God's will. The real question we should be asking ourselves is, "Lord, what do You want me to do?"

Fr. Brighenti: On another note, if you keep all the Commandments, do the best you can, love God with all your heart, soul, and mind, then you can go to Heaven one day and ask God all your "why" questions.

15. Free Will in the Garden

Why did God allow the serpent to enter Eden and tempt Eve? While I understand that Eve had free will, why would God allow her to be tempted? Wasn't Eden a perfect place of happiness surrounded by God's protection before the Fall?

Fr. Trigilio: We have to bear in mind that not only do we have free will, but God, in His infinite wisdom, put His rational creatures to the test. The angels, too, were put to the test, and only two-thirds of them passed. Now, Adam and Eve were not in Heaven; they were in Paradise, which was a physical place where they could have dwelt forever in "natural happiness." In order to get to Heaven, the species or beings had to pass a test, and not something arbitrary like a driver's license test, but more like taking exams at medical school to become a doctor. Once you've been certified, you're now worthy, in a sense, of calling yourself a true disciple of the Lord, where you submit to the will of God by being obedient. Disobedience is the big test here. Lucifer disobeyed. Adam and Eve disobeyed. Why did God let the serpent in? Because the serpent had free will, Adam and Eve had free will, and God wanted them to prove themselves, just as Jesus chose Judas to be one of His twelve disciples, even though He knew he was going to betray Him. At any moment, Judas could have said no to the temptations he was receiving from the devil. Instead, he embraced them.

Fr. Brighenti: Also, God didn't directly intend the serpent to enter the Garden, but He allowed it so that a greater good could spring forth from it. All God wants from us is an act of love made in our free will. He doesn't want us to be robots. Hopefully, what we do with our lives is to choose the Lord freely and make a commitment to Him in an act of love, rejecting sin and rejecting evil. Only God can fix this mess, and He did so by bringing in His Son, Jesus Christ, Who died for us and opened up the possibility of Heaven. Through Baptism, our souls receive sanctifying grace where we seize the promise of everlasting life, which is greater than anything Eden could have been. In fact, the Scriptures even tell us that there will be a new Heaven and a new earth.

Fr. Trigilio: There's a poetic reference to Jesus being the New Adam and Mary being the New Eve. While the old Adam and Eve rejected God's commandments, Jesus said, "not my will, but thine, be done" (Luke 22:42). Mary said, "Behold, I am the handmaid of the Lord; let it be to me according to your word" (Luke 1:38). The *fiat* of Jesus and Mary transformed the human condition, whereas Adam and Eve's disobedience is what got us into trouble.

16. Wrong Choice before Original Sin

If we make wrong choices because of our fallen nature due to Original Sin, how did Adam and Eve make the wrong choice of eating the fruit of the forbidden tree prior to receiving Original Sin?

Fr. Trigilio: This is a very profound theological question, because the fact that Adam and Eve were without a fallen human nature means that their sin was even more heinous than ours. They did not bear the effects of Original Sin that the rest of us inherit; and not only do we inherit sin, but we also inherit the negative effects of sin. We now have what we call concupiscence, which is a proclivity to sin. We have a darkened intellect and a weakened will, and our lower passions are disordered. Sometimes, as most of us know, our anger or lust gets the better of us, whereas Adam and Eve were in complete control of their emotions because they had no inclination to do wrong. This factor heightens the impact and severity of their sin. Now, when we commit sin, it's not because of Original Sin. Original Sin makes us more vulnerable, but it would be wrong to say that we commit sin because of Original Sin, and this is proved by the fact that both the angels and Adam and Eve sinned prior to the existence of Original Sin. Neither the angels nor Adam and Eve were created in the state of sin; they were created in the state of grace, and both of them fell. We don't want to make it sound as if it's Original Sin which is the cause of our disobedience. Original Sin makes disobedience possible, and it certainly makes disobedience more probable as we become more prone to it; however, this makes God's grace all the more wonderful, because it heals the wound that sin has made while strengthening the will, enlightening the intellect, and motivating us to do better.

17. Mother Church

During Mass, we affirm our belief in God and the Catholic Church. I believe in God, but to me the Church is only a conduit that provides us with an opportunity to get closer to Jesus. Please help me understand why we believe in the Church.

Fr. Brighenti: I've never heard the Church referred to as a conduit before, but if we could play off that word, we can easily show that the Church is a vehicle or way of salvation. When we talk about the sacraments as an outward sign instituted by Christ to give us grace, we can also talk about the Church itself as the primordial sacrament. It was created by Christ to confer grace like a conduit, a vehicle, or a way to salvation. Christ established the Church through St. Peter, saying, "And I tell you, you are Peter, and on this rock I will build my church, and the powers of death shall not prevail against it" (Matthew 16:18). Christ gave St. Peter the keys, so to speak; a symbol of the authority to bind and loosen as the pope, the Vicar of Christ, here on earth. The Church was instituted by Christ as an outward sign, a visible institution as a means to give us grace.

Fr. Trigilio: The Church is not separate from Christ, because She *is* the Mystical Body of Christ. Too often, people see the Church as extraneous or peripheral. But as Popes Benedict, Francis, John Paul II, and so many other popes and saints have conveyed to us, the Church is a living organism. It's something that we all belong to, and it's not just a club or an organization, and it's not just an institution either. This is the Bride of Christ. There's this sort of personality involved, and there's a relationship. Just like you have a relationship with your friends and family, you have a relationship with God. You also need to have a relationship with the Church, because the Church was founded by Christ. It's His Mystical Body, and the Church is therefore part of Jesus in a mystical sense, and that's why the Head of the Church—the pope—speaks for all of us, and you and I are like different parts of this Body. If there were just the pope and no one else, the Church would only be a decapitated head. We need the whole body together to make this work.

Fr. Brighenti: I'd recommend people read the beautiful encyclical by Pope Pius XII called *Mystici Corporis Christi*, or *The Mystical Body of Christ*. It should be available for free online, and it would be a wonderful source of meditation in regard to this topic. The Church provides the opportunity to be closer to Jesus, because He is the Head of the Church. The Church is also where we encounter the doctrines of our Faith, the truths of Sacred Scripture and Sacred Tradition, the teachings of Christ, and where the Seven

Sacraments are celebrated as well. We encounter the Triune God in every one of those sacraments that we worthily receive. We get closer to the Father, Son, and Holy Spirit through the vehicle of the primordial sacrament called the Church.

Fr. Trigilio: In addition to *Mystici Corporis Christi*, I also highly recommend the Vatican II document *Lumen Gentium*, because it explains the Church's idea of how She sees Herself as the Light of all peoples. That's what *Lumen Gentium* means. She also uses terminology like "a Pilgrim People." We are on a pilgrimage. There are so many different analogies and metaphors for the Church, which is also described as a ship at times, with the pope as the captain, and we're the crew. Fr. Levis had a show on EWTN called *The Voyage of Faith* where he had this motif of a ship.

Fr. Brighenti: Chapter eight of *Lumen Gentium* also speaks about Mary as the Mother of the Church, so that's a very enlightening and wonderful section to meditate on, because it's always been a Catholic teaching that we get closer to Jesus through the intercession of Our Lady.

18. Purgatory, Part 1

I read a sermon recently by a Protestant pastor who declared the following to his congregation: "Sometimes nuns and priests say that they will pray to have God release souls from Purgatory. But I tell you the truth, whether you believe me or not, there is no such place as Purgatory. Purgatory was invented by men; it was invented by the popes. The Bible clearly says that there is a Heaven and a real Hell." Could you please clarify these things for me? I don't want to go to Hell.

Fr. Trigilio: Well, we certainly don't want you to go to Hell either. Whenever people say to me, "I can't find that in the Bible,"

I always respond with, "Well, I'll show you where that is after you show me where the word 'Bible' is in the Bible," because the word "Bible" can't be found in the Bible. The word "Bible" was invented by the Church, as St. Jerome and Pope Damasus used that word to describe the collection of books of Sacred Scripture. Technically speaking, to call this book the "Bible," you're not using a word that's actually found in the Bible, but that's okay, because the words we use don't always have to be in the Bible. This is the case with the word "Purgatory," although the very concept of it is found in the Book of Maccabees where we find the practice of praying for the dead.

Fr. Brighenti: Maybe you could explain a little about the Book of Maccabees.

Fr. Trigilio: Well, Maccabees is one of the seven deuterocanonical books that Martin Luther had pulled out of the Old Testament at the time of the Protestant Reformation. These books were present from 250 B.C. all the way up until the time of Christ and for the first fifteen hundred years of Christianity. Maccabees mentions these Jewish soldiers who died while bravely defending Israel, but unfortunately, when they were burying their bodies, they found these pagan lucky charms on them. They therefore died in sin, but they also died defending Israel. The idea was present that since these Jews weren't in Heaven but also not really in Hell, there must be some state in between and some ability to cleanse them. So, they made an offering for the dead to expiate their attachment to former sins, so long as these sins were not mortal sins that they died unrepentant of. This ancient practice of praying for the dead goes back to day one of the Church, which offered up Masses for the deceased. If the dead are in Heaven, then they don't need the prayers, and if they're in Hell, the prayers can't help them anyway. So, there must be a middle ground, a state of cleansing where they can sever themselves from those attachments to sin and the temporal punishment due to sin. This idea is found in Scripture, it's part of our Tradition, and therefore it's in the *Catechism*. In the Bible, Jesus says, "He who hears you hears me" (Luke 10:16). He never said, "He who reads this," but He said, "He who hears you." Jesus gave the apostles the magisterial teaching authority, and He gave the keys of the Kingdom to St. Peter and his successors when He said, "I will give you the keys of the kingdom of heaven, and whatever you bind on earth shall be bound in heaven, and whatever you loose on earth shall be loosed in heaven" (Matthew 16:19). The teaching authority was given to the Church, not to a book. The Bible was entrusted to the Church to be preserved and taught from. Sacred Scripture and Sacred Tradition work together, not in competition against each other.

Fr. Brighenti: It's important to note that in the scholarly non-Catholic Bibles, like the Oxford Revised Standard, the deutero-canonical books are now included in the back.

Fr. Trigilio: These Catholic books were included in the First Edition of the King James Bible as well, although an act of Parliament eventually had them removed. The Gutenberg Bible, the first one with movable type, was an edition of the Latin Vulgate that included the seven deuterocanonical books. When we look at these doctrines, there is a scriptural foundation to them, but they're not always explicitly stated in the Scriptures. Like I said, even the word "Bible" comes from an extra-biblical source.

Fr. Brighenti: All Protestants are Trinitarian, but you won't find the word "Trinity" in the Bible, and it's not fully explained in the Bible either. When they accuse us of these things, they themselves often rely on extra-biblical sources, too, and they accept plenty of terms that you won't find in the Sacred Scriptures. We have the full message of revelation contained in both Sacred Scripture and Sacred Tradition. In fact, the Bible we have today only exists because of the Catholic Church, which has carefully preserved it throughout the centuries.

19. Purgatory, Part 2

What is Purgatory, and where is it found in the Bible? In the first act of Shakespeare's Hamlet, *the ghost of his father, the king, appears to Hamlet, saying, "I am thy father's spirit, doomed for a certain term to walk the night, and for the day confined to fast in fires, till the foul crimes done in my days of nature are burnt and purged away" (I.v.14-18). Is it possible to find comfort with such a dreary fate?*

Fr. Trigilio: For starters, you've got to realize that Shakespeare, like Dante Alighieri, was using a literary device to describe something that's spiritual. It's not a doctoral explanation, but it's a poetic way of describing a reality. When we look to the *Catechism*, we see the official doctrine on the existence of Purgatory, which merely means that the temporal punishment due to our sin must be remitted in some way for those people who still have an attachment to sin, whether they had venial sins that weren't forgiven before their death, didn't express true sorrow for their sins, or still had some pleasant memories of those sins that they had confessed. They need to go through a time of *purging*, and that's where Purgatory comes in. It's not eternal punishment like Hell, but it's a cleansing for Heaven. There is the temporal punishment for sin because of Divine Justice. Yet, in Divine Mercy there is the medicinal pain to bring about healing. Here's an analogy: When I was a hospital chaplain and had to visit someone in the intensive care unit, the staff would require me to wash my hands, scrubbing away all the dirt until they were almost red. It wasn't always a pleasant experience, but it was necessary, as I was now clean and able to enter that patient's room safely. Purgatory is also a period of cleansing, in the spiritual sense, and we get this idea from the Book of Maccabees, where some soldiers who had died defending Israel were found with pagan lucky charms on their corpses. After their death, they were prayed for, and the Church continues this ancient practice of praying for the dead.

Fr. Brighenti: Another analogy that Sr. Mary Pious taught us in second grade is that Purgatory is the porch to Heaven. If we died as a friend of God, we will go to Heaven, but we have some cleaning up to do first. When we were children who would often get filthy from playing outside, our parents would have us take a bath before coming to the dinner table. Before we go to the big Eucharistic banquet table that Christ has prepared for us, we need to take a bath as well, a purgation or cleansing of our attachments to sin. St. Catherine of Genoa had written a fair amount on Purgatory and stated that we could serve our time in Purgatory here on earth. There are different stages for this: the purgative, the illuminative, and the unitive. Once you get to the unitive stage, you won't even have a fond memory of your former sins, as the very thought of them will be distasteful to you. We can pass through these stages by living a penitential life, and the Church reminds us every Lent about taking on penances, encouraging us to live our whole lives this way. There's a lot of preparation to do before entering Heaven, but we can be working on it right now, here on earth.

20. Death, Part 1

When a person dies, will he go immediately before the Lord? 2 Corinthians 5:8 tells us that to be absent from the body is to be present with the Lord. If a person has received or rejected Our Lord Jesus Christ, will he go to Heaven or Hell on that same day?

Fr. Brighenti: In the study of eschatology, there are four last things: death, judgment, Heaven, and Hell. When we die, we each individually immediately undergo the particular judgment, where Our Lord Jesus judges us on our merits, our words and actions, and how we lived our lives. If we died in a state of grace, we are friends of God, and He will then bring us into the afterlife. Those who rejected the Lord in their free will, even to their last breath, will be left in that terrible state, and that is what we call going to Hell. Following the particular judgment is the general judgment, which takes place at the end of the world, and that might be where the confusion comes in, due to this delay. We need to remember that God doesn't live in time; God created time.

Fr. Trigilio: I think a problem is that when people hear about judgment, they tend to envision a typical court scene where you can make an appeal, and if the state court passes something or rejects it, then you can go to the federal court and then to the Supreme Court. But this isn't an appeal. No one in Heaven who's been judged will be thrown out, and if you're judged in Hell, you're not going to get out. There's no appeal. The general judgment is then a ratification so that those who are in Heaven know why they're there and why the ones are in Hell are where they are. Death, judgment, Heaven, and Hell are the four last things, and then there's also the Second Coming of Christ, the resurrection of the dead, the general judgment, and the end of the world. People are so fixated on this second grouping instead of the first, yet it's your particular judgment that is more important, as it pertains to where you're going to spend eternity as opposed to when the world's going to end. Only the particular judgment concerns your personal salvation through Jesus Christ. So many people are obsessed with whether they're going to be raptured or not, but we don't know if there is even going to be a rapture. What there is going to be is a Heaven or a Hell, and that's what we need to stay focused on.

21. Death, Part 2

What happens when we die?

Fr. Brighenti: Upon death, your soul separates from your body, and it undergoes what we call the "particular judgment." It's not anything like a classic court scene where you'd plead your case with a lawyer before Jesus, Who is the Supreme Judge. Rather, you are judged based on your merits and the state in which you died. If you die as a friend of God, and your merits prove it, then you go to Heaven. If you die as an enemy of God, then you go to Hell. Now, we can also die in the state of grace, as a friend of God, but with some imperfections, which would mean that we didn't finish our purification or cleansing of our forgiven sins here on earth. If that's the case, then we are not pure enough to enter Heaven, and we must go through Purgatory, which is a temporary state of cleansing. We here in the Church Militant can help these souls in Purgatory get to Heaven by praying for them and offering up Masses for their sakes. Think of Purgatory as the porch of Heaven. When you go there, you are on your way to Heaven, but you need to be purged of any attachments to sin and pay for any past sins that have been forgiven but weren't atoned for here on earth.

Fr. Trigilio: Sometimes, people get the idea that we become angels when we die. In reality, when a human being dies and goes to Heaven, he becomes a saint. An angel is a separate created entity that, after passing their test of obedience to God, went to Heaven, like St. Michael, St. Gabriel, and St. Raphael. You're also not going to come back as another person. Jesus died for you as an individual, not as a recycled soul in some kind of factory.

Fr. Brighenti: Reincarnation is another trick from the devil that says you'll have more chances. You don't. You're given only one life and one chance. The old *Baltimore Catechism* tells us to know, love, and serve God, and to prepare ourselves in this life to be with Him in the next. That's what we should be focusing on right now while we're on earth, because we only have one chance to do this.

Fr. Trigilio: Sometimes people also buy into these New Age ideas where, when we die, we join together in this great nebulous consciousness and we all become God, no matter how we've lived our lives. This is wrong; our choices matter, and we've only got one chance at making them.

22. Calling a Priest "Father"

Why is a priest addressed as "Father"? Protestant denominations call their clergymen "Brother," "Pastor," or "Reverend." Are priests on another spiritual level?

Fr. Brighenti: Let's answer the second part of this question first. Within the Catholic Church, "Brother" is a title that refers to someone in a religious community. Because religious orders, such as the Franciscans and the Dominicans, include both brothers and priests, "Brother" is used to refer to a member of the order who is not ordained. The term "Pastor" can be applied to a priest, as that would denote his position as the pastor of a parish, or he can be called "Parochial Vicar," which would be an assistant pastor or the pastor of two parishes. The final term, "Reverend," is a formal title used to address a priest, but you wouldn't casually call him "Reverend" as you would a Protestant minister.

Fr. Trigilio: If you were addressing a priest on a card or in a letter, you would put "The Reverend" followed by the name of the priest.

Fr. Brighenti: To answer the main point of the question now, "Father" carries with it a spiritual connotation of the term. As ordained priests, we share in the priesthood of Jesus Christ, and thus in the sacraments, especially Baptism where people are re-born by the regenerative waters in sanctifying grace. In this sense, we are spiritual fathers, and it's most beautifully represented in the relationship between a pastor and his parish. Every soul in a pastor's confine, be it a church or territory, is his spiritual child. Some Protestants misinterpret the passage in Scripture where it says "And call no man your father on earth, for you have one Father, who is in heaven" (Matthew 23:9) as a denunciation of the priesthood, but in Scripture we see Our Blessed Savior say the name, "Father Abraham" (Luke chapter 16). Jesus Himself indicates that "Father" is a term that we can use.

Fr. Trigilio: Fr. Levis always reminded us that if you take a text out of context, you end up with a pretext. If you take the text "do not call anyone your father" out of context, it could liter-ally mean that you can't even call your dad "Father," and you couldn't call George Washington the father of our country. If this was the case, then Jesus Himself would have been guilty of breaking His own axiom, because as you've already pointed out in the parable of Dives and Lazarus, He uses the name "Father Abraham." Even St. Paul refers to himself as a "spiritual father" in one of his epistles, and he addresses the fledgling Christians in Corinth and Galatia as "my children." When Jesus taught us not to call anyone on earth father, he was warning us not to let anyone replace that special relationship of God the Father in our spiritual lives, whereas priests as "spiritual fathers" reflect the fatherhood of God in our sacred ordained ministry.

Fr. Brighenti: A beautiful patron for priests would be St. Joseph, who was the chaste foster father of Our Blessed Savior. Certainly, Jesus would have used the term "Father" to St. Joseph, who raised Him, taught Him how to be a carpenter, and brought Him up in religion. St. Joseph was also a role model for Our Blessed Savior in all those quiet years that the Gospel does not account for. St. Joseph is the patron of the universal Church, and he's a good example of a spiritual father, and we model our priesthood and our lives after St. Joseph. The term "Father" does not replace or take away anything from God Our Heavenly Father, but it's a title that can be used to denote a special relationship with our spiritual children, which are the souls that are entrusted to us as priests of Jesus Christ.

Fr. Trigilio: There was also a phenomenon in Jesus' time where Judaism was split into various sectarian groups led by particular rabbis, and the Jewish people would call them "Father." While these sects were not cults, they were very isolated and became more parochial and less communitarian. That's what Jesus was opposing: this disintegration and lack of unity within the faith.

23. The Suffering of Our Blessed Mother

I often read that Mary suffered the same Passion with Christ. Does this mean she suffered the same as Him physically, emotionally, or both?

Fr. Brighenti: First, we need to remember that Mary's *fiat* of "Thy will be done" was not temporary, but it applied to her entire life. When Our Lord was presented in the temple, St. Simeon the Prophet told Mary that a sword would pierce her heart. On Good Friday, Mary spiritually entered into the sufferings of her Son at the foot of the Cross. She didn't have to make up for the Sacrifice, as Christ's suffering is complete for all people, but Christ allowed Mary to do this in her *fiat*. It was a way to teach us that we, too, can unite our sufferings with the Lord and let it change our crown of thorns into a crown of victory.

Fr. Trigilio: Mary's anguish was emotional, not physical, yet I recall reading in one of the spiritual classics that Mary herself would have likely passed out or died from the emotional strain alone if not for a special grace God had granted her to persevere. When my brothers passed away, I remember seeing the effect it had on my parents. While not on the same level as physical pain, the empathy one may have for the suffering of a loved one can be very close. You and I both know as priests that when we go to hospitals or nursing homes, relatives of those who are dying undergo an extreme amount of stress and anxiety even though it's not physical. Mary united herself with Jesus on the Cross, not because it had to happen that way, but because Christ invited her and she accepted.

Fr. Brighenti: Again, the *fiat* is not temporary. It's an ongoing "Thy will be done." When we call her Our Lady of Sorrows, we're not saying she's "Our Lady of Despair." Rather, we're recognizing that at the foot of the Cross, she did experience sorrow, and who wouldn't? The image of Our Lord on the Cross is not just some knickknack that we hang on the wall but a very bloody and gruesome picture. This was the scene Our Lady witnessed of her own innocent Son, Who had committed no sin, yet was being crucified between two thieves. She is also Our Lady of Hope, because she knew in her heart that Good Friday would be turned into Easter Sunday, and we all have to go through Good Friday in order to reach Easter Sunday.

Fr. Trigilio: The devotion of Our Lady of Sorrows is so wonderful. It's called The Seven Sorrows, and there are two sorrows in particular that I've always had an affinity for. The first is where Jesus was missing for three days, because that is a parent's worst nightmare. Your twelve-year-old is missing; is he dead, is he alive? Is he hurt, was he kidnapped? All the scenarios you'd think of today, Mary thought of two thousand years ago. The other sorrow is seeing Him die on the Cross, and those two alone not only show us the depth of Mary's love but also her participation. As you said regarding despair, it's not doom and gloom. Mary got through those, she weathered those sorrows by God's grace, and this should inspire us. If God would give Mary the grace to ride out her seven sorrows, then we're going to be given the same grace to ride out all of ours.

24. Angels and the Fall

How many archangels were in Heaven before the Fall? Since Lucifer may have been an archangel prior to rebelling against God, could there have been more archangels that fell, and how many?

Fr. Trigilio: We don't have a precise understanding, so to speak, of the angels. St. Thomas Aquinas wrote in his *Summa*

Theologica[5] that it would boggle our imagination, because each angel in and of himself would exhaust a whole species, and they're so beyond us in terms of their power, agility, and intellect. We find the teaching that one-third of the angels rebelled against God in Scripture where it speaks of the one-third of the stars that fell from Heaven, and we can deduce that two-thirds of the angels remained good. St. Michael the Archangel is depicted in Scripture as the one who vanquished the great dragon, who is synonymous with the devil. St. Raphael the Archangel is mentioned in the Book of Tobit, which is one of the deuterocanonical books, and St. Gabriel is the archangel who announced to Mary that she was to be the Mother of God, and who also told Zechariah that his wife Elizabeth was going to have a child — St. John the Baptist. We do not know the names of any other angels besides these three. To help make sense of the positions and authority of the angels in Heaven, St. Thomas Aquinas listed nine choirs of angels, but these are not part of dogma; they're only theological speculation, meaning you don't have to believe it, although we do find the names of these angelic choirs in Scripture. For instance, there are the seraphim, which are considered the highest level. These are the angels who praise and adore God all day long, and you may see this choir of angels referenced in our hymns. There are then the cherubim, thrones, dominions, principalities, powers, virtues, archangels, and lastly angels, which are the lowest of the ranks and could be assigned as our guardian angels, for example. A fact I want to highlight is that you do *not* become an angel when you die; human beings who have been saved by Christ become saints in Heaven. Angels remain angels, and the good ones are

---

[5] *Summa Theologica*, I, q. 12.

in Heaven, and the bad ones are in Hell. These fallen angels are called demons. The angels were not originally in Heaven, because once you're in Heaven you can't turn your back on God. In Heaven, you would be so fulfilled by the Beatific Vision that you couldn't possibly choose wrong, so the angels existed outside of Heaven and were put to a test. Scripture talks about a great war that ensued in the heavens, and while we don't know what that entailed since we're dealing with spiritual beings, it must have been the mother of all battles, considering that these spirits are so powerful that just thinking about them boggles the mind.

Fr. Brighenti: There's a feast day for St. Michael the Archangel on September 29, although today they've combined it with St. Raphael's and St. Gabriel's, but St. Michael's Mass was famous in the fall semester and was commonly called "The St. Michael Mass Semester." There's also a feast day for the guardian angels on October 2. There's a votive Mass that a priest can offer up to the angels, and there are some private devotions you can offer in the form of beautiful prayers to your guardian angel or a litany to the angels in general. The days of the week used to be divided up with themes, too, where angels would be celebrated on a Wednesday, for example, and that's when a votive Mass could take place if there were no feast planned for another saint on that specific day. It's important to remember that the Lord gives us our guardian angel to guide, to protect, and to inspire us, and that last one is the most underused gift that we receive from them. Too often, we think that guardian angels are just for little children, but in reality, our guardian angels go with us through our entire lives. It's beneficial to have a healthy devotion to your guardian angel, because in turn you'll be more tuned in to the Lord.

Fr. Trigilio: Sacred Scripture makes it clear when Jesus says there are angels in Heaven and to plead their cause. We had a professor back in seminary who told us that there was a spreading rumor that angels didn't really exist. Angels are indeed real beings, but they are independent beings in the sense that we cannot control them. New Age religion tends to have this angelology that tries to come up with names for the other angels. I know of one supposed angel, Uriel, who is mentioned in the apocrypha (*pseudepigrapha* in Protestant bibles) and maintained in the Anglican and Episcopalian traditions, and there could very well be an angel named Uriel, but he's not listed in the canonized list of Scripture. There are several other names that have come from many other bizarre sources, but I tell people not to worry about those angels, because the ones that we do know, Michael, Raphael, and Gabriel, are all mentioned in the canonized text of Scripture, and it's not so much that you need to know the name of your guardian angel but that you know he's there.

25. Did Mary Have Free Will?

How many women were selected by God for the birth of Our Lord? I ask because the Blessed Mother, the Immaculate Conception, was born without sin — a dogma of the Church. If the angel had asked her if she would be the Mother of God, and if Mary had said no, who would be the next in line to fill in for her? The women hand-picked to be the Mother of God would have to be virgins born without sin and part of the lineage of David. If there were no other women selected, then God, Who is all-knowing, would not have allowed Mary to exercise free will, and this would mean that she really did not have any.

Fr. Trigilio: The way this is worded, it almost sounds like there was some kind of spiritual beauty contest going on, and Mary won.

Fr. Brighenti: First of all, Mary's role in the Catholic Church is so important because of her *fiat* where she said, "Thy will be done." That's how we should live our whole lives. God knew beforehand that Mary would say yes, and that did not take away her free will simply because God is all-knowing. He knows all things, and nothing can be hidden from Him, and He also exists outside of time, whereas we are working these things out. The Blessed Virgin Mary was part of His divine knowledge, and He knew that she was going to say yes, but let's not ignore the lesson here: the importance of Mary's *fiat* is that she didn't quite understand at that moment how everything was going to pan out and that she would be the Mother of God, yet she said, "Thy will be done." She placed her trust in the Lord and knew that everything would work out. That's the lesson she teaches us.

Fr. Trigilio: That's the key. When people get hung up on the divine foreknowledge of God, I usually give them this analogy: Say you're in an airplane and you can see all the street traffic below you. You spot a car on collision course with a truck, but they can't see each other because their view is obstructed by the way the road bends. Neither party realizes that they're going to crash, but you can see exactly what's going to happen from above. In one sense, you have foreknowledge even though you're not causing the collision to occur, nor are you impacting the fact that one of the drivers could swerve out of the way. Likewise, God saw in His divine foreknowledge that Mary was going to say yes. He didn't force her to say it, but because He infallibly knew she would say yes, He prepared her beforehand with the gift of the Immaculate Conception. Imagine stepping into a time machine and finding out that in the future your son or daughter was going to be a great scientist and discover the cure for cancer.

Back in your time, your kid may only be in diapers, but knowing the future now you would certainly start putting money away to send your child to medical school. You're not going to force him to go, because you already know what he will become, and when your child says, "Daddy, I'd like to go to medical school," you're not going to pass out because you don't have the funds. You knew ahead of time, and you prepared. In a sense, that's what God did. He knew ahead of time because of being able to peer into both Mary's future and her past. He gave her participation in His divine plan ahead of time, where Jesus' Redemption on the Cross retroactively applied to Mary at the very moment of her Immaculate Conception. She was as much saved by Christ as you or I, but that moment for her occurred at conception, while ours takes place at Baptism.

26. The Perfection of the Blessed Mother

Was Mary perfect? How can we identify with her if she is so high above us? I feel sorry for St. Joseph, if he had to live with two perfect people.

Fr. Brighenti: I'd like to make two distinctions about this. First of all, the perfectionism that the question is referring to is more of an ontological type of perfectionism, such as that of an obsessive-compulsive disorder. That's not what we're saying about Mary. On the other hand, we also are talking about an attribute of God. God is One, an infinite perfection! With Mary, we're talking about a finite perfection that God created within her, and this is in regard to sin and the life of grace. We can say that the origin of this is the Immaculate Conception of Mary in the womb of St. Anne, where she was preserved from Original Sin. This happened because she was to be the Mother of God and to provide a pure and immaculate Vessel, a Body, to the Second

Person of the Blessed Trinity Who would redeem us from sin. In regard to the Immaculate Conception, Mary is perfect and was always free from sin. But even though she was preserved from Original Sin in sanctifying grace, her free will was never obliterated. She could still freely choose to follow or not to follow God. We know that Mary will always freely choose to follow God, and this is beautifully proclaimed at the Annunciation with her words, "Thy will be done," and in the prayer of the Magnificat: "My soul proclaims the greatness of the Lord."

Fr. Trigilio: When we hear the word "perfection," we tend to think of the caricature of someone who's obsessed with meticulous perfection, which you'll never find in this world. With Mary, it's a moral and spiritual perfection, as St. Gabriel the Archangel greeted her with the words, "Hail, Full of Grace," which is from the Greek word *kecharitomene*. If she was full of grace, then there was no room for sin. On the spiritual, moral level, Mary is at her zenith because of the Immaculate Conception. That doesn't mean, however, that she never made a mistake in the sense of a slip of the tongue or spilling something while cooking. When we think of perfection, only God is without any defect both morally and ontologically. With Mary, it's all purely moral and spiritual. In terms of her physicality, it doesn't mean that her body was at absolute perfection to the point it couldn't have looked any better, but it's of moral character. This is encouraging for us, as we ourselves may not be able to attain a certain level of material or outward perfection, but it's the interior one that counts. My spiritual relationship with God is what matters the most.

Fr. Brighenti: Also, both Mary and Joseph freely chose the will of God in their lives. In this way, we can relate to them when we choose the Lord every day and increase the level of grace in our lives as Mary did. We can turn to the Holy Family as an example for all Christian families. Instead of seeing it as a hindrance, we should see it as a model. I believe Pope St. John Paul II brought this concept out so brilliantly in his encyclical on family life, *Familiaris Consortio.*

Fr. Trigilio: I also can't see St. Joseph being bummed out that he had to live with Jesus and the Virgin Mary. It was a privilege for him.

27. The Immaculate Conception

As a new convert to Catholicism, the role of the Virgin Mary in the Church is very difficult for me to grasp. I have read that the Immaculate Conception became official Church doctrine in 1854, and I am curious to know what the Church taught prior to this date.

Fr. Trigilio: Many times when people learn that Pope Pius IX defined the dogma of the Immaculate Conception in 1854, they wonder what the belief was for all the centuries prior. It's not that the Immaculate Conception wasn't taught, but that the doctrine itself was not in question. There was no great opposition or controversy regarding this doctrine, and the only time some questions arose was back during the Middle Ages, most prominently by St. Thomas Aquinas. Now, St. Thomas Aquinas was a theologian with one of the greatest minds the Church has ever seen, but he was not a pope or a bishop and therefore didn't have the fullness of teaching authority. He had a brilliant mind, but he was limited in that he could not participate in any way in terms of the infallibility of the Church; he was only able to explain what the Church had already taught. Since this specific doctrine had not yet been infallibly defined, it had the leeway for theologians to discuss it, and his only issue stemmed from the

Aristotelian biology that was commonly accepted in his time. From the time of Aristotle, which was prior to Jesus Christ, there was this bizarre biological concept which speculated that human beings developed within the womb first as a plant, then as an animal, and then they became human so that they would have passed through the different levels of being within their mothers. The thought concluded that once they were human, God would then infuse the soul. We know now from modern science that this is not the case. As soon as the egg is fertilized at the moment of conception, the child's DNA becomes distinct from the mother's. It's similar so that you can tell from whom the DNA derives, but it's also different so you know it's not the mother's. The fertilized egg, the embryo, the fetus, the zygote — this is a distinct individual human being. It's not plant DNA, and it's not animal DNA; it is human DNA, and it's a brand new person. If St. Thomas Aquinas had understood the biology that we have access to today, he would have no problem with the Immaculate Conception on a biological level. The basis is that Mary was preserved from Original Sin from the moment of her conception within her mother's womb, and that's the moment the soul was infused within her. St. Bonaventure didn't have any issues with believing in the Immaculate Conception because he had a slightly different understanding of biology, but St. Thomas Aquinas was unfortunately limited in this one area. Remember, they didn't have sonograms or x-rays back then, and even doing an autopsy was considered an improper thing to do by society's standards, as it was deemed offensive to the integrity of the human person. It was only during the Renaissance that people like Leonardo da Vinci and others literally cut the corpses of people open and drew these very intricate drawings, which they still use for medicine today.

Fr. Brighenti: Like you mentioned, the Immaculate Conception was commonly believed all the way down from the time of the apostles, so St. Thomas Aquinas was in the minority. Private devotions that have been accepted by the Church also prove this teaching. When Mary appeared to St. Catherine Labouré in the 1830s on the Rue de Bac in Paris at her motherhouse chapel, she said to construct what we know today as the Miraculous Medal, which reads, "O Mary, conceived without sin, pray for us who have recourse to thee." That is the title of the Immaculate Conception in prayer form. St. Bernadette then received the apparition of Our Lady in Lourdes, France, and when Bernadette asked her who she was, Mary replied, "I am the Immaculate Conception."

Fr. Trigilio: That occurred in 1858, only four years after the doctrine had been defined.

Fr. Brighenti: It shows that even our private devotions, the ones that have been accepted as authentic apparitions of the Church, point to this magnificent doctrine of the Faith.

28. Mary's Other Children

Did the Virgin Mary have any other children with Joseph after Jesus? If so, can you tell me their names, and if not, was Mary a virgin all her life?

Fr. Trigilio: We get this question a lot, especially as priests, and particularly when I'm at the airport or out in public, people will ask me about the brothers and sisters of Jesus Christ, whether these were Mary's other children or Joseph's kids from a previous marriage. The *Catechism* states that she remained a virgin and that her virginity was always intact. We even use the phrase "Ever

Virgin" to describe her. The brethren of Jesus that are referred to in Scripture are not biological siblings, and they're not half or step-siblings either, but they are instead relatives. The ancient Hebrew, along with other ancient languages, did not have the refinements that we take for granted today. To give you an example, we're told explicitly in the Book of Genesis that Abraham and Haran were brothers and that Lot was the son of Haran. Well, we can say then, in our modern English tongue, that Abraham was the uncle of Lot and that Lot was his nephew. They didn't have the words "uncle" and "nephew" back then, but they instead had a word that encompassed everything, such as the word "relative." My brother is my relative; if I had a nephew, he would be my relative; and my dad is my relative. Any relationship would be a relative, and so the word that they used in the Hebrew was אח (ach), which is translated in the Greek as *adelphos*, which can mean brother in the sense of sibling, or it could mean a cousin, nephew, uncle, or any other type of family relationship. In Genesis, the King James Bible reads, "Abraham and his brother, Lot." Now, Lot is not Abraham's biological brother, but this particular translation is due to the fact that they were translating from the Septuagint, a Greek version of the Old Testament which used the word *adelphos*. When it says that Jesus' *adelphoi*, which is the plural form, are outside, it's just like with Abraham and his *adelphos*, Lot, who is not his brother but instead a relative. Now, Jesus had cousins, such as John the Baptist, and Joseph may have had brothers who had children, but what if one of his brothers had died and left some children behind? Those children would have likely moved in with Joseph. So, in the neighborhood or even in the household, there were relatives who were under Joseph's care though they were not his biological children, and thus these *adelphoi* were not Jesus' biological brothers and sisters.

Not only do we have the language barrier refuting any thoughts to the contrary, but at the Crucifixion Jesus told St. John the Evangelist, "Behold, your mother!" (John 19:27). Jewish law was so strict and tradition so steep at the time, that if Mary had any children whatsoever, even if they were stepchildren, they would have been obligated to take care of her. Why weren't they present at the Cross? Why would Jesus have given His Mother to John? Because she had nobody else to care for her, for Jesus had no siblings.

Fr. Brighenti: It's only by taking a verse out of context that one can arrive at the faulty conclusion that Jesus had literal brothers. You always need to take in the broader picture. When Our Lord said in Matthew 12:48, "who are my brethren?" He was talking about His disciples and those who were following Him.

Fr. Trigilio: It was a spiritual relationship. When you take a verse out of context, it's like a jigsaw puzzle; one piece of Scripture alone could mean anything.

Fr. Brighenti: You also have to consider that in some languages, especially among Italians, we often refer to a friend with a title that would otherwise indicate a relative. For example, the children might call a close friend to the family "aunt" or "uncle" even though they're not related to them.

29. Jesus as God

Is there anywhere in Scripture where Jesus refers to Himself as God?

Fr. Trigilio: Strictly speaking, Jesus never said, "I am God," but He does identify as the Son of God. At one point in Scripture, Jesus makes the bold statement: "Before Abraham was, I am" (John 8:58). He is identifying Himself as divine, and again when

He says, "I and the Father are one" (John 10:30) or when He tells Philip, "He who has seen me has seen the Father" (John 14:9).

When we see the text written, the "I AM" is capitalized. This says volumes for people who are students of Scripture, because we read in the Old Testament that when Moses encountered the burning bush, he asked, "If I come to the people of Israel and say to them, 'The God of your fathers has sent me to you,' and they ask me, 'What is his name?' what shall I say to them?" The voice of God replied, "I Am Who I Am" (Exodus 3:13-14), which is the English translation of the Hebrew word that we sloppily translate as *Yahweh*. This was the sacred name only whispered by the high priest on the Day of Atonement in the Holy of Holies. No one else was allowed to speak it.

Ancient Hebrew had no vowels, so, when they ran into the letters spelling out the sacred name of God, YHWH, they would change the vowel to avoid saying "Yahweh" and would instead say "Jehovah" or substitute the word with "Adonai," meaning Lord, or "Elohim," meaning God. Even though the sacred name was mentioned in Scripture, it was so sacred that they would never drop it casually. Jesus was thus making a significant claim when he said, "Before Abraham was, I AM." The high priest then tore his clothes in two, because in the minds of the Jews at the time, to say what Jesus had said was counted as blasphemy. Yet Jesus, while He never said the sentence in English, "I am God," does appropriate the Divine Identity by saying, "Before Abraham was, I AM."

Fr. Brighenti: This is, of course, the claim that the Jewish leaders used to condemn and crucify Him.

Fr. Trigilio: Especially the Sanhedrin, as that was the last straw for them. When Jesus started saying that He was the Son of God, they were just beginning to understand what implications that actually had for them. That's the beauty of Scripture. Sometimes things are said that are so subtle, and they require you to read into them in order to grasp their full meaning. That's why the context of Scripture is so important.

Fr. Brighenti: It even took the apostles a while to see the big picture. That's why Jesus had a seminary of sorts for them, the three years of study to understand this concept of God and Messiah. Indeed, they were put to a test and trial on Good Friday, and many of them fled, their faith shattered. It really wasn't until the Resurrection that they understood, and until the Feast of Pentecost where they were enlivened to go spread the message of salvation. This was an ongoing process for them.

Fr. Trigilio: When you consider the scene of Jesus' Baptism at the Jordan River, the voice from Heaven declared, "This is my beloved Son" (Matthew 3:17). No one else in salvation history was given that address. Mary's commandment to "Do whatever He tells you" is a perfect parallel to this. It's like when a mother and a father are on the same page.

30. The Order of the Mass

I am a Catholic and have a lot of non-Catholic friends. They often ask me questions about Catholicism to which I do not have the answers. For instance, why do we have an order for celebrating the Mass, which seemingly leaves little room for the Holy Spirit to operate within us? They also say that the Catholic Church's claim to be the only Church of Christ is wrong because the Church of Christ is comprised of all who have the Spirit of God, wherever they may be. Because of questions like these, I don't say the Hail Mary anymore. Please help me with these questions.

Fr. Trigilio: The way we celebrate Mass is commanded to us by Jesus at the Last Supper, in Luke 22:19-20: "Do this in remembrance of me." He used wheat bread, He used grape wine, and the exact words that Jesus Christ Himself spoke, which are contained in the Gospels as well as in the Epistle of St. Paul, are: "This is My Body. This is My Blood." We've followed that tradition meticulously for two thousand years. Now, it's true that we've added some other aspects to the Divine Liturgy, but the essence of using bread and wine along with Christ's words comes directly from Jesus. We follow what the Church says because Jesus said to Peter, "And I tell you, you are Peter, and on this rock I will build my church" (Matthew 16:18). The Church, built by Christ, was given the authority to speak in His name, and that includes instructing us how we are to worship the Lord Our God. You and I, as members of the Church, then participate in that work of Christ's continuing role to sanctify, to teach, and to govern.

Fr. Brighenti: Since the time of Moses and up to the time of Christ, Jewish worship of God consisted in Temple and Synagogue. The Temple in Jerusalem was where the Ark of the Covenant resided, and where sacrifice was made by the priests (the tribe of Levi), culminating in the High Priest sacrificing the lamb at Passover. Synagogues were local places of worship where the local rabbi read the Hebrew scriptures (the Torah, the Prophets, and so on). Christianity united both temple and synagogue in the Holy Mass where both Scripture (the Liturgy of the Word) and the Holy Sacrifice (the Liturgy of the Eucharist) are celebrated together.

Fr. Trigilio: The earliest name for what we now call the Holy Mass was the Breaking of the Bread. Recall that the disciples on the road to Emmaus did not recognize the Risen Lord until the "breaking of the bread." St. Paul recounts with precision how the early Christians worshiped by obeying Jesus' command to "Do this in remembrance of me" (1 Corinthians 11:24). The "this" He is referring to is the Lord's Supper where He took, blessed, broke, and gave the bread and wine which had become His Body and Blood. It is Catholic practice that the priest imposes his hands over the chalice filled with grape wine and the plate (paten) where the host made of wheat bread is placed. It is at that moment called the Epiclesis that the Church teaches the Holy Spirit is invoked and comes down for the transubstantiation (the changing of the substances of bread and wine into the substances of Christ's Body and Blood). So, the Holy Spirit is indeed at work in the Holy Mass. He is invoked along with the Father and Son at the beginning of Mass, and at the end of Mass as well.

Fr. Brighenti: Just look at the rubrics, which are those instructions in the Roman Missal written in red to show the priest how to celebrate the Mass in a proper form. If we were left to our own devices, people would not be in unity at the Mass. We've seen just how different the ceremonies are for non-Catholic denominations when they are left to their own inventions. In the Catholic Church, these rubrics safeguard the Sacrifice of the Mass. The public liturgy belongs to the Church, and therefore there are rules and regulations on how to follow it, and it has the potential to become even more prayerful if there are no distractions due to a loosely improvised worship. In the past, there have been some priests who tried to improvise at the Mass, and we've seen just how destructive it was and how it negatively tampered with peoples' spiritual lives.

Fr. Trigilio: This malpractice was forbidden at the Councils of Trent, Vatican I, and Vatican II, which said that no one under their own authority has the right to change what the Church has officially stated is mandatory.

Fr. Brighenti: Yet some priests choose to do so out of their own pride. The Roman Missal is there to safeguard the liturgy.

Fr. Trigilio: I recently read in one of Pope Benedict's books, from back when he was a cardinal, about Moses when he went to see Pharaoh. If you ask most people what Moses said to Pharaoh, the majority will only get it half right by responding with: "Let my people go." But there's a comma in the text, and the full sentence reads: "Let my people go, that they may serve me in the wilderness" (Exodus 7:16). God was very meticulous on exactly how the Hebrews were to worship Him. He did not leave it to their own devices. He instructed them specifically, not just for the Passover meal, but for when they were in the desert and when they were building the temple, because Divine Worship is the worship of God. He designed it. Likewise, at the Last Supper, it was Jesus Who instructed the apostles in the Holy Sacrifice of the Mass. He didn't just say, "Hey, guys, work something up, and I'll let you know if I like it or not." No, He gave them the Mass. It belongs to Christ, and it was entrusted to the Church to safeguard.

Fr. Brighenti: Besides the Mass, the Benediction of the Blessed Sacrament, the Liturgy of the Hours, and the sacraments themselves all have rubrics explaining how they are to be celebrated, because again these are public liturgy, not private devotions like our praying of the Rosary and the Litany of the Saints. Could you imagine if a game like basketball or football didn't have any rules and regulations, and everyone was left to their own design in the gymnasium or on the field? It would be a total mess. Or consider if they didn't have rules and regulations on how to run a school, where we wouldn't have to follow the criteria set forth by the state. The rubrics are in place to safeguard the Divine Liturgy for the people to experience an authentic moment of worship.

Fr. Trigilio: I'm always impressed whenever we have a military funeral and I see the meticulous way in which they fold the flag, and they do it exactly the same way every time. It's done with reverence as they present the flag to the widow or widower and say the words, "On behalf of a grateful nation." It's inspiring, even though it's not a religious ceremony. It's fraught with symbolism, and all that the flag represents is entrusted in that one act where it's given to the fallen warrior's husband, wife, or child. How much more in our faith should we use poignant symbolism to convey what's in the deepest recesses of our hearts!

Fr. Brighenti: I would suggest a rediscovery of the documents on the liturgy, the conciliar and post-conciliar documents, in which there's an abundance of them, and Pope St. John Paul II's document on the Eucharist during the Year of the Eucharist would be wonderful for meditation as well.

Fr. Trigilio: Pope Benedict has written a number of books on the topic, too. *The Spirit of the Liturgy* gives fantastic insight, like the passage I shared previously about Moses speaking to Pharaoh.

Fr. Brighenti: Scott Hahn also states in his books that the Bible contains the rubrics for worshipping.

Fr. Trigilio: When you consider how the Bible came to us, it was first designed because people needed to hear God's holy, inspired Word at worship. Most people only heard the Word of God as it was read to them at the sacred liturgy, whether in the Hebrew form or in the Christian form. Now, to address the other part of the question regarding the Catholic Church as the True Church: *Dominus Iesus* is a wonderful document that you can find in our online library; in it, the Holy Father makes abundantly clear that the Catholic Church is the True Church and that people are saved through the Church and through Christ. Now, it is possible for people to be saved by the Church and by Christ who may not know it. The only ones who are culpable are those who know this and consciously, deliberately reject it. If somebody isn't aware of this and is living a good life of faith, is following their conscience, and seeking to do what the Lord wants him to do, and he does not know that the Catholic Church is what the Lord set up and established, then he's not consciously rejecting it, and therefore he's not culpable. That's why when Fr. Feeney got on the radio and said that if you're not a card-carrying Catholic then you're damned to Hell, the Church excommunicated him. He later repented and was reconciled with the Church, but he had no authority to have made that statement.

Fr. Brighenti: He had become the very product of what he was preaching.

Fr. Trigilio: Exactly! But the teaching that "outside the Church there is no salvation" doesn't mean that just because you're not a member of the Church and weren't baptized, you won't be saved, but that you must be consciously rejecting the Church. In God's universal salvific will, as St. Augustine would phrase it, He gave everyone sufficient grace, and it only becomes efficacious to the ones who cooperate with it. You can implicitly cooperate with God's grace and not be aware of it, and that's why we believe that God wants as many people as possible to get to Heaven. This doesn't mean that you and I don't have the obligation to evangelize and to catechize, as it's not enough to figure people can get into Heaven by the bare minimum. We want people to have the fullness of grace and the fullness of truth, so we must reach out and evangelize, and that's why we are striving for more Christian unity. We can't just assume there's a safety net to catch everyone. That would be like leaving people on life support when they could be out of bed, walking around, and feeding themselves.

31. Receiving Holy Communion in the Hand

Is it true that receiving the Holy Eucharist in the hand was properly approved by the Vatican in 1977? It seems that this practice was not a prevailing method in the Church at the time and was a means of receiving the Holy Eucharist prior to the Vatican's approval.

Fr. Brighenti: Permission was officially given by the Vatican in 1977 when it approved the American Bishops' petition for an indult to allow the option of receiving Holy Communion in the hand. It didn't suppress receiving Communion on the tongue, however, as that is still universally normative. The Eastern Catholic Church, however, gives Communion by mouth, though not on the tongue and not in the hand. The priest drops consecrated bread (the Precious Body) into the chalice of consecrated wine (the Precious Blood) and administers the Eucharist with a spoon by placing it inside the opened mouth (with tongue kept back). The Eastern Rite uses leavened bread cut up into cubes, whereas the Latin Rite uses unleavened, flat hosts in the shape of discs.

Prior to 1977, Holy Communion on the tongue was normative and mandatory in the West since around A.D. 900, if not sooner. The ancient Church before that allowed Communion in the hand, but in the Middle Ages stopped the practice to prevent potential sacrilege by nefarious persons and possible dropping of the sacred host onto the floor.

Fr. Trigilio: And just because things were done illicitly or without permission doesn't mean that they can't be recognized after the fact. So, now it's legitimate, but it is up to each individual bishop and each episcopal conference or conference of bishops to decide if they're going to allow it. For instance, in the city of Rome during the reigns of Pope St. John Paul II and Pope Emeritus Benedict XVI, the pope (being the Bishop of Rome) decreed that Communion on the tongue would be the only way of receiving. Yet when people line up at the Papal Masses with their hands out, nine times out of ten they're going to receive Holy Communion anyway. Pope Francis has not stipulated only one method for receiving in his diocese.

Fr. Brighenti: When we gave out Communion on Epiphany Sunday in Rome one year, they told us to just give It to the people if they had their hands out, since it's the custom in their dioceses. But that was just what the English-speaking priests were told. The priests who spoke other languages were told to give only on the tongue.

Fr. Trigilio: I would like to remind everyone that if you go to the Byzantine or other Eastern Catholic Church, deacons therein do not distribute Holy Communion as ours do in the Western Church.

32. Reading Sacred Scripture

I am a college student who is reading the Bible and enjoying it very much. What advice do you have for me in how to read the Bible from a Catholic perspective? I don't know what to take literally or figuratively.

For example, Mary of Magdala, upon seeing the Lord resurrected from the dead, could not touch Him, for the Lord had not yet ascended to God the Father. Eight days later, Thomas touched Him and even put his hands inside His wounds. Had the Lord then ascended before the encounter with Thomas? What about the Ascension forty days after His Resurrection?

Fr. Trigilio: The thing about the Gospels is that they were not written presuming that the reader was going to get his or her hands on another Gospel. Each individual Sacred Author was inspired by the Holy Spirit without knowing that another one was going to write a Gospel as well. That said, each Gospel is going to give you a different perspective, and you cannot compare them as if they were in a contest to see who had the least alleged discrepancies, because each one is written for a particular audience from a particular perspective. To glean the fullness of Scripture, you need to read all of it in its proper context. Regarding interpretation, there are some excellent Catholic commentaries out there. I highly recommend the Navarre Bible series that's published by Scepter Publishers, which is a vehicle of Opus Dei. Liturgical Press in Collegeville, Minnesota prints the Ignatius Bible based on the Revised Standard Version, and this is excellent for studying purposes due to the commentaries it includes. These are going to be quite helpful to you, as well as reading Bible commentaries from the Fathers of the Church. You'll also see how scriptural passages are used at Mass and on feast days throughout the year.

Fr. Brighenti: There are a couple of handy apps that you can download as well, assuming you have a smart device. The first is Laudate, in which (in addition to the many prayers and devotions they provide) you can also receive the daily Mass readings. The second app is Catholic Daily Reflections, which usually includes a reflection on the first reading from the Mass and also a reflection on the Gospel. These could help you in what we call *Lectio Divina*, where you pray Scripture. The app provides you with a little commentary and puts the passage into context along with key points to think about.

Fr. Trigilio: Remember, Catholic Bibles have all the inspired books of the Bible. There are forty-six books in the Old Testament, while Protestant Bibles only have thirty-nine. Both have twenty-seven books in the New Testament. The discrepancy is not that the Catholic Church added seven books, but that Martin Luther and the Protestants removed seven books. Martin Luther was a Catholic Augustinian monk before he broke from Rome and started the Protestant Reformation. Before the year 1517, there was only the Catholic Church in Europe. Hence, for 1,500 years (that is, fifteen centuries), there was one Bible and it had forty-six books in the Old Testament. When Luther started his own religion, he removed seven books for various reasons. For example, one of them was the book of Maccabees, which is the biblical foundation for the doctrine of Purgatory. Ironically, many Protestant bibles (other than the King James Version) include those seven books, but list them as Apocrypha in the back of the text.

Fr. Brighenti: And Catholicism does care about the literal sense of Sacred Scripture. That means, what do the words actually say? She demands accurate translations from Hebrew, Greek, and Latin. Literal translations (that is, formal correspondence) must sometimes yield to dynamic equivalence. Idioms and figures of speech often become difficult to understand, so a word for word translation may need to be paraphrased in very specific cases.

For example, in English we often ask, "are you pulling my leg?" A literal interpretation would mean that someone is trying to physically tug at your lower limb. The real meaning, then, is "are you trying to fool me?" Since the text itself does not always and explicitly let the reader know if he or she is to interpret literally or figuratively, it makes sense that Jesus established His Church as *the* authority to decide authentically what the text means.

Fr. Trigilio: So what you're saying, Father, is that Catholics do promote a literal sense of Scripture but not a literal interpretation exclusively to every word and phrase. In other words, the Church interprets the biblical text *faithfully*, which often is literal but sometimes is figurative. Like when Jesus says, "If your right eye causes you to sin, pluck it out and throw it away; ... And if your right hand causes you to sin, cut it off" (Matthew 5:29-30). Christianity never advocated amputating or blinding sinners. Yet, the Church does interpret Jesus' words "this is My body.... This is My blood" (Matthew 26:26-27) literally. Without a Magisterium (that is, teaching authority), it would be left to each individual person to interpret the biblical text as he saw fit. That could get messy.

Fr. Brighenti: Catholic Christians ask, what does the text *say* and what does it *mean*?

Fr. Trigilio: And as my beloved mentor and your predecessor on this show, Father Bob Levis, always used to say: "if you take the text out of context, you get a pretext." Seeing the words, phrases, sentences, paragraphs, and so on, before and after the text in question, help give proper context. Also, seeing what the other three Gospels say helps, too. Since all of Scripture (the whole Bible) is divinely inspired, then no text can contradict another text. St. Augustine said any perceived contradictions are really a mistake in the reader, not the author.[6] The Holy Spirit inspired the Sacred Authors. You and I, on our own, can come to false conclusions. That is why we need a Church founded by Christ Himself: "he who hears you, hears me" (Luke 10:16).

Fr. Brighenti: It must also be made clear that Catholicism believes Divine Revelation comes to us from God in *both* Sacred Scripture (the Bible) *and* Sacred Tradition. The biblical text never gives a list of books that belong. The publisher created a table of contents. The ancient manuscripts did not. So, how do we know there are forty-six books in the Old Testament? That there are only four Gospels (Matthew, Mark, Luke, and John)? The Church made those decisions.

Fr. Trigilio: Not to mention chapter and verse. The original manuscripts written in ancient Hebrew and Greek had no punctuation and no chapter and verse, let alone any pagination. Cardinal Stephen Langton, medieval Archbishop of Canterbury, devised the chapter numbers for the Bible in the thirteenth century. There were none before that. Thirteen centuries with no chapter identifications. Robertus Stephanus, in the sixteenth century, came up with the verse numbers in each chapter. Both were Catholics. A purist would insist there not be any chapter and verse if he totally believed in *Sola Scriptura* (scripture alone) as the text is silent on this matter. Even the word "bible" is not found even once *in* the Bible. Pope Damasus, in the fifth century, used the term *biblia* (Latin for "books," and taken from the Greek *biblos*) when St. Jerome translated all the Hebrew and Greek Scriptures into Latin and combined them

---

6   St. Augustine of Hippo, *The Harmony of The Gospels.*

into one volume (around A.D. 400). So, the Bible is actually a book of books.

Fr. Brighenti: Not every verse in the Bible has one and only one explanation. Some passages do, as in the words Jesus spoke at the Last Supper over the bread and wine. Lots of biblical texts have more than one meaning and many also remain mysterious.

33. Scripture and Tradition

Why do Catholics need Tradition in addition to Scripture? I think the Bible has all the answers in there for us to find. As 2 Timothy 3:16 says, "All scripture is inspired by God and profitable for teaching, for reproof, for correction, and for training in righteousness."

Fr. Trigilio: What you say is absolutely true in the sense that all Scripture is helpful, but nowhere in Scripture does it say that only Scripture is helpful. The phrase *"Sola Scriptura"* that Martin Luther coined in the sixteenth century is not found in Scripture. So, if Scripture was to be the only source of revelation, then I think it would have said so. We see divine revelation coming directly from God through two fonts or channels, one being Sacred Scripture and the other being Sacred Tradition. They're not in opposition to each other, and they're not in competition. It's just as Pope Benedict has said so many times throughout his pontificate: our religion is not one of *either/or*, that you have to choose Sacred Tradition over Sacred Scripture or vice versa, but it's *both/and*. Just like a coin has two sides, heads and tails, it's still one coin. So, too, divine revelation comes to us through both Sacred Scripture and Sacred Tradition. The word "bible" isn't in the Bible, so why even call it the Bible? Where in the Bible do we get the terminology of calling it a bible, or the list of what books should be in there, their arrangement, and the sequence of Matthew, Mark, Luke, and John? Why not put John before Luke in the Gospels? The Bible doesn't give us these guidelines. They came from the Church, as the Church is given guardianship of revelation and has authority over both Sacred Scripture and Sacred Tradition. Again, it's not that you have to choose one over the other, the Bible over Tradition or the Church over the two of these, as they are all established by God. We believe Jesus founded the Church and that He gave His Church the authority to interpret Scripture authentically, and it was within the confines of the Church that the message of the Bible was even given. For fifteen hundred years, people learned the Bible by going to Mass. It's only a recent phenomenon that people actually have their own copy of the Bible that they can read at home, which is a laudable opportunity today, but in early times either you weren't literate or you couldn't afford a copy of the Bible, so you went to Sunday worship and had it read to you.

Fr. Brighenti: It's also very important to note that Sacred Tradition is with a capital S and a capital T and is not to be confused with lower-case t traditions, which are manmade customs. Rather, Sacred Tradition is part of revelation that has been revealed through the Holy Spirit to the apostles, the last being St. John the Beloved. The era of public revelation then came to an end. After that, we have had refinements, which are the terminology used to describe what we believe as language develops, but they are the same doctrine and the same beliefs that were given to the apostles. Out of this oral tradition to St. John came this written Scripture, and both Scripture and Tradition work together; they're not in competition with each other but give us the full message of God's plan for us and for our salvation. If you were to shut off one of the fonts to this water, then you wouldn't receive the full message.

Fr. Trigilio: It's like how Pope Benedict and Pope St. John Paul the Great often referred to the relationship of the Western Church and the Eastern Church as breathing with two lungs. We can use that same analogy for revelation. You need both lungs, Sacred Scripture and Sacred Tradition. There's a distinction between lower-case *t* traditions which accumulate over time into what the Pharisees had, but then there's Sacred Tradition. As St. Paul says in 1 Corinthians 11:23, "For I received from the Lord what I also delivered to you." In this sense, "to deliver" is "to hand on," and in the Latin is *traditio,* from where we get the word "tradition." The apostles received the verbal words of Jesus, like at the Sermon on the Mount, yet the earliest of the Gospel records were not written down until at least A.D. 50. That's at least twenty years where everything done and taught by Christ was oral. Nothing was written down, except for maybe St. Paul's epistles.

Fr. Brighenti: It's very interesting that there are Christians who do not subscribe to Sacred Tradition, when the canon of Scripture—the books of the Bible—only came about because of Sacred Tradition. There were nearly seven hundred ghostwriters who claimed to have written the most authentic Gospels, and the Church had to decipher that Matthew, Mark, Luke, and John were the only ones inspired by the Holy Spirit. If it weren't for the Church's oral Sacred Tradition, we would not have the Canon of Scripture or the Bible as we know it today. We owe the Bible itself to our Sacred Tradition. I point this out to our non-Catholic brothers and sisters who claim only to believe in the Scriptures. Well, we hold to the Scriptures, thank God, through our Sacred Tradition.

34. Catholic Bible Translations

What is the best Bible for modern-day Catholics to use for reference and study?

Fr. Brighenti: The question alone makes a good distinction by separating reference and study Bibles from devotional Bibles. I always like to read the Douay-Rheims Bible, and especially for the Psalms, because of the way it was translated. While it's an elegant and literal translation, it's not very practical today in terms of studying, due to the language style it contains, but there are a number of excellent modern translations available. There's the Revised Standard Version Catholic Edition, which is the one I have on my shelf, and the Ignatius Bible is a great copy of this translation which includes insightful commentaries. The Navarre Bible series is excellent as well, and I use them when I prepare a homily; I find their exegesis and commentary quite helpful. Concerning reference, there's a powerful electronic study software called Verbum, which both Fr. Trigilio and I have on our computers. Logos is the parent company, and Verbum is the Catholic edition. It allows you to access all these Bible translations online, and you can delve even deeper into the scriptures by enabling Greek translations, commentaries, lectionaries, and the Lives of the Saints if it's included in your software package.

Fr. Trigilio: At one time, there was the option to use several of the translations that the publishers offered, including the Jerusalem Bible and the Revised Standard Version, but now the liturgy is exclusively done with the New American Bible. This means that if you use the Revised Standard Version Catholic Edition, or what they call the Ignatius Bible, the Jerusalem Bible, the Douay-Rheims, or the Knox Bible, some of the words are going to vary with the readings. But these translations can still be excellent tools for study, reference, or devotional purposes. Archbishop Fulton Sheen used to rely on the New English Bible for his personal study. Fr. Brighenti and I like the Douay-Rheims Bible for the Psalms as well as for the Gospels, because it makes some of those phrases stand out and resonate with us so much more. I remember when I was in minor seminary and read when Jesus was confronted by the high priest who asked, "I adjure thee by the living God, that thou tell us if thou be the Christ the Son of God." And Jesus said, "Thou hast said it" (Matthew 26:63-64).[7] This translation gives formality to the text, but not everyone may like that; as the Latin saying goes, *"De gustibus non disputandum est,"* which means "There's no argument in taste." You may prefer the New American Bible, someone else the Douay-Rheims, and another fellow may like the Jerusalem Bible, which is the translation Mother Angelica used when she had her TV show.

Fr. Brighenti: The Jerusalem Bible was actually translated from French, too.

Fr. Trigilio: If you want to expand your horizons, get familiar with the other Catholic translations, and start dabbling with some of these interlinear translations that have the Greek or Latin text with the English underneath. It's not that you'll be able to read Greek fluently, but you'll get a better sense of the words. In the software, you just hover your cursor over a Latin or Greek word and it will tell you what the word means.

Fr. Brighenti: Verbum is a fairly economical software, too, especially if you're studying. If you're a student taking Scripture

---

[7] From the Douay-Rheims Bible.

classes, this would probably be an excellent package to consider. I like to use the Douay-Rheims Bible for *Lectio Divina*, which means "Divine Lesson," and it's a form of prayer where we meditate on passages from the Gospels. The Douay-Rheims is sometimes very expressive in the English language, so it lends to the meditation, and after a quiet moment of contemplation to let the Lord speak to you, you finish with a devotional prayer. For preparing homilies or for studying purposes, I think the Revised Standard Version Catholic Edition, or the Ignatius Bible, and the Navarre Bible series are the best options.

Fr. Trigilio: A quick point on the Latin: while most people may be a little shy of the Vulgate because they can't read Latin, it's the original text that St. Jerome translated from the Old and New Testaments in the year A.D. 400, and reading it is not limited to clergy and seminarians. Many people are adept at languages, and there are some very memorable lines, like when Jesus is confronted by Mary Magdalene, and He says, *"Noli Me tangere,"* or "Don't cling to me" as just a Teacher. Again, some of these phrases in either the Old English or in the Latin stick in your mind, and Fr. Rutler is famous for giving these wonderful Latin quotes from Scripture. They stand out there and grab your attention. The common language is good, too, and that's why the Bible has been translated into the vernacular tongue. Some things I stay away from though are those cutesy, watered-down translations for the modern man that change the text and sometimes make Jesus appear like a hippie. You want an authentic text that's been approved by the Catholic Church and is true to the original text. The New American Bible, the Jerusalem Bible, and the Revised Standard Version Catholic Edition are the three main Catholic translations that are available to you.

35. Name Changes in the Bible

Why did the names of certain apostles change in the New Testament?

Fr. Trigilio: Even in the Old Testament, we have the instances where God changed Abram's name to Abraham, Sarai to Sarah, and Jacob to Israel. In the New Testament, this doesn't happen nearly as often, but we still have Jesus saying to Simon, "And I tell you, you are Peter, and on this rock I will build my church" (Matthew 16:18). Saul of Tarsus was also later called Paul. But beyond those two, there aren't many other times in the New Testament where names are changed. Usually, when there's a name change in the Bible, it marks the start of a new mission. Abraham and Sarah had become the patriarch and matriarch of a new nation; Saul was going to become an apostle; and Peter became the first pope of the Catholic Church. There are subtle name changes in the Bible, too, as some of the characters were called by different names, such as Bartholomew, who has also been identified as Nathanael, the latter being a Hebrew name and the former a Greek one. The Gospel of Mark was written by Mark, but his technical name was John Mark. However, he went by Mark, as he was writing for a Roman audience, and Marcus was certainly more of a Roman name than John.

Fr. Brighenti: There were also the missionaries Simon and Jude, possibly identified with Thaddeus.

Fr. Trigilio: People will also confuse Judas Iscariot with another apostle named Judas, the son of James, and there are then James the Lesser and James the Greater, but the changing of the names generally indicates a new mission. That's why the popes have maintained the custom of changing their names, though they don't have to; but this has been the practice for over one thousand years. In ancient times, the first pope to change his name did so because he deemed his former name of Mercury as too pagan.

Fr. Brighenti: It's inspiring to consider the signal of a new mission, like Peter, of course, whose mission was to be the head of the Church. Paul had a great conversion and went from Saul to Paul, and his mission was to be an evangelist. Those two are very important, as they are the Pillars of the Church. It's also interesting that their relics were found together under St. Peter's Basilica. Paul's relics were then transferred to the Basilica of St. Paul Outside the Walls, where he had been martyred. It was in 1947 when Pope Pius XII encouraged the excavation underneath St. Peter's baldachin where they found these relics, and where St. Peter and St. Paul were both buried. There was a red wall down there with writing upon it that said, "Here are the remains of Peter and Paul." In the ninth century, a church had been built over the location, and in the fifteenth century another church had been built over that one. It was always commonly believed that Sts. Peter and Paul were buried under the baldachin, and that's exactly where they found them. You can book the Scavi Tour today and explore the excavation site. They only take twelve people at a time, and it's simply fascinating.

36. Gospel Witnesses

There are a number of instances recorded in the Gospels where there were no witnesses besides the individual to whom an event was happening. Three of these happenings are when Jesus was alone in the desert being tempted by the devil; when the angel Gabriel appeared to Mary to tell her she was going to bear the Christ Child; and when an angel appeared to Joseph in his sleep to tell him that Mary was going to have a baby conceived by the Holy Spirit and that His name would be Jesus. How do biblical scholars explain how these events were made known to the authors of the Gospels?

Fr. Trigilio: In a world revolving around social media, people are so used to videos going viral and things being tweeted or shared on Facebook as soon as they happen. We're so accustomed to seeing and hearing about things right away, but this was not the case in ancient times. People first heard news by word of mouth, because it took a while for the bearers of news to get around. It was told to one person, who told another person, who then told another person. That being the case, when the Sacred Authors wrote the Gospels, we believe they were led by the inspiration of the Holy Spirit. When you read the Church documents, they firmly teach of a process of how this took place. At first, Jesus said and did these things. Oral tradition then took place where people told each other. Most of the things that St. Paul knew about Jesus, for example, he had received from second-hand sources. Then came the actual writing of the sacred texts. When we read these things today, like about Jesus being tempted in the desert, of course we realize no one else was there to witness the event. But Jesus was there, and He must've then told His apostles, who told others. Bear in mind that St. John writes that not everything Jesus said and did is contained in Scripture. I can imagine Jesus and His disciples sitting around the campfire one night, and Him telling them about various things that had happened. Then later on, Matthew, Mark, Luke, and John wrote these things down under the inspiration of the Holy Spirit. Luke wasn't an apostle, but he probably got the information from the Blessed Mother, and Mark probably got it from St. Peter. This is how the Gospels came to be. They didn't come about the same way news is transmitted today.

Fr. Brighenti: It's crucial that we don't read the Bible as we would read a particular genre in its linear format. Today, we read a newspaper as a newspaper, a novel as a novel, and a history book as a history book. The Bible, however, includes several types of genre, as there are many ways to convey the message of truth. It's not a history book by our modern understanding, but it's a book of salvation history. The Bible includes historical events, but relaying history is not its primary role. It's the events for our salvation that are important. Yet while it may not be a historical account, everything that is recorded in the Bible is given under the umbrella of the Holy Spirit's inspiration, and it is therefore both accurate and valid. That is an important thing to remember, even though there may be some minor differences among the four Gospels.

Fr. Trigilio: When we were in the seminary, Fr. Heidt was teaching us Scripture, and he said it's like when our grandparents came over from the old country and we asked them their story. We would ask, how did they come over here? They'll tell us a story about being on the boat. The story is accurate, as this is how it happened, but there are going to be a lot of details they had to account for and fill in the blanks. Was it on a Sunday or a Monday, spring or winter when they left the old country? That's irrelevant. What's important is that they left the old country and came to the new world. Who was with them? Who wasn't? A lot of the little details, like what they had for lunch, are not critical and won't be remembered so many decades later. However, they might say they ate macaroni for lunch, because that's what most people consumed while they were over there. Sometimes people get so absorbed into the little details while missing the big picture. *Every word of Scripture is inspired*, and the Bible is both infallible and inerrant. But the inerrancy of Scripture only means that it doesn't contradict the Faith. This doesn't mean that everything in the Bible is to be taken in a literal context. For example, we are not to believe that the sun revolves around the earth simply because the Bible says that the sun rises and sets. The point of the sun rising and setting in Scripture is not to teach us cosmology, science, or astronomy; it's to say that God's love is timeless. It should be noted, however, that even today we still use the terms "sunset" and "sunrise" when the sun doesn't do either. It's a figure of speech and not meant to be taken literally.

37. "Extra Books" in the Catholic Bible

What is the difference between the Catholic and Protestant Bibles? The Catholic Bible contains additional books in the Old Testament. Can you tell me when and why these books were added, or when and why they were removed?

Fr. Brighenti: For the bulk of Christian history, there was only one Bible, and it was the Catholic Church that compiled the biblical canon, including the Old and New Testaments. It wasn't until the Protestant Revolt in the sixteenth century that this canon was challenged and these "additional" books were taken out. Part of the reason as to why the Catholic Church has the fuller account of Scripture is because we use the Septuagint, which is a Greek copy of the Old Testament, and it includes more books in the Old Testament. The Protestant Bible uses what they call the Hebrew Scriptures, which is a shorter version.

Fr. Trigilio: Now, some people might hear this and wonder why we gravitate toward the Greek text when Christianity descended from the Hebrew religion. What they forget is that in the third century B.C., two-thirds of the world's Jews were scattered during what's called the *diaspora*. They were in exile, and only one-third were left in the Holy Land at that time. Over the course of three hundred years, the Jews were no longer able to read or speak Hebrew anymore because it was against the law; but they were fluent in Greek, which was the *lingua franca* (that is to say, the common language) at the time. The seven additional books found in the Catholic Bible were written at this time when most of the Jews were dispersed from the Holy Land. The Jewish faith accepted these books as inspired, and these are books that the Jews were reading at the time of Jesus Christ. So naturally, the first Christians also read and treated them as the inspired Word of God. The entire Old Testament, including these seven additional books, were carried straight over to Christianity. It wasn't until A.D. 70 when Jewish theologians removed those books, after Christianity had become an independent religion and the temple in Jerusalem was destroyed by the Romans. The Jews wanted to expunge anything that was not purely Jewish or Hebrew. By this time, Christianity had already separated and accepted the full list of the Old Testament books, which were known by Our Savior and quoted from by the Church Fathers. There was only one Christian Bible, including these seven books in question. Then came the Protestant Revolt one-and-a-half millennia later, where Martin Luther chose to use the newer, shorter list of Old Testament books, simply because he didn't agree with the Book of Maccabees.

Fr. Brighenti: The reason why Martin Luther didn't care for the Book of Maccabees was because it includes a reference to our doctrine of Purgatory. In this book, Judas Maccabeus had an expiatory sacrifice offered in the temple for the dead Jewish soldiers who were found with pagan amulets on their possession, picked up on the fields of victory following previous battles. It was forbidden in Jewish law to possess these amulets, so Judas had this sacrifice offered, which involved praying for the dead. This is where we get our doctrine on Purgatory, but it was something that Martin Luther didn't go for.

Fr. Trigilio: Yet as an Augustinian monk, he knew there was this other list, even though it was not the list used by Christians for the first fifteen hundred years. The Gutenberg Bible, one of the earliest printed Bibles, contained all forty-six books in the Old Testament, just as we have in the Catholic Bible today. In fact, even the first King James Version of the Bible included those seven books in the back, even though the Protestants called them the "apocrypha." It was only after an act of parliament that they were completely removed from Protestant Bibles. However, the fact that the Protestants were hesitant to pull them out beforehand reveals that they were not totally convinced that these books weren't inspired. Except for today's King James Version, you may even find the "apocrypha" included in the back of some modern Protestant Bibles.

38. Finding Faith in a Broken World

I am a man who works in the streets, and I see all the despair and danger. I have been away from the Church for many years, and now I am trying to find true faith. It is difficult for me, because all I see is the worst in man, and it is impossible for me to trust anyone. What can I do to find true faith?

Fr. Brighenti: First of all, what a beautiful thing you are doing by helping the underprivileged in our society. You are indeed in contact every day with the raw reality of sin in our world and the effects of peoples' sin in the lives of others, yet you're cooperating with grace at that moment as you help these people and bring hope through the light of Christ into their hearts. The important thing to remember is that true faith is given to us by Our Lord, and we receive that in Baptism. This is embodied in our Catholic Faith, as we profess the four marks of the True Church of Christ in our Creed as "one, holy, catholic, and apostolic." By your very question, I think you're researching to come back home, which is our Faith, and I encourage you to develop your interior life, because if we just do works of charity without involving our Faith, then we become no more than a social worker. But when our works of charity flow from the faith of our spiritual life, it's God's working through us to reach other people. A great book I recommend is *The Soul of the Apostolate*, by Jean-Baptiste Chautard, and it talks about the interior life and the importance of prayer to God and the flowing out of that prayer into our works of charity. You see this represented most beautifully in Mother Teresa's religious sisters, who have to make a Holy Hour before going out into Calcutta or Newark or wherever they're stationed to meet these people who are despairing on the streets. The sisters bring their faith, and God works through them to alleviate the suffering so powerfully that the people feel as if they've been touched by the Lord in those works of charity. That becomes a lively faith. So, you're on the right path, but I encourage you to plunge deeper and explore your Catholic Faith in its fullness.

Fr. Trigilio: One thing that can be quite helpful is knowing that the Church looks at faith in a very specific way as an act of the intellect. It's accepting intellectually what God has revealed, and it's considered a form of knowledge. It's not rational knowledge in the sense that we reason on our own, but it's theologically accepted because of Who has revealed Himself. Whereas the act of charity, sometimes called love, is a function of the will. Love is faith put into action. There's philosophical truth but then there's also theological truth, and it's the goal of every Christian to know the truth and put that faith into action by performing acts of love and charity.

Fr. Brighenti: St. James tells us so clearly in his letter that faith without works is a faith that is dead (James 2:26). In other words, our faith has to be alive through the corporal and spiritual works of mercy, and the man who posed this question appears to already be doing the corporal works of mercy. He now needs the nourishment to continue to work in these difficult situations, and that only comes from the Lord, from the Sacred Word, and from the Holy Eucharist. These will fortify you and everyone else to meet the obstacles they will have in this life. As Jesus says in the Gospel of Matthew, "But he who endures to the end will be saved" (Matthew 24:13).

Fr. Trigilio: Even though you've seen a lot of the dark side of human nature, there is also the light side. God never ordains evil, but He permits it so that a greater good can come from it. When there is a natural disaster or tragedy or when there is an act of evil committed by man, there are always some people who do nothing, or even some who participate, but there are also those who come to the plate and do good. Pope St. John Paul II often said that one does not conquer evil with evil; one overcomes evil by doing good. The terrorist attack on 9/11 was a horrible act of human evil. We also saw great bravery and heroism among the first responders, the firefighters, and the police.

39. The Consciousness of Christ

Did Jesus always know that He was God?

Fr. Trigilio: In one sentence, you spoke volumes. This is a question which theologians really had to battle with in the Ancient

Church; what was the knowledge of Christ? Jesus Christ is the Second Person of the Holy Trinity, but He has two natures: a human nature and a divine nature. Therefore, He has a human intellect and a divine intellect. In His divine intellect, He knows everything that God the Father knows and everything God the Holy Spirit knows, because all three share the same intellect that knows everything. His human intellect is finite by definition, because it's created and is still a human intellect that's united to His divine Person. The Church infallibly defined at the Council of Chalcedon that Christ has two natures, human and divine, hypostatically united to His one divine Person. Each nature has an intellect and will. Hence, Jesus has a divine intellect and a divine will, and He has a human intellect and a human will.

Even though Jesus has a human intellect and a divine intellect, this doesn't mean He has a split personality. He didn't have an identity crisis. He did not "discover" Who He was, as He's always known. We see this when Mary and Joseph found Him in the temple when He was twelve years old, and He said, "How is it that you sought me? Did you not know that I must be in my Father's house?" (Luke 2:49). He already knew what He was doing: His Father's business. Who was His Father? He was obviously talking about God the Father. He wasn't dissenting from Joseph, His foster father, but He was showing His consciousness. Fr. William Most wrote a most beautiful, succinct, and easy-to-read book called *The Consciousness of Christ* which explains the human knowledge of Jesus in His divine Personhood.

Fr. Brighenti: When we were going to seminary back in the 1980s, there was this awful time in Christology where they had the theology from "below" (low Christology) and theology from "above" (high Christology) and all this nonsense. Holy Mother

Church teaches us that we must believe that Jesus was and is true God and true Man. He has a full divine nature and a full human nature. Neither a fifty-fifty nor a hybrid, He is mysteriously fully both at the same time. Low Christology over-emphasizes the human nature and in some cases even proposes weaknesses like concupiscence. Some of these "theologians" maintain Jesus had a wounded human nature with a darkened intellect, weakened will, and disordered lower passions.

Fr. Trigilio: Adam and Eve, after the Fall, and all their descendants (that is, the human race) had such a wounded nature, but Jesus was preserved from Original Sin because of the Incarnation and the Immaculate Conception. That preserved His humanity. Arianism is the heresy that Jesus Christ only shared a similar but not the same divine nature as God the Father. It falsely taught that Christ was adopted by divinity.

Fr. Brighenti: Likewise, High Christology over-emphasizes the divine nature and makes Our Lord's humanity more like pretending, as is erroneously taught by the heresy of Docetism. The first seven centuries of the ecumenical councils dealt with these and other Christological heresies, so I don't know why they had to rehash them in different terms. The hypostatic union consists of one divine Person in human and divine nature, so what Our Lord chose to learn in His sacred humanity, He already knew in His divinity.

40. The Beginning of God

When did God begin? If He is eternal, how did He have a beginning? If He didn't have a beginning, how does He exist?

Fr. Trigilio: I think whoever posed this question is going to be a good lawyer someday, because it's apparent he's got a keen mind.

At first glance, it may seem confusing and almost contradictory, but when we say God is eternal, we mean He has no beginning or end. That is because He exists outside of time and space, and He is the source of all being. He is the cause of why everything is, and if there were no God, then there would be nothing. Things cannot exist by themselves, so there must be a Creator. We listen to scientists today tell us the age of the universe. Well, the age of the universe tells you there had to have been a beginning, a time when there was the universe and then a time when there was not the universe, otherwise you cannot ascribe an age. You can't say it's forty billion years old, because what are you counting if there's no beginning? With God, because He is pure spirit, intellect and will, He can't have a beginning or an end; He is the source of being itself. If there were a time when there was no God, then how did He become God? Who created God? There would have to be another supreme being. You can't have an infinite regression, because that would contradict the laws of logic. Outside the created universe, there must be something else, an intelligent designer who sets these things in motion but also keeps them going. God's divine providence, being in and of itself, sustains everything. St. Thomas Aquinas, the thirteenth-century philosopher and theologian extraordinaire, explained that God, as the Supreme Being, is the Uncaused Cause, the Cause of all Causes, the Necessary Being, and Prime Mover.[8] He has no beginning since He is the Creator and is the source of being (that is, existence itself).

Fr. Brighenti: Consider the simple liturgical prayer: "Glory be to the Father, and to the Son, and to the Holy Ghost; as it was

---

[8] *Summa Theologica*, I, q. 1, arts. 1, 2; q. 4, art. 26; q. 45, art. 7.

in the beginning, is now, and ever shall be: world without end."
This certainly speaks to our belief in God's eternal being. It should
also be mentioned that our human language falls despairingly
short to describe the divine. Therefore, we can only speak in
analogies to convey what we believe concerning such. However,
our articles of faith are all reasonable. While we may not be
fully able to explain them in our limited human vocabulary, our
articles make rational sense to the human mind, because God
can neither deceive nor be deceived.

41. Death and Suffering

I know God is my Lord and Savior, but for the last three years my
health has been in steady decline. I recently got diagnosed with irrevers-
ible kidney failure and severe anemia as a consequence. I am having
a very difficult time finding blood donors. I know God can and has
done great miracles for many people, but how can I keep and grow in
my faith when the odds are so greatly against me? If it is His will for
me to die in this life, then how can I prepare myself for that day and
be ready for His calling?

Fr. Trigilio: This is a very profound question, and we will certainly keep you in our prayers as you carry these heavy crosses.
Speaking from personal experience as a priest and in my own
family, there are many times where innocent people suffer. I
had a brother with muscular dystrophy and he only lived to be
twenty-six years old, and there are then the various illnesses that
afflicted my parents. There's a choice that's made when people
are suffering, and it's not just whether to offer it up; it's also if
you allow this suffering to transform you. When you visit people
in the hospital as a priest, you can see the difference. There are
people who become bitter, resent God, and are mad at the world

because they feel that an injustice has been done to them. "Why did it have to happen to me?" they ask. "Why aren't I getting better? How come other people have these miraculous cures or timely donors?" Then there's that other person who says, "Thy will be done. If it's God's will I get better, then I'm certainly asking for it. But if not, then I will bear this cross with dignity and respect." These are the people who ask you how things are going, or they'll want to have a conversation, and not just about their aches and pains. There are then those people who don't want to complain but at least want to share. They'll say, "Father, I'm having a rough day." You listen to them tell you what went wrong that day. Instead of thinking, "Oh, no! Here comes another litany of aches and pains," you just let them know that somebody cares. Sometimes that's all they need, because the doctor and nurses are too busy, and the family members aren't present. So, by being an ear, you can be transformative, because once they get it out there, they can look at their sufferings and say, "You know what? Despite what I'm going through, when I look at the Cross, I know my suffering is nothing compared to His."

Fr. Brighenti: The question mentions miracles, and I think this person is seeking guidance in regard to those. We are still in the time of miracles, and they take place all the time in Lourdes, France, and Fátima, Portugal, and even here at home. Miracles aren't just for the person receiving one, but they're for everyone, as miracles are a testimony that God is with us and is trying to ignite the Faith in people. A healing miracle has not only a private reason, but is part of a broader issue of why it took place, and it's usually to encourage the faithful. God often works through the intercession of the saints in Heaven, and their initial miracles are confirmed by the Church for canonization. There are very specific requirements for miracles that are used for the beatification ceremony and canonization: there can be no other reason under the laws of nature as to why something miraculous, such as a cure, took place; and it has to be immediate. This doesn't mean, however, that other miracles do not take place in our lives through the intercession of the saints. There's a very inspiring book I highly recommend called *Nothing Short of a Miracle* by Patricia Treece. She takes a look at twenty of the most popular saints or those who are on the path to sainthood, some of whom are in our own country, and there are interviews with people who've had a miracle happen to them or one of their family members, and the stories they tell are those that brought reassurance to their faith. Another wonderful book is *Arise from Darkness* by Fr. Benedict Groeschel, CFR, which deals with human suffering.

Fr. Trigilio: The miracles involved in the canonization process of the saints are incredible stories themselves. I did a little research into the miracles accredited to St. Juan Diego. In one case, a very devout and pious woman had a son who was suicidal and abusing drugs. One day, he either fell or jumped out a window and smacked head-first into the pavement and wasn't expected to live. His mother prayed to Juan Diego, who was the one that Mary appeared to in Guadalupe, and her son was immediately and miraculously cured. You might wonder why this individual was picked to receive a miracle, and since his mother was very religious, you might figure it was only natural her prayers would be heard. But in reality, God chooses, and it's not because He doesn't love those of us who don't receive miracles. When you think of all the people Jesus healed, keep in mind that there were plenty who didn't get healed. We tend to focus on the paralyzed man who was lowered through the ceiling, but what about the people who didn't make it into the Gospel account? There might have been people right next door who were still blind or deaf and didn't get healed. Why not? We don't know.

Fr. Brighenti: Sometimes, the miracle itself is perseverance, or the strength to carry your cross in that time of tribulation, and even people who go to Lourdes will come back saying they didn't receive a physical cure but a spiritual one. They'll tell you that they feel so much stronger in their fight, encouraged that they can bring their sufferings to the Cross and not lose heart and fall into despair. The life of Pope St. John Paul II is such an incredible example for us. Here's a man who suffered to the bitter end with Parkinson's disease and other complications, and while he never experienced a healing miracle to alleviate his struggles, he was undoubtedly given the miracle of perseverance; and what a wonderful teaching he gave to us all. These physical miracles are certainly there to inspire us, but sometimes the miracle might be of holy perseverance.

Fr. Trigilio: I was thinking of our friends, Fred and Maryanne Fisher, who take wounded soldiers to Lourdes. Some of them receive miraculous healings, while others find the perseverance to carry on. They get the integrity restored in their lives, which have otherwise been turned upside-down. Everyone who goes to Lourdes comes back a better person, whether they're physically healed or not, and that's why I always encourage people to visit a place like Lourdes or Fátima, if they can. If it's too far or too expensive for you, they have these "virtual pilgrimages" where they'll bring you a whole setup with videos and slides you can watch, and it's to the point it almost feels like you're there in person. It's similar to how St. Francis of Assisi designed the Stations of the Cross for people who couldn't make it to the Holy Land.

Fr. Brighenti: Another kind of miracle we see in the lives of the suffering is the encouragement they bring to others to engage in works of charity. There was one wounded warrior on Staten Island who needed a handicap ramp and a special pool to swim in, yet he didn't have the money for either of these things. Well, the whole community came together and fundraised for this person. It was a very beautiful and inspirational event; this one fellow changed the lives of so many through his suffering. Never underestimate the power of your perseverance, the power of your suffering, and the power of your cross. Also, read about the lives of some of these wonderful saints, as they will inspire you and give you the strength to carry on, and hopefully their intercession will make the crosses you bear a little lighter.

42. Being Catholic Is Being Christian

I am a Christian who is very lost, and I want to explore the Catholic Church. What are the key differences between being a Christian and being a Catholic?

Fr. Brighenti: I hope it's not a shock to anyone out there, but Catholics *are* Christians. As we profess in the Creed every Sunday, the Church is "one, holy, catholic, and apostolic." The word "catholic" means universal, as the Catholic Church is meant for all time, and it will be here until the end of time, as Jesus said, "and the powers of death shall not prevail against it" (Matthew 16:18). The Church is the vehicle and means for our salvation. It is missionary, meaning we go out to the ends of the earth, as Jesus also instructed us to baptize all nations. In every sense of the word, Catholics are Christians, because we believe in Jesus Christ. However, in our contemporary milieu, many use "Christian" to denote Protestants, and "Catholic" has become a specific title to refer to Roman Catholics. All Christians (Catholic, Protestant, and Eastern Orthodox) who are baptized in the name of the Father and of the Son and of the Holy Spirit are members of the Catholic Church, though they may not be in full communion with it.

Fr. Trigilio: Many don't realize that they're part of the Catholic Church, but that doesn't change the fact that they are. When it comes to being a Christian and a Catholic, it's never a question of either/or but both/and, as we often say. And we don't see it as if Catholic Christians are right and Protestant Christians are wrong. Rather, it is that Catholicism has the fullness of grace (all seven sacraments), the fullness of truth (Sacred Scripture and Sacred Tradition), under the leadership of one shepherd (the pope). Protestantism has some of the truth (the Bible) and some of sacramental grace (Baptism and Matrimony) and they have local shepherds (pastors). That is why we refer to a Protestant Christian becoming a Catholic Christian as being "brought into full communion."

43. The Difference Between Catholics and Protestants

What is the difference between Christians, Catholics, and Baptists? Aren't they all children of God? Why do you have to be brought up in the Catholic Church?

Fr. Brighenti: First of all, I think it should be noted that Catholics are Christians.

Fr. Trigilio: We need to dispel that one right there.

Fr. Brighenti: There's no competition between the two. The word "catholic" has the understanding of universality, and it came into use during the first few centuries in the Church. The term in no way ever took the place of "Christian." Catholics are Christians, and I know for a lot of non-Catholics this can be a big shock. In fact, Catholics are the first Christians, and within our communion we have the four marks of the true Church, "one, holy, catholic, and apostolic," all of which reside and exist in the Catholic Church. Baptists consist of various denominations who have broken away from the Protestant Church, which eventually ties its own roots with breaking away from the Catholic Church. If a Baptist receives Baptism with the correct, Trinitarian formula which includes the words, "I baptize you in the name of the Father and of the Son and of the Holy Spirit," and water is placed on them in a threefold fashion, then they become members of the Church, although they are not in full communion. When a validly baptized person wants to become a Catholic, we call that becoming in full communion as opposed to saying they want to convert. A convert would be someone who has not been baptized and is coming into the Church, but if a non-Catholic denomination doesn't baptize with the valid formula, then we have to baptize the people coming into the Church from that denomination. Usually your baptismal certificate will say if you've been baptized under the right formula, and we know in the case of Baptists, they generally don't get baptized until they're teenagers or older.

Fr. Trigilio: The question asks why we need to be brought up in the Catholic Church, and I think Pope Benedict and Pope St. John Paul the Great made it very clear that while we believe the Catholic Church is the One True Church, there are people who, through no fault of their own, aren't aware of this truth. It is still through Christ and through the Church that people are saved, but they may not realize that they are part of the Catholic

Church when properly baptized. This might be a poor analogy, but if you're living in one of the fifty states but don't know there is such a thing as the United States of America, you're still a part of it whether you realize it or not. Your recognition of it doesn't determine the reality. This same rule applies to being a part of the Catholic Church, and there are many people who are anonymous members of it, meaning they are unaware of their membership. It's Christ through His Church Who gives us the grace we receive at Baptism, as long as it's valid. That's why we are not allowed to re-baptize anyone coming in from a non-Catholic denomination that uses the Trinitarian formula.

Fr. Brighenti: Let's also address conditional Baptism, as this question comes up from time to time.

Fr. Trigilio: If you're in the RCIA (Rite of Christian Initiation of Adults) process, sometimes a conditional Baptism is required for those who may have been baptized but possess no documentation to prove it, or if there's a question concerning the validity of their Baptism, because maybe the pastor didn't use water or didn't use the Trinitarian formula or only put water on your foot and not your head. In this case, the priest or deacon would say, "If you are not yet baptized, I baptize you." He has to include that conditional word "if." Now, if you've got a baptismal certificate and can vouch for the fact that you were properly baptized under the Trinitarian formula, as shared by Methodists, Baptists, Presbyterians, and Episcopalians to name a few, then your Baptism is valid. This is why we don't call people catechumens who are coming into the Church from these denominations. These are separated Christians who are coming into full communion. With a valid Baptism, they at least have partial communion with the Catholic Church.

Fr. Brighenti: In a nutshell, this is why you want to be brought up in the Catholic Church, because you will have full communion; the fullness of revelation, grace, and truth. Christ is Our Head, and we are the Mystical Body.

44. Catholics Are Christians

Are Catholics really Christian? A Southern Baptist friend in college said she honestly didn't know that Catholics were Christians. Pentecostals and charismatics teach that you must be "born again" in the Holy Spirit. How do we meet the requirements to be considered Christian?

Fr. Trigilio: This is a common question that particularly comes up for young Catholics who go to college and meet Christians of various Protestant denominations who, as soon as they learn you're Catholic, will say you're not Christian. This attitude stems from a misnomer. Technically speaking, someone who professes that Jesus Christ is the Son of God; believes in the Trinity (that God is one God in three Persons: the Father, Son, and Holy Spirit); and is baptized is *de facto* a Christian. Christianity is the belief in the Triune God, and specifically in the divinity of Jesus Christ. This is something unique to Christianity. It distinguishes us from Judaism and Islam, which are the two other major monotheistic religions. Within Christianity, there is Catholicism, Eastern Orthodoxy, and Protestantism. Catholic Christians and Protestant Christians share the same belief in the Holy Trinity and that Jesus Christ is the Son of God, but we deviate on several other issues, including the seven sacraments. We, as Catholics, firmly believe that Jesus Christ founded His Church on the rock of St. Peter, the first pope. We believe in the teaching authority of the Church, which is called the Magisterium. We believe in the intercession of the saints and the Blessed Virgin

Mary, and we believe in the Marian dogmas. People talk about being born again; Catholic Christians are born again through Baptism. Nicodemus had asked Jesus in the Bible how a man can be born again, and Jesus said to him, "Truly, truly, I say to you, unless one is born of water and the Spirit, he cannot enter the kingdom of God" (John 3:5). When the priest or deacon pours the water at Baptism and says the words, "I baptize you in the name of the Father and of the Son and of the Holy Spirit," we believe that's when a person is literally regenerated and becomes a child of God, although they will later need to assimilate the Faith. In the Protestant tradition, there's this conviction that when you personally accept Jesus as your Lord and Savior, this is the beginning of being born again. We, as Catholic Christians, certainly want people to accept Jesus as their Lord and Savior, but we don't make that the pivotal moment in our lives. We believe that the moment of salvation takes place at Baptism and that it must be continued.

Fr. Brighenti: Fr. Sullivan taught us theology in the seminary, and he would use his famous line: "What is conversion? It's turning away from sin and turning back toward God." Sin is turning away from God (*aversio a Deo*) and turning toward a thing instead (*conversio ad creaturam*). That's a lifetime process and thank God we have the sacraments to help us along the way, as well as the doctrines of our Faith and the intercession of the saints. Now, the question at hand made a reference to Pentecostals and charismatics. Pentecostalism is a division of Protestantism. They are charismatic in their worship, where they become "slain in the Spirit," so to speak, and they're very vivid in their prayer life. There are also Catholic charismatics, who are in full communion with the Catholic Church. The Catholic Church is a large

Church, and we have many different expressions of our Faith. When I was pastor in an Italian parish, we had processions of the saints through the streets and various litanies and novenas, as was tradition in our parish. I was also assigned as an associate to a parish that was more charismatic in nature, and they had "healing Masses" where people would come up to the priest to be prayed over, and many of them experienced being "slain in the Spirit" and so on.

Fr. Trigilio: Now, where does the word "charismatic" come from?

Fr. Brighenti: It comes from the Holy Spirit, as we receive the gifts (charisms) of the Holy Spirit at Baptism, and they're then strengthened in Confirmation. They're called charisms, and they're the seven gifts of the Holy Spirit (Wisdom, Understanding, Counsel, Fortitude, Knowledge, Piety, and Fear of the Lord) that are there to help us in our daily conversion as we turn away from sin and turn toward God. The Church has been guided by the Holy Spirit from Pentecost Sunday to our present time, giving us these gifts to help us on our spiritual journey toward Heaven.

45. The Roots of the Catholic Church

I am currently a history student in college and have been searching for answers on Christian history. Being Christian, I realize that my real roots are from the Catholic Church, and I want to know more about these roots. When was the Church first called the "Catholic" Church, and what does this term mean?

Fr. Brighenti: I always get a little chuckle when people insist Catholics aren't Christians. The Catholic Church has existed since the time of the apostles, and we are disciples of Christ. Obviously, we are Christians as well, and that's a term we've always used. There were other terms in the Early Church, as the Church Fathers mentioned the Church being called "the Way" for many years, but let's look at the Nicene Creed, which includes the words "I believe in one holy, catholic, and apostolic Church." This term has persisted from a very ancient time and was refortified in the Nicene-Constantinopolitan Creed, which we profess at Mass on Sundays and on holy days of obligation. The word "catholic" means universal, as the Church's mission is universal. St. Ignatius of Antioch, in A.D. 100, was the first to use the word "Catholic" formally, but the concept of a universal Christian Church originates with Christ Himself when He sent the Apostles to preach to all the nations. The Catholic Church is for the salvation of souls. It's not a particular ethnic group, and it's not a particular time or place, as we've seen plenty of other churches splinter off from the Catholic Church that have flourished for a spell in limited areas before dying off. Catholic means universal, and we can be found on all seven continents. The Great Commission to go out into all the world has really taken effect. There is also the universality of the Church, considering that when you go to Mass in the United States or in Rome, although the language may differ, the structure of the Mass can still be observed and followed along in your own language in your Missal.

Fr. Trigilio: It's important to point out that just because a word comes into use later on, this doesn't mean that the thing it refers to didn't exist prior to the word. For instance, Jesus never used the word "sacrament," but we believe that He instituted the seven sacraments, and we can trace all seven of them back to the Scriptures. While Jesus didn't use the word "sacrament," the Church gave that name to the sacred rituals that Jesus Himself intended.

Fr. Brighenti: The Trinity is a good example of this as well.

Fr. Trigilio: The terms for both the Trinity and the Bible are not found in Scripture, and I always point this out to our Protestant brethren. They'll then say, "Well, the Church came up with these words later on." Exactly! The Church came up with the word "Bible" to describe the Scriptures in the fourth century when St. Jerome, in A.D. 400, put together for the first time a one-volume collection of the Old and New Testament in one language. He translated the Hebrew and the Greek into Latin, and they used the term "Bible" from the Greek word *biblos*, which means a collection of books, and the term stuck. But it wasn't the text itself that instructed us to call this collection of books "the Bible" any more than Jesus told us to call these sacred rituals "the sacraments." Things often exist prior to the ascribing of a particular name. The Catholic Church existed before it was called Catholic.

Fr. Brighenti: Catholic refers to one of the four marks of the True Church of Jesus Christ, as we mentioned in the Creed, "one holy, catholic, and apostolic Church."

46. Jesus' Birthday

Was Jesus really born on December 25? I always hear different answers. Either the Church doesn't know, or the Church just set that date as His birth.

Fr. Brighenti: This is a great question, and believe it or not, it's asked in many different situations, either in the RCIA (Rite of Christian Initiation for Adults) process or in religious education programs for children.

Fr. Trigilio: Or when you're Christmas shopping.

Fr. Brighenti: That, too! Now, we don't really know the exact date of Christ's birth. The early Christians highlighted the Easter season for the first few centuries, and it was only later on that Christians also wanted to highlight the birth of the Savior. They used December 25, which coincided with a pagan Roman feast day, to confuse their persecutors because the Roman Empire martyred Christians at that time; and they were not allowed to celebrate any religious festivals or have any public display of religiosity. This way, the Christian celebration of Christ's birth could be celebrated publicly and without any hindrance because the Romans would also be celebrating their own festival. If you want to look at this biblically, consider the gospel passage where St. John the Baptist says, "He must increase, but I must decrease" (John 3:30). Jesus says He is the Light of the World. Hence, we commemorate St. John the Baptist's birth on June 24, as the day's amount of sunlight decreases from that day on in the Northern Hemisphere; and starting December 25, the day's amount of sunlight begins to increase. This is how we started to get the liturgical calendar, and if you count back nine months from December 25, you get the Annunciation on March 25.

Fr. Trigilio: So, in the absence of an actual date, the Church wanted to have a day for the birth of Christ. As St. Augustine explained regarding the positioning of the sun and when daylight starts to increase, symbolizing Christ as the Light of the World, the date plays off of what's happening in the natural world. We have the changing of the seasons coinciding with Advent, Lent, Easter, Christmas, and Ordinary Time. The Church wouldn't just pick some arbitrary date for such a special celebration, but instead She gave it careful consideration.

Fr. Brighenti: This is also how we get the seasons of preparation. The season of Lent prepares us for Easter, and the season to prepare us for Christmas is Advent. Slowly but surely, the liturgical calendar started to fill out. As you mentioned, the liturgical calendar is sort of like the different seasons that we have in nature. We have Ordinary Time and then Advent, Christmas, Lent, and Easter, along with the different celebrations within those seasons.

Fr. Trigilio: Let's also consider Mary, as we don't know when her birthday was. There were no leftover birthday cards from St. Joseph and Jesus wishing her a happy birthday, but she obviously had a birthday, and the Church wanted to honor that day. So just as they selected the birthdays of St. John the Baptist and Jesus Christ, they chose Mary's birthday to be nine months after the Immaculate Conception. This fits in with the schema, and it's a beautiful way in which the Church honors Jesus, Mary, and John the Baptist, the only three for whom we celebrate their natural birth. For all the other saints, we honor the day they died and went to Heaven.

Fr. Brighenti: Also, the liturgical calendar, the feast days, and the liturgy itself teach us the doctrines and the dogma of our Faith. It's not just a celebration for its own sake, but it's a teaching tool for us, to show us an article of our Faith or a part of revelation.

Chapter 2

Liturgy

1. Holy Water and Blessing of the Home

Who can bless a home? When things are not going well at home, I spread holy salt along the perimeter of my property. Each night, I spray each room with holy water and bless each family member.

Fr. Brighenti: In my old parish where I was pastor, I had to provide little bottles of holy water on Holy Saturday and Easter Sunday. I would get about two thousand of them, and the parishioners would clean me out of Easter water and take them home, because it's a custom to sprinkle holy water on your pillows at night or during thunderstorms. But the question here concerns the distinction between Holy Orders and the actual blessing of a home, versus spreading blessed salt or sprinkling holy water around the home, which anyone can do. Think of it as wearing a medal or carrying your rosary or obtaining blessed oil from the Shrines of St. Anthony and St. Padre Pio, where they have these little vials of holy oil that you can bring home and bless yourself with. But as far as blessing a home or any other object, only a man in sacramental orders can do so. A deacon or a priest would commonly come and bless your home, especially around the Epiphany, which is a beautiful time commemorating the manifestation of the three kings during the Christmas season, and they commonly bless homes again during Eastertide.

Fr. Trigilio: Another opportune time would be when somebody buys a new home.

Fr. Brighenti: Priests and deacons can go to the home and bless it either on the day the new owners are moving in or around that time, and they can bless new cars, too. Just the other day, someone came up to the seminary and had a whole car full of candles that they wanted blessed because they were going to pass the candles out.

Fr. Trigilio: Another example would be the blessing of pets on St. Francis of Assisi's feast day.

Fr. Brighenti: Medals, rosaries, statues—all these things can be blessed by a priest or a deacon, but not by a layperson.

Fr. Trigilio: In order to bless these sacramentals, one has to be what we call a cleric or a clergyman, which means that this person received the Sacrament of Holy Orders. A layperson is allowed to bless these things under certain circumstances as specified in the *Book of Blessings*. They don't make the Sign of the Cross, but when a priest or a deacon or a bishop does, these items become sacramentals. I believe it's also mentioned in the *Book of Blessings* about the practice of sprinkling holy water around the home, as it serves as a reminder of our Baptism, and it's also a great way to chase away evil spirits and put the devil on notice that we're with God.

Fr. Brighenti: Blessed salt is good as well. I'm reminded of Mother Teresa, who would take blessed Miraculous Medals and go by abortion clinics or pornography stores and scatter these medals around. Some places had such deep conversions that they were no longer in resistance after that. Mother Teresa would take these medals, blessed by priests, and she would throw them right at the entrances to these places.

Fr. Trigilio: I recall a happy memory of a friend of ours, Fr. Michael Scott; he used to work with Mother Teresa when he was a seminarian. On one occasion, she threw a Miraculous Medal into one of these abortion clinics at night when nobody was there, and the whole building fell into itself. No one was hurt, thank goodness.

2. Indulgences

What does it mean to gain an indulgence?

Fr. Brighenti: This is a topic that caused a lot of confusion back in the sixteenth century when Martin Luther had left the Church because of his misunderstanding of the official teaching of the Magisterium. For starters, an indulgence is the remission of temporal punishment due to forgiven sins. So, for example, if I committed a sin, then went to Confession, and the priest instructed me to say an Our Father, a Hail Mary, or a Glory Be, while making a valid confession and reciting those prayers would obtain forgiveness for my sin, they don't really take the insult of that sin away. Remember, the ramification of your sin can continue on and on until the end of time. We're called to live a penitential life to make up for our sins and to prepare ourselves for the future. In His infinite mercy, Jesus gave us this treasury of merit that we can tap into. One of the ways to do this is through an indulgence. An indulgence means that we would perform a specific act that is recognized by the Church to lessen the penalty of our sins, such as a pilgrimage, for example. If we're in a Year of Faith, you can go to your church of Baptism and recite prayers at the baptismal font, pray for the Holy Father, go to Confession and receive Communion within a certain timeframe, and you then gain a full, plenary indulgence. Another example would be if you read the *Catechism* during this Year of Faith, or studied parts of the documents of the Second Vatican Council; you can receive plenary indulgences for those as well.

Fr. Trigilio: Yes, and these are not "get out of jail free" cards. They're not an excuse to misbehave, and they're not a wink or a nod.

Fr. Brighenti: And you cannot buy them.

Fr. Trigilio: That's right, they cannot be bought. They are an application of the infinite merits bestowed upon us by Jesus, Mary, and the saints.

3. Relics of the True Cross

When the priest kisses the altar in celebrating the Mass, I always believed he did so out of respect for the piece of the True Cross that I thought was enclosed within every church altar. I later realized that, with the construction of so many churches, it would be impossible for every altar to contain a piece. Are the relics of the True Cross removed from older churches to be recycled, or has this practice been abandoned overall?

Fr. Brighenti: First of all, if every altar featured a relic of the True Cross, then I think the True Cross would be as big as a skyscraper at this point. It would simply be impossible to have a relic of the True Cross for each and every altar throughout the whole world. But more than just a relic of the True Cross can be placed inside an altar. Under the old Code of Canon Law, there was what they called an altar stone set inside the altar, which would contain five relics typically from early Christian martyrs. This goes back to the time of the early Roman martyrdom in the first century when Mass was being said in close proximity to the tombs of those who had been killed for their Faith, and especially so on their feast days. The Church has carried on that connection to the intercession of the saints and martyrs by placing these relics in the altar. Today, it's no longer mandatory for an altar to include a relic stone, although plenty of new altars still have them. When I restored the church at St. Ann's in Raritan, New Jersey, where I was pastor, we placed five relics inside the altar. They weren't set inside a stone but within the altar itself, and these were relics from saints who were not martyrs. As for the priest kissing the altar, he does so because the altar is a symbol of Christ, Who is represented in the altar. In the Byzantine liturgy, they have what they call an altar cloth, which has an image of the Dead Christ of it, and five relics of the True Cross are placed within it.

Fr. Trigilio: Yes, the relics are embedded in the cloth, into the antimension itself. The antimension is a Byzantine corporal with a relic sewed inside, so it acts like a marble altar stone used in the Roman Rite. I think that it is quite rare for an altar to have a relic of the True Cross inside of it. You'd be more likely to see a relic of the True Cross in a reliquary on top of the altar for veneration. It would be considered a privilege for an altar to contain a piece of the True Cross, but they usually contain relics from either ancient martyrs or contemporary saints. We also don't want people to get stuck with the idea that every altar must have a literal piece of wood from the True Cross, as it's impossible for every altar to share a relic from this same source, and it would make no difference regarding the use of the altar for the Mass since, metaphysically speaking, it's the same Sacrifice of Calvary.

Fr. Brighenti: I'd like to note that if you do happen to come across any older altars that have unfortunately been dismantled, there is a chance that there could be that square stone with the relics still inside. These relics should be carefully removed and properly venerated.

4. The Sign of the Cross

What does the Sign of the Cross mean, and why don't Protestants use it?

Fr. Brighenti: I suppose it's because many of the Protestant churches, particularly the mainstream evangelical ones, don't display signs or symbols in general. You would think they would be more open to the idea of making the Sign of the Cross, as it's plainly an open profession of our shared belief in the Trinity as we trace ourselves saying, "In the name of the Father, and of the Son, and of the Holy Spirit." Making the Sign of the Cross is also a symbol of our salvation.

Fr. Trigilio: In the Protestant tradition, they believe that we're saved by Jesus' sacrifice on the Cross, and they typically believe in the Holy Trinity as well. However, making the Sign of the Cross falls in line with several Catholic religious gestures, such as genuflecting, and there was a rather anti-popery movement in England, particularly during the time of the Protestant Reformation, where anything that looked too *Roman* was deemed as idolatry, on the level of venerating saints with statues. You could tell if an Englishman was Roman or if he was Anglican based on whether he would make the Sign of the Cross. There's nothing theologically offensive to a Protestant Christian in making the Sign of the Cross, and when you explain that we're invoking the Blessed Trinity when we make the Sign while also affirming the fact that it's the Cross by which we were saved, that should make sense to most Protestants. However, the Sign of the Cross is not explicitly mandated in the Bible, and that's where a lot of animosity due to misunderstanding can arise.

Fr. Brighenti: This misunderstanding on the part of Protestants stems from the false notion of iconoclasm that was seen during the Reformation and experienced as well in the ninth century in the Eastern Orthodox Church, where even the emperor had gotten involved. There's even a feast now called the "Triumph of Orthodoxy," which celebrates the restoration of the icons that were being removed by forces both inside and outside the Orthodox Church. Today, those who are not Catholic and who devoid their churches of these religious symbols mistakenly think that we worship the pictures and statues we put up, and the truth is that we simply do not worship them. These icons are symbols, used to help us remember and honor the Trinity, the Blessed Virgin, and the rest of the saints in Heaven. It's no different than a photograph of Mount Rushmore with the presidents. You'd be hard-pressed to find anyone who would accuse Americans of worshipping the faces carved into the side of that rock, as those faces were only placed there in their honor.

Fr. Trigilio: It's just like when you put your hand over your heart when you say the Pledge of Allegiance or sing the National Anthem, or when you're at the cemetery and they're playing "Taps" for someone, and the soldiers give their salute — it's a gesture and nothing more.

5. Last Rites

*My husband received Communion every day while he was hospital-
ized, but he then died suddenly. Should I have called for a priest
after he died?*

Fr. Brighenti: First of all, my condolences to you on the death
of your husband. It appears by the question that he was a very
devout Catholic, seeing as he wanted to receive Communion
as frequently as he did. What's not clear in the question is, during the husband's hospitalization, did a priest come and anoint
him? Did a priest hear his confession? I would assume that both
of those sacraments were administered, since he was receiving
Communion on a daily basis. The sacraments are for the living,
and that's the important thing. If he received the Sacraments
of Confession and the Anointing of the Sick, there's a short,
beautiful prayer called the Apostolic Blessing that can also be
given, and Holy Communion administered at the time is called
the "Viaticum," which is food for the journey when a person
is in the dying process. What can we do after he's dead? If the
body is still warm to the touch, then a priest can still anoint it.
However, if rigor mortis is setting in, then we believe that the
soul has departed, and a blessing can be given instead. A priest
can still bless the body, but it's not necessary, as it appears that
the husband has been fully prepared during the last few days
of his life. A blessing at that stage would be done more for the
comfort of those who mourn him.

Fr. Trigilio: What is crucial is that people let the priest know
ahead of time if someone needs to be anointed. No one in the
hospital may have asked, or perhaps they didn't have the opportunity to ask because the patient was unconscious, or maybe
he just never said anything. It's important to ask your loved

ones if they would like you to get a hold of a priest. If there's no chaplain available at the hospital, then contact your parish priest, but more often than not there's a priest in the area assigned to every hospital. Calling your parish priest might take longer, and he could arrive too late to administer the Sacrament of Anointing of the Sick. Don't be embarrassed to request that service right away. Too often we get called to anoint someone after they're already dead.

Fr. Brighenti: That's not to say that you shouldn't call your parish priest; of course, he wants to know so he can come visit and offer prayers for the sick and dying, but the hospital chaplain should be the first priest you call, as they'll be there immediately.

Fr. Trigilio: Time is of the essence, because we cannot anoint a dead person. We can only anoint the living. "*Sacramenta propter homines*," or, sacraments are for men (that is, human beings), as St. Thomas Aquinas put it in part III of the *Summa Theologica*.

6. Being a Priest

What is the hardest thing about being a priest?

Fr. Brighenti: Well, every vocation has its benefits as well as its challenges, and they each have their sacrifices as well. Take married life, for example, where a man and wife are brought together for the purpose of helping each other get to Heaven. But there are many sacrifices involved in married life. They can get on each other's nerves. My parents, who will be married for sixty-four years, would probably say that their difficulties today are a lot different than they were when they first married. When they were first married, the hardships were probably related to making the financial ends meet while raising the children and making sure they had a good Catholic school to go to. For me, the hardest thing in the priesthood is obedience.

Fr. Trigilio: I imagine some people would expect you to say celibacy, but as we're both middle-aged now, celibacy is not so much of an issue as it was back when we were younger.

Fr. Brighenti: But with obedience, we're sometimes asked by our superiors to do things we don't always want to do, like move to a new parish. After serving the people at one parish for a number of years, you may really come to enjoy it there, but then the bishop sends you to another parish because it needs to be fixed. It's situations like these where obedience comes into play. We must obey the bishop, as he is the voice of the Lord in our lives. This doesn't always make obedience easy at times, but just keep in mind that the Lord will help you and that He always provides, and sometimes what happens is even better than what you expected.

Fr. Trigilio: When you look in hindsight at certain situations, you'll often see where the Lord knew more than He was telling you. It's all part of His Divine Wisdom, and we just need to be obedient and trust in Him. Over time, a priest gets used to things like celibacy, poverty, and living a simple life, but obedience takes time to adapt to. On the bright side, one of the most rewarding aspects about being a priest is the effect you have on so many souls. It's like when a doctor knows that he or she is saving lives. There is nothing more important in the universe than to save souls, and it's not me doing it but Jesus through His divine grace. By offering the Holy Sacrifice of the Mass, hearing confessions, and teaching others, I find that saving souls is the most rewarding aspect of my ordained ministry.

Fr. Brighenti: Also, once you realize that saving souls is the result of your obedience, it really sets you free inside. Yes, I still struggle with it, but the decision has been made, and God's going to provide me with the grace to get through whatever I need to do.

Fr. Trigilio: Likewise, when you ask a married couple what the happiest part of their married life is, they look to their children and grandchildren. When they ask what's the best thing about your priesthood, you think of all the people you've affected. Both Fr. Brighenti and I have recently celebrated our twenty-fifth anniversaries as priests, and there are people from several parishes who have remained a part of our lives over the past twenty-five years. These kinds of friendships are more than just acquaintances.

Fr. Brighenti: These are excellent points. And at your twenty-fifth anniversary as a priest, there were so many people who attended that you had to host it at the Cathedral. In regard to obedience, Fr. Frederick Miller's book *The Grace of Ars* states that St. John Vianney tried to leave Ars as many as three times because he thought he was doing a poor job, and three times he was brought back to Ars. He finally realized that Ars is where God wanted him to be, and by following the obedience of God and his bishop, he later became a saint.[9]

Fr. Trigilio: When people see that you're happy being a priest, and not necessarily because Father's always got a smile on his face, it truly shows that you like what you're doing. It's not that you necessarily enjoy all the craziness, nonsense, red tape, and bureaucracy that will sometimes come your way, but people can

[9]   Frederick L. Miller, *The Grace of Ars* (San Francisco: Ignatius Press, 2010).

tell if you're content with your vocation. When you're celebrating Mass, when you're preaching, or when you're anointing the sick, they can tell if you find joy in what you do or if you're just going through the motions. When they see that you truly love the priesthood, that encourages them, and that's where you may get some vocations to follow in your footsteps.

7. Discerning Monastic Life as a Vocation

What is the difference between a sister and a nun? I believe God is calling me to be a nun and I feel Him pulling me toward a particular contemplative cloistered monastery. I am fifty-seven years old and need advice on how to chase away the spirit of cowardice and claim the "spirit of power, love, and self-control" that God gives us in 2 Timothy 1:7.

Fr. Trigilio: A nun is a religious woman who typically resides in a monastery. Her religious life is a consecrated one that requires taking the vows of poverty, chastity, and obedience, but her apostolate is much different than that of a religious sister who lives in a convent. Most sisters work as nurses and doctors in hospitals or in schools as religious teachers. There are the Religious Teachers Filippini, which is an order of sisters who predominantly teach, as well as the Sisters of St. Joseph and the (Nashville) Dominican Sisters of St. Cecilia. Then there are the cloistered nuns, such as the Poor Clares, which we have here in Hanceville, Alabama. Now, most of the communities have an age cutoff at forty to forty-five, so that's going to greatly limit your choices, although the cloistered Carmelite nuns in Erie sometimes take women who are a little bit older. This is something you need to carefully discern by going on a retreat and having a confessor and spiritual director whom you can trust and who will help you through this discernment, just like the men in the seminary who spend anywhere from four to eight years discerning if they have a vocation to the priesthood. Having a vocation to religious life is no different in that you have to discern. You don't say one day, "I want to join the convent," and suddenly you're a sister.

Fr. Brighenti: Finding a trustworthy spiritual director is by far the first step. You need to be honest with the Holy Spirit in discerning your vocation. I would also suggest going over the fourteen rules for discerning spirits by St. Ignatius of Loyola. Since the presenter of this question seems to have a Carmelite's cloistered spirituality, she should see if there is what they call a "Third Order of Carmelites," or "Lay Carmelites," that she can join. We have a very good friend, a doctor at Hershey Medical Center, who belongs to the Lay Carmelites, who meet every month to pray the Divine Office, and they keep up with similar prayer obligations as well. Besides their monthly meetings and annual retreats, they also wear a full-size scapular of Our Lady of Mount Carmel at their gatherings, and what's beautiful is when this doctor's mother passed away, all of the Lay Carmelites came and prayed the Liturgy of the Hours along with the Rosary, followed by the Mass the next day where they each wore their scapulars so everyone knew they belonged to the Third Order. There are third orders for the Dominicans and Franciscans, too, so if you have either of those three types of spiritualities, you can look into those groups as well. These third orders might be a good place to start at fifty-seven, even if it's different than the cloister, which is far more intense.

Fr. Trigilio: There's also the option of becoming a hermit, which is a simplistic way of life that a few women in my diocese have pursued; they live by themselves and lead a whole life of prayer and offering penances. There's also the religious community that a sister founded after she converted from the Jewish faith that's particularly for older women. But step one: you need to pray about this; you have to discern. You need guidance, and that's where a good spiritual director and confessor is indispensable. You can't do this alone, because even though you might feel God is calling you, how can you be sure of that? It's through Holy Mother Church and Her representatives that you'll find confirmation. That's why the men at the seminary spend so much time discerning their vocation before the bishop finally puts his hands on their heads.

Fr. Brighenti: After finding a spiritual director, it may be wise to join a branch of the Lay Carmelites first. Then you can make a retreat with the actual Carmelite sisters and see if they'd let you in and what their daily routine in life is about. At fifty-seven, entering this way of life may be strenuous for you. These sisters grew into it over the years, but for some who are just walking in, it could be quite the challenge. There are some extremely strict groups that won't even eat meat except for a few high-regarded holy days.

Fr. Trigilio: Most Carmelites do not eat meat at all, even on holy days.

Fr. Brighenti: Some of them rarely ever use heat as well, even in the cold of winter. There is an enormous amount of penance being done by these sisters, and you need to see it before you join. Going on a retreat with them would be the smart thing to do so you can observe their daily life. For us men, we can go to Spencer, Massachusetts and live the Liturgy of the Hours with the Trappist monks. You get up in the middle of the night and join them for prayer. You can't reside within the cloistered monastery, but you can participate in their liturgical cycle so you can see what it's like and discern if God's calling you to it.

Fr. Trigilio: I made a retreat once at the Benedictines' Mount Savior Monastery up in Elvira, New York, and at four o'clock in the morning there was a knock on the door, and Brother Pier asked if I wanted to milk the cows. I said, "No, thanks, Brother. I'll pray and have my milk at breakfast."

8. Pursuing the Priesthood

I am a new convert to the Catholic Church, and I hear the calling to become a priest though I am forty years old. Is it too late to pursue the priesthood? Did either of you have these feelings of being inadequate before pursing your vocations?

Fr. Brighenti: First off, welcome to the Faith. I think you're experiencing the joys of it, and this is why you would like to pursue the priesthood. It's very important for you, as you deepen your spiritual life, to find a spiritual director, whether it's a priest in your parish or another one that you're comfortable with, to start discussing these matters with so he can help you discern. A good book to read, which will help you deepen your interior life, is *The Soul of the Apostolate*, by Jean-Baptiste Chautard. Forty years is not too old to enter the priesthood; God could certainly call you at that age. I'm not going to say that formation will be easy, because as we get older, it becomes harder for us to take orders from others. When we're in the seminary, we're putting ourselves at disposal during the formation of our spiritual, human, intellectual, and pastoral pillars.

Fr. Trigilio: At Mount St. Mary's, where Fr. Brighenti is Vice Rector, there are a few seasoned gentlemen there, and also at the Holy Apostles College and Seminary in Connecticut where I remember seeing a poster that read, "God calls you to the priest-hood at any age." St. Ignatius of Loyola was in his forties when he finally felt a calling to the priesthood.

Fr. Brighenti: The last part of the question asks about feeling inadequate. I don't think any priest who goes to the altar to be ordained ever feels quite adequate. We certainly believe that God's grace is working within us and calling the poor instruments that we are to the priesthood, but we never feel that we're always right for the occasion, and there's always room for improvement.

Fr. Trigilio: Absolutely. Not a day goes by where you don't feel that you could be a better priest, just as every husband and father should be saying, "I could be a better husband. I could be a better father." Something else I want to underscore are the challenges involved with an older vocation. Some dioceses won't take you if you have too much debt, for example, because you need to be debt-free, as the diocese could be financially responsible. Your overall health is also important. The bishop doesn't need you on sick leave just after he ordains you.

Fr. Brighenti: These are some valid points, and your education plays a pivotal role, too. At forty years old, you might already have four years of college under your belt, but you still have to go through two years of what we call "pre-theology," which would meet the philosophy requirement. There's then the spiritual formation that's occurring at the same time, and once you get your philosophy credits, then you can proceed to theology, which is still another four years. So, if you start at forty, you'll probably be forty-six by the time you will be ordained—and that's still not old. If you didn't finish your college education, you'll still have to, but you would finish it while majoring in philosophy.

9. Celibacy for Priests

Is celibacy necessary for priests? It seems a priest would be so lonely with no one there just for them, as they give and give yet receive so little in return, and they go home to an empty house after being with the entire parish at Mass. Does celibacy in the priesthood come from doctrine, or is it a discipline, and why? Does it have to do with Mary and Joseph's virginity in attending to the Son of God?

Fr. Trigilio: It could certainly appear to be a lonely life, and it's definitely a solitary life in many regards. However, one thing that you have to keep in mind is that celibacy is not a dogma; it is a discipline in the Latin Church going back to the Synod of Elvira in A.D. 309, which made priestly celibacy the normative. It later became mandatory in the eleventh century, under Pope Gregory. In the Western tradition, this has been consistently followed, but in the Eastern Catholic Church they've had married clergy this whole time except in the episcopacy, and this applies to the Eastern Orthodox Church as well where all bishops are celibate. Married priests do not advance any further up the ecclesiastical ladder in the Eastern tradition. In the Latin Church, however, priests are mostly celibate, except for former Anglican priests who join the Church and discern the priesthood. That being said, the seminarians prepare themselves for an entire life of celibacy, they take a vow of celibacy when they become a deacon, and this vow is renewed at their ordination for priesthood.

Fr. Brighenti: We have wonderful discussions on celibacy from the moment these men join the seminary. Celibacy, simplicity of life, and obedience are three critical things that we go over during their four years of theology, plus an additional two years if they're taking pre-theology. It's a decision that they consciously know they are making. If you're called to be a priest in the Latin

Church, then you're also called to be a celibate. When we try to explain, teach, and live this, we're showing that we're joyful celibates. We're not sorrowful or depressed, because we are well aware that even in married life couples are forsaking something else, whether it be another person or celibacy itself. For our sake, we're forgoing married life, but we're receiving so much more in return. For the seminarians and ourselves, St. Joseph is such a beautiful model of spirituality. Although he was not the physical father of Our Blessed Savior, he was certainly a father to Him in so many different ways. He taught Jesus carpentry, and He taught Him religion. Likewise, as a priest, while we may not have physical children, we instead have spiritual children.

Fr. Trigilio: That's why they call us "Father."

Fr. Brighenti: We're shepherds of souls. Our parish becomes our spiritual family, and we have a wonderful spiritual relationship with them. Because of them, we're not alone, and we don't feel loneliness in that regard. In fact, by the end of the week when I've had so much going on, I look forward to some quiet time so I can research and work on my studies. We're not lonely, so don't worry about us. We're happy, joyful celibates.

10. Entering the Seminary

I am a thirty-year-old college graduate, and I would love to enter the seminary. At what stage of the seminary would I start since I am a college graduate, or would I start at the beginning?

Fr. Trigilio: I entered the seminary right out of grade school, so I went to high-school seminary, college seminary, then finally seminary. It was a total of twelve years of seminary for me, but that's certainly not the norm. Typically, men go into the seminary after college, and a college degree is essential to begin with. If you don't have a philosophy degree or background in philosophy, they may require a certain number of credits that you must perform. If you didn't major in philosophy, then you may still need to spend two years in what they call "pre-theology" to get acclimated to seminary life. There's also going to be at least four to five years in major theology, because you may need to take an extra "pastoral" year, depending on the diocese, your education, and your debts.

Fr. Brighenti: There's also the formation of the spiritual, human, intellectual, and pastoral pillars that's taking place as well. Since some of the seminarians are coming in from secular colleges and universities, there is also some catching up to do with the basic catechetical tools during those two years in pre-theology. Sometimes people haven't heard anything about their Catholic Faith outside of Mass and receiving the sacraments. After that two-year period in pre-theology, they would then enter what we call major seminary, which takes four years before ordination. As stated, there are some dioceses that require a pastoral year in between your second and third year of theology. It's all there to help the seminarian discern his vocation and to ensure that he has the proper tools and knowledge to teach and administer the sacraments. In our seminary, we offer a master's degree in philosophy; in other words, if you're a graduate, then you've got two years of philosophy to complete. What you can do is apply through the university and get your master's in philosophy. Many of our seminarians do this so it's not a waste of two years on the academic timetable, although we know that spiritual and human formation is progressing during that period.

Fr. Trigilio: What's also important besides the theological academic component is the pastoral formation period, because as the late Cardinal Bevilacqua once mentioned, a lot of men joining the seminary today are under bigger strains and face greater challenges than previously, because so many of them are coming from broken families or are dealing with other modern issues. A lot of them have fought emotional and physiological battles that the older crowd didn't have to. When you look at Catholic grade school and see how many kids are on medication today or require counseling, and their parents are in their fourth or fifth relationship, there is an impact on the individual who needs to get that worked out and resolved before they can start helping other people.

Fr. Brighenti: In Philadelphia and the Archdiocese of Denver, they have a mandatory program called a "Spiritual Year." It's not a pastoral year, and there's no academic system in play, but it's where the seminarians are together and focus on their prayer techniques, spiritual confidences, and interior life.

11. Discerning a Vocation

I'm a twenty-six-year-old Catholic, and I want to be a Jesuit priest, but at the same time I also want to get married. What should I do?

Fr. Brighenti: At twenty-six years old, you're not unlike many other young men who are also experiencing a call; but remember: it is a call either to be a priest or to be married. You cannot be both. Right now, you're in an act of discernment, which is wonderful. There are a couple things I would suggest to help you through it, and the first is to get a spiritual director. Since you're interested in the Jesuits, contact the Jesuit community in your area and see if one of the priests would be available for spiritual direction. Secondly, start actively praying for what God wants you to do in life, because when we do God's will, no matter what it is, we will be most happy in this life. You have to start emptying yourself out of "me, myself, and I, and what I want" and filling it with what God wants for your life. Get yourself in the habit of going both to daily Mass and to Holy Hour. Archbishop Fulton J. Sheen always preached about the importance of Holy Hour every day. If you're too busy, he said you can spend half an hour in the morning and the other half in the afternoon, although this isn't optimal. Spend no less than that half hour, because it takes that long to get into prayer. I will also suggest some very traditional devotions during your Holy Hour: pray the Rosary to Our Lady and practice *Lectio Divina*, where you take a Scripture reading and meditate on it. This could be from the daily readings at Mass, from the *Magnificat* book, from the Laudate app on your smart device, or *The Word Among Us* magazine which includes meditations on the daily readings as well. Spend at least fifteen to twenty minutes performing what we call "contemplation," and that's when the Lord speaks to us in the quietness of our soul, though He's not going to speak to you in an audible voice like a person would. You may get very distracted during those twenty minutes, but take your time and keep practicing, and it will change you, and you'll become subtly open to the Word and if He is calling you to a specific state in life.

Fr. Trigilio: Isn't there an Ignatian spirituality he could start to familiarize himself with outside the spiritual exercise? There's a Jesuit technique that can assist you in your discernment of spirits.

Fr. Brighenti: St. Ignatius of Loyola developed fourteen rules for discerning spirits. You never make a decision when you're upset or in distress; that's rule number five. You only make a decision when you're in a calm state of mind and after much prayerful reflection.

Fr. Trigilio: He should also make a Jesuit retreat, if possible. The best one is thirty days, though not everyone can afford to take an entire month off from work. But there are many Jesuit retreats you can go on, and some are only five days long or even just a weekend. It'd be good for him to at least get in contact with a Jesuit. Jesuits go to school for a long time, longer than the diocesan, and longer than the Dominicans or Franciscans. He'll be going to school for at least twelve or fifteen years and will have a master or doctorate's degree before ordination. For a Jesuit, there's going to be a lot of studying involved, as their way of life is very academia-based. You could then be sent on any number of assignments, because it's a very global-oriented vocation as well. I would encourage him to look into it along with other religious communities, because if you're not the academic type, then the Jesuits might not be the way to go. One thing I also want to point out is that being a Jesuit is mutually exclusive; you cannot be a Jesuit and married. If he had been a Byzantine Catholic, he could get married prior to being ordained, but in the Latin Rite you're limited to being a married or single layperson, a religious, or a priest, and I think it's wonderful that he's discerning the full spectrum of vocations. Those are the four vocations that we see in the Second Vatican Council documents, and sometimes when people hear the word "vocation," they only think of a priestly or a religious vocation, but we want people to know that all four are legitimate, authentic vocations. Vocation comes from the Latin word *vocare*, which means calling. God is calling you to a particular state in life.

12. The Liturgical Year and Feast Days

Why does the Church have a liturgical year? Don't all these secondary feasts detract from Christmas and Easter? Some churches simply have a Christmas play on Christmas Day. Is all this celebrating really necessary for salvation? Fasting before Christmas and Easter is unheard of outside the Catholic Church, however, some people choose to fast on Sunday before hosting a church service at their home. Can you explain how liturgical seasons and fasting bring spiritual benefit to believers?

Fr. Brighenti: We address the liturgical year in greater detail in our book *Catholic Mass for Dummies*, and it's quite beautiful to see how it came together. The oldest celebration is of course Easter, and the preparation of Easter is Lent. The next big feast would be Christmas, and its season of preparation is called Advent, and from there on the liturgical year began to fill out. Why do we have them? Well, why not? They don't distract us from Our Lord and Savior Jesus Christ. Rather, as we mention in our book *Saints for Dummies*, saints bring us closer to the Lord because they are modeled after the Gospel to its perfection. Saints are not only available to us for their prayerful intercession, but they inspire us as heroes and role models as well. The liturgical calendar was developed over many, many centuries, and it's still being updated today to include new saints who have been canonized. The liturgical calendars are not always the same for all regions. For example, while the English martyrs from the Protestant Reformation era are on the English Catholic calendar, they are not found on our American calendar, yet they are all part of the general Roman Martyrology. The Feast of the Annunciation, which is on March 25, was calculated at nine months before Christmas, and the Nativity of St. John the Baptist on June 24, the longest day of the year, which was selected due to the passage in Scripture that reads, "He must increase, but I must decrease" (John 3:30). Christmas Eve was placed on December 24, which is the shortest day of the year, and from that day on the light increases, as the Lord becomes the Light of the World. The Feast of the Immaculate Conception of Mary is on December 8, and then we have the Nativity of Mary on September 8, nine months later. This is how some of these feast days became added to the calendar.

Fr. Trigilio: Because we're so used to seeing things on our smart devices, it's easy to forget that while the calendar is often used today as a reference for when you schedule appointments, in ancient times up until the modern industrial era it was crucial to the agrarian life, as the growing season was so much more relevant to the common people. The calendar told you when to plant and when to harvest, and the Church in Her wisdom decided to utilize this standard concept that the people were already attuned to, and She divided the year into two principle ideas: Christ, Our Light, and Christ, Our Life. Christ Our Light focuses on Christmastime, where nature is pierced by a dark winter followed by increasing light, and Christ Our Life on Easter, as the new life of spring follows immediately afterward. The cycle of all the other feasts are then inserted into this calendar. I remember that Fr. Heidt, a Benedictine priest who taught us liturgy at Holy Apostles Seminary, used to remind us that the liturgical year was not only a catechetical means to teach the people the Faith, but to also encourage them to live moral lives in addition to coming to the sacraments and to Mass. It was the liturgical celebration of salvation history that also provided guidance to the people with a moral impetus to lead good and holy Christian lives.

13. Holy Communion

Why is it that after the Consecration, Our Lord's Body and Blood are referred to as the "Bread" and "Cup" instead of the "Body" and "Blood"? I find it very confusing to keep changing the words back and forth, and it seems that those who do not believe that the bread and wine have become the actual Body and Blood of Christ would have reason to doubt the Real Presence even more so when the wording is not always consistent.

Fr. Brighenti: This can be very confusing, and we are thankfully seeing more informative catechisms today that better explain the true nature of transubstantiation. We studied with the old *Baltimore Catechism* back when we were growing up, and there was a period of time from the late 1960s up to the early 1980s where the catechisms were kind of weak.

Fr. Trigilio: They weren't even called catechisms when we were kids. They were called "religion books," and they had no religion in them at all.

Fr. Brighenti: Today, more children are studying what transubstantiation means. Through the words of Consecration, the bread and wine cease to exist, and they become the Body and Blood, Soul and Divinity of Jesus Christ under the accidents or appearances of bread and wine so that you and I may receive Our Lord. Now, the wording the question addresses was corrected by the Church in the sacramentary, now known as the Roman Missal. The Blood of Christ is not referred to as "the Cup" anymore, but instead as "the Chalice." "The Bread" comes from the more ancient terms such as "the Bread of Life" and "Heavenly Manna." The beautiful hymn "Panis Angelicus," which means "Bread of Angels," has been sung for many years in church, and some of the newer hymns have actually been corrected to refer properly to Our Lord in the Blessed Sacrament.

Fr. Trigilio: I remember when we were newly ordained, that even before the third English edition of the Missal, they tweaked the Eucharistic Prayer because it referred to "one Body and one Cup" or "one Bread and one Cup." They changed it to "one Bread and one Body," because they wanted to refer either to the Body or the Blood, but they didn't want to use "wine" after the Consecration, because while Jesus said, "I am the bread of life" (John 6:35), He never said, "I am the wine of life." We don't even prefer to use the term "consecrated wine," because people can be confused by that. I personally get a little upset when some of the extraordinary ministers of Holy Communion say, "Father, are we having wine at Mass today?" I tell them, "Well, I use wine at Mass, but we never give out wine. We give out the Precious Blood, and if you can't refer to It as such, then you have no business being an extraordinary minister of Holy Communion."

Fr. Brighenti: There are some wonderful opportunities throughout the liturgical seasons to preach on this topic. During the lectionary cycle B, we'll read the sixth chapter of the Gospel of John where Jesus multiplies the loaves of bread and says, "I am the Bread of Life." Another time would be on Holy Thursday as well as Corpus Christi Sunday, and a priest can always explain the significance in his homilies during the Holy Mass to instill reverence inside of the church by teaching the people to genuflect before the Blessed Sacrament in the Tabernacle if that practice has been lost. Our catechetical programs and catechisms today seem to be doing a better job of teaching the students about transubstantiation and what that entails. It's a big word that just needs to be broken apart and taught to the children, and it would be wise for the catechetical teachers to learn this as well. Every so often, Rome has wonderful celebrations, like the Year of the Eucharist, and these are opportunities to bring out the mysteries of the Blessed Sacrament in a fuller way.

In addition to the theology and catechesis behind it, there's also the very practical reemphasis that we have in the nomenclature. We don't refer to the Blessed Sacrament as wine once It's been consecrated; we call It the Precious Blood. If there is any leftover Precious Blood at the end of Mass, It must be consumed instead of being poured down the sacrarium, a special sink in the church sacristy used for cleansing sacred cloths and vessels. It goes straight into the soil of the earth so that nothing from these sacred items may enter the sewer system.

People notice these things, and if they see how reverently we treat the Sacred Elements after the Consecration by mindfully placing the sacred hosts into the tabernacle and carefully consuming any leftover Precious Blood, this teaching is reemphasized by our piety. By doing this, we convey to the people the real Eucharistic theology that the Church has consistently taught for two thousand years.

Fr. Brighenti: Something that's helping many to understand the literal Presence of Christ in the Eucharist is that many churches are putting the Blessed Sacrament back in the center where Our Lord belongs, and reinstructing people about what is the proper mode of entering in and out of the pews with proper genuflection. The little things that we do to honor Our Lord reflect our reverence for Him.

Fr. Trigilio: The new Missal also no longer allows the use of glass Eucharistic vessels, as for a while we used clay pots and cheap glass, and some argued that this was an impious sign of poverty. Mother Teresa of Calcutta had lived among the poorest of the poor, and she said that the people in India expected nothing less than the best for God, so they used a gold chalice and paten, which wasn't to show off as being wealthy, but these items belonged directly to God, as this was truly sacred worship. The people would have been offended if you put out plastic cups and plates. There's sometimes that false kinship, like Judas when he scorned the woman who cried at the feet of Jesus, claiming that the costly perfume could have been sold and the proceeds given to the poor. Yet Jesus said that the poor will be with you always. He was not denigrating the point that we must help the poor but was telling us not to be stingy or lackadaisical when it comes to Divine Worship.

Fr. Brighenti: Sometimes as a parishioner, for example, you'll notice that the church linens are tattered and need to be replaced. Don't just donate money for them, but actually go out and buy new linens and bring them in. We were blessed at my parish, as we had the sisters who cleaned the linens, first by washing them in the sacrarium, so if there was any Particle of the Blessed Sacrament left behind in the material It would be reverently drained into the ground beneath the church. After the first washing, the sisters would then bring the linens back to the convent where they were washed and starched. The altar was always neat and clean, and we were a blue-collar parish, not some wealthy parish. But the people saw to it that the church was immaculate, and the altar was the best we could afford. The tabernacle veil, which refers back to the Holy of Holies in the Jewish Temple, featured a different color for each liturgical season, and it really added a sense of mystery. We even had veils over the ciborium, which is what contains the sacred hosts in the tabernacle, and we also placed a pall over the chalice, which is a little square that covers the mouth of the chalice, so no foreign particles fall into the Precious Blood. There was then the burse, which carried the folded corporal, which is the white cloth that we place underneath the chalice and the paten for the Consecration at Mass, and that would match with the appropriate liturgical season as well. We used bells at the moment of Consecration, too.

Fr. Trigilio: If you watch the Mass on television on EWTN, you'll see all those things utilized as well. It's not so much that we're using expensive things, but that we're using them reverently and with good taste. What I find offensive is when priests use cheap equipment for the Mass. I have heard of parishes that use paper towels as purificators, which is forbidden, and yet the priest is driving a BMW. If Father is driving an expensive car and going to Hawaii on his vacations but he can't spend money on the Divine Worship, then there's something wrong. One of the things that we have to do as priests, as deacons, as bishops — as clergy — is to celebrate the sacraments with reverence and dignity. When people see that, it reemphasizes that we're doing something special and that what we're doing is for God.

Fr. Brighenti: When I was pastor, we held classes for our Extraordinary Ministers of Holy Communion as well as our lectors at least two to three times a year. We would go over the beauty of the liturgy to update their understanding of and fuel their devotion for the Mass. People look to the Extraordinary Ministers and see what they're doing and how they dress, because they are a part of the sanctuary when they're distributing the Precious Body and Blood of Our Lord Jesus Christ.

14. Vestment Colors, Part 1

What do the different colors of the liturgical vestments represent? Can priests ever make a change of color for variety's sake? Can they ever use gray instead of black, or just wear plain clothes?

Fr. Brighenti: Liturgical vestments and the colors that we have today are more of a recent innovation from perhaps the last two hundred years. I remember visiting Christopher Columbus's chapel in Boalsburg, Pennsylvania, where they had some funky kind of vestments of all kinds of colors and patterns. Back in the day, wealthy matrons would use their expensive clothing for one season and then donate the material to the nuns to be sewn into vestments. The colors that we have today are rich with symbolism. During the seasons of Advent and Lent, we use purple or violet, which symbolizes penance, and we also use it for the Sacrament of Confession. It can also be used at funerals and for Mass on All Souls' Day as a potential reminder. We then use white or gold for festivities, the Christmas and Easter seasons, for saints who are not martyrs, and also at funeral liturgies for the Mass of Christian Burial. White or gold can also be used in the Sacrament of Baptism, the celebration of First Holy Communion, Holy Orders, and Holy Matrimony as well. Red is used as a twofold symbol. It could denote blood, which is why red is used for the Passion on Good Friday as Christ shed His Blood for us. It's used on Palm Sunday, the beginning of Holy Week in the Passion of Our Lord. It's used in solemnities of martyrs, because they shed their blood for Christ. It also denotes tongues of fire, so it's used for Pentecost and the Sacrament of Confirmation. We have the color green which symbolizes Ordinary Time, which would be the Sundays falling outside of the Lent, Advent, Christmas and Easter seasons. Green would also be worn during the week in Ordinary Time if there's no votive Mass to a saint being celebrated. Rose color is worn two times a year, the first being on Gaudete Sunday, which would be the third Sunday of Advent. *Gaudete* means "rejoice," and it comes from the entrance antiphon (introit) of that day, *Gaudete in Domino semper*, "Rejoice in the Lord always" (Philippians 4:4). Rose is also used on Laetare Sunday, which also means "rejoice," from its entrance antiphon on the fourth Sunday of Lent: *Laetare, Ierusalem*, or "Rejoice, Jerusalem." The use of these colors on those Sundays symbolizes that the preparation is almost over. Black is the final color and was used exclusively before the Second Vatican Council for funerals. It can still be worn at funerals and on All Souls' Day, and it remains a valid liturgical color that reminds us of sorrow and our empathy for the mourner, especially Holy Mother Church mourning the death of one of her spiritual sons and daughters. Today, black, purple, or white can be worn for Funeral Masses.

Fr. Trigilio: While not as commonly practiced in the United States, there's what we call a "clerical gray" shirt that a lot of the European priests wear, and especially the Italian ones. There's also navy blue. Though typically when you see a priest in real wild, vibrant colors, that's usually a sign that he's not a Catholic priest; he's probably a Protestant minister, as obviously they have no restrictions. Anglican bishops and priests will often wear very bright purple or violet, whereas our standard color is black. Colors were expensive back in the old days, so black was a common color of dress for a person of modest means, and clergy are expected to live a modest lifestyle. In the Gospels we have Lydia, who was a dealer in purple dye, and purple was a sign of aristocracy. At one point, only Caesar, or perhaps someone from the Roman Senate, was allowed to adorn himself in purple. Whereas, black was more typical of the poor common folk, and consequently black became the color of the clergy, and predominately among the lower clergy. As you climbed the ecclesiastical ranks, the colors of your cassock would change. A monsignor's buttons would be a different color, either red or purple, a cardinal wears a scarlet-red cassock, and the pope is the one who wears all white.

Fr. Brighenti: The tradition of the pope wearing white began with Pope Pius V, who was a Dominican.

Fr. Trigilio: In the Byzantine or Eastern Catholic tradition, their use of colors is different from ours. If you go to a Byzantine church and see the priest wearing green, it's not because it's Ordinary

Time. For them, green is worn for Palm Sunday and Pentecost. Red is worn for Martyrs (as in the West) but also for Advent and for Holy Thursday. Light blue is for the Theotokos (Blessed Virgin Mary, Mother of God). Gold can be worn anytime there is no other required color; and white is worn at funerals, Christmas, and Easter.

Fr. Trigilio: If you see someone outside the liturgy dressed in white robes, for example, he could possibly be a Dominican. If he's wearing brown, he's probably a Franciscan.

Fr. Brighenti: Let's address a priest wearing lay clothes. There's no problem for a priest to wear lay clothes if he wants to just relax and have supper or watch a movie. But even when a priest is not in his clerical clothes, he should never be in a situation where he would be embarrassed to wear his clerical clothes. A priest is on duty twenty-four hours a day, because it is his sacramental character. He doesn't work nine to five then take the collar off and have a brew. He's a priest, whether he's wearing his cassock, wearing his clerical clothes, or just wearing plain lay clothes. Once, two other priests and I went to a winery. We didn't have our clerical clothes on, and the person pouring the wine wanted to know what line of work we were in. When we told her we were priests, she exclaimed, "I knew it!" Upon asking her what gave us away, she told us that it was by the way we acted. You see, it's important for a priest to make sure that when he's not wearing his clerical clothes, he always exhibits a priestly character.

15. Ordinary Time Feast Days

What are some of the feasts that we celebrate during Ordinary Time? Could you share some information about those special feasts?

Fr. Brighenti: First of all, I would suggest obtaining a copy of the Roman Missal, as that would include all the feasts that we celebrate on our liturgical calendar in the United States. We have some particular American feasts that would not necessarily be on the Italian calendar or the English calendar and so on, and they have feasts that wouldn't necessarily be on ours. For example, St. Elizabeth Ann Seton would be celebrated on the calendar in the United States but not over in Poland or France, as she is a canonized American saint. There are then feast days during our liturgical year that we celebrate universally, such as those of St. Francis of Assisi, St. Clare, St. Dominic, and St. Anthony of Padua, among countless others. There are some feasts that also appear during the Advent and Christmas season or Lent and Easter season that are not related to those particular seasons. One example would be the Immaculate Conception of Mary on December 8, which occurs during the Advent season even though it's not part of Advent. And it is the patronal feast of the United States of America.

Fr. Trigilio: St. Joseph's Day sometimes falls during Lent, too. If we ever want to analyze the liturgical calendar, we'll see the year starts with Advent and culminates with Christmas, and this period is followed by "Ordinary Time." Then comes Lent which culminates with Easter, and then you go back to Ordinary Time.

Fr. Brighenti: The Liturgical Year is bookended by Christmas, which emphasizes Christ Our Light, and Easter, which focuses on Christ Our Life. Advent prepares for the former, and Lent for the latter.

Fr. Trigilio: So, Ordinary Time is that in-between time when it's not Advent, it's not Lent, it's not Christmas, and it's not Easter.

But there's that small peppering of feast days for the different saints even during those seasonal aspects, and we refer to this as the "Sanctoral Cycle." This is a way the Church sanctifies not just days or periods of time on the calendar but also these feast days for saints who reflect aspects of Jesus Christ or the Blessed Mother. It's a wonderful ongoing complementary. I think a drawback with the term "Ordinary Time," though, is that it sounds too pedestrian. One of the things I appreciate in the Extraordinary Rite is that they would call it the "Fifth Sunday" after Easter, Pentecost, or what have you. In the Byzantine Rite, they title the Sundays after the Gospel, so you'd have the "Sunday of the Man Born Blind" or "Sunday of the Samaritan Woman." When we speak of Ordinary Time, people can get the false notion that it's not an extraordinary period of time or that it's just a lesser season on the liturgical calendar, but that's not what the Church means by the term. Ordinary Time simply means that it's not Lent, Easter, Advent, or Christmas. Ordinary does not mean boring, however.

Fr. Brighenti: Beautiful feasts and solemnities occur during Ordinary Time, some of them being the Feast of the Transfiguration and the Assumption of Mary in August; the Exaltation of the Holy Cross in September; and the Solemnity of All Saints in November. The feast days of Saints Peter and Paul often fall outside of the Easter season, and these are wonderful feast days that we celebrate throughout the year. They continue the message of faith, and we celebrate it in a liturgical fashion to help bring these divine mysteries closer to us. We do this through prayer and through the readings at Mass. Again, the Roman Missal will probably be the best place to start so that you can become more familiar with these feast days.

Fr. Trigilio: While you can find the Roman Missal in print format by Scepter Publishers, you can also download an app to your smartphone. It's important to keep in mind that the whole idea of consecrating time is such a strong Christian aspect that we used to have "ember days" and "rogation day" where the farmer was planting and harvesting. It was this idea that we were sanctifying our human work, and it wasn't just more time you spent in church, but your whole life was consecrated to God. We recognize this consecration in this concept, as well as things like the blessing of throats celebrated on the feast day of St. Blaise; the blessing of candles on Candlemas the day before; the May Crowning; Corpus Christi; and Forty Hours' Devotion. A little piece of Catholic trivia I'd like to mention at this point is when a solemnity, like that of St. Joseph or the Annunciation, falls on a Friday in Lent but not during Holy Week, you're dispensed from abstaining from meat. They sing the "Gloria" at that Mass to show that this is an important celebration, even though we're in the midst of a penitential period. Now, if it's also the patronal feast of your diocese, St. Patrick being the patron in our diocese as well as in Ireland, you're automatically dispensed, which I know many of the Irish are quite happy about so they can get their corned beef and cabbage for St. Paddy's Day.

Fr. Brighenti: It's also beautiful to see how the liturgical calendar came about. If you look at the birth of Mary on September 8, her Immaculate Conception on December 8 is nine months earlier. The Annunciation is on March 25 when the "Word became flesh," and Christ's birth is on December 25. There's then the Feast of St. John the Baptist on June 24 and the expression that "I must decrease so that He [Jesus Christ] may increase."

The days get shorter up to Christ's birth, and the days get longer immediately after the Winter Solstice, symbolizing the Light of the World.

Fr. Trigilio: Each coincides with the longest day and the shortest day in the Northern Hemisphere.

16. Vestment Colors, Part 2

Why does a priest put on a purple stole for hearing confessions? What is its purpose and significance? Except for the white collar, why do priests wear black? Could they wear other colors?

Fr. Brighenti: To answer the first part of this question, there are certain colors that priests wear during the liturgical seasons. Purple is used for the Advent and Lenten seasons, for penitential purposes, and for the Anointing of the Sick. This is why we wear a purple stole in the Sacrament of Confession, because it symbolizes penance. We priests (and deacons) wear white for celebrations of the sacraments, such as the Eucharist, Baptism, First Holy Communion, Holy Orders, weddings, and the Christmas and Easter seasons. We wear red for Confirmation and for the Feast of Pentecost, as red represents the Holy Spirit; and it's also used for martyrs, symbolizing the shedding of blood. Green is then worn for Ordinary Time, which would be from after Pentecost to the first Sunday of Advent, and especially on Sundays where there's no special feast. White, purple, and black are three colors that the Church allows a priest to use for funerals. Now, why do priests wear a black clerical shirt or cassock, and do they have to wear black? If you go to Italy, you'll see a few colors that clergy wear, depending on the culture that they come from. I know people in our seminary from down south who are given special permission to wear a white cassock with black buttons because of the heat, and this is common in Africa, too, or anywhere where it's really hot. However, black is normally the color that we wear because it's a denouncing of the things of this world and a professing of the things of the world to come. It used to be that a priest would wear a cassock, but permission was given way back in the 1800s in America to wear suits since it's not necessarily a Catholic country. Wearing a cassock to the grocery store might seem kind of strange, so it's reserved more for liturgical use, around the rectory, in the church, or in the parish school.

Fr. Trigilio: Black was also an easy way of identifying the rank of a clergyman in the Church. For instance, if you saw a simple black cassock, you would assume that was a priest. A purple cassock, on the other hand, would be a monsignor or a bishop, and a red cassock would be a cardinal. The pope then wears the full white cassock. But the color black was not extravagant. It was easy to get and easy to make. St. John Vianney, the Curé of Ars, had a very simple black cassock that he would wear with the purple stole when he heard confessions. The color of the black cassock doesn't mean what some people today sometimes deem as derogatory. It's a sign of somberness and an official status that just takes getting used to. I saw a vocation poster once with guys wearing collars and sunglasses, and it said, "The New Men in Black." When we're in Rome, we sometimes encounter bishops and cardinals wearing just a plain black cassock. Now, how can we tell that they're a bishop or a cardinal? By the color of their socks. The bishops will still wear purple socks, and the cardinals wear red socks, yet they'll wear the simple black cassock if they want to go in and out without people grabbing them on the street to have their picture taken. Cardinal Ratzinger was famous for wearing his black cassock.

Fr. Brighenti: We had a friend who was made metropolitan Archbishop in Pittsburgh, and when we were in Rome, we bought him a pair of purple socks. He got a good kick out of that!

17. The Consecration at the Mass

When do the bread and wine become the Body and Blood of Jesus during the Mass?

Fr. Brighenti: The most important part of the Mass is the Consecration. When we begin to kneel right after the preface and the "Holy, Holy, Holy," there's a gesture that the priest does called "the epiclesis," where he calls down the Holy Spirit to change the substances of bread and wine into the substances of the Body, Blood, Soul, and Divinity of Our Lord under the appearances (accidents) of bread and wine so that you and I may receive It. We then have the separate Consecration, in which the priest speaks the word of Consecration over the bread, elevates it and genuflects, and does the same with the chalice. This separate Consecration, the separating of Body from Blood, denotes the sacred Passion and death of Our Lord, and the mingling of the Body and Blood is performed after the "Lamb of God," also known as the *"Agnus Dei,"* symbolizing the Resurrection since we're receiving the Whole Risen Savior. It's this part, where we kneel through the Eucharistic Prayer, that is the core part that the Mass is building up to through our preparation in the readings and homily. After the Consecration (followed by the Lord's Prayer and the Sign of Peace) is our reception of Holy Communion and then our dismissal to take Our Lord, Who is now in our soul, out into the world.

Fr. Trigilio: In the Eastern Byzantine or Orthodox tradition, although they have the Consecration as we do in the Latin Rite, they look at the whole, contiguous Eucharistic Prayer. While we have it broken up into different sections, such as the epiclesis, the preface, and the Consecration, they would not pinpoint as we do in the Latin Rite to the very moment of the Consecration. However, it's forbidden for us to consecrate without the rest of those parts. At this particular point, it's true to repeat the words of St. Thomas Aquinas that it's at the Consecration where the transubstantiation takes place. You can never do it outside the Eucharistic Prayer, and you can't do the Eucharistic Prayer outside of the Mass; both are integrated and must be followed through in their proper context. Even in an emergency, I can't just take some bread and wine and say, "This is My Body. This is My Blood." I have to do it within the context of the Holy Sacrifice of the Mass.

Fr. Brighenti: It's such a beautiful time. On high holy days, we'll hear the tower bells ringing here at Mount St. Mary's Seminary where we both taught, and this event harkens back to when the Church was the center of the village and people were out in the fields. At the moment of Consecration, the tower bells would ring, and people would literally stop their work, put down their sickles and baskets, and kneel until they heard the second set of bells ringing, which is when they knew the Consecration was over. When I hear the tower bells at the seminary ring at the Consecration, I think it's such a beautiful sign that we're announcing to the whole world that God is made present and that Heaven and earth are miraculously united here on that altar.

Fr. Trigilio: It's a profound moment, because you realize that the Mass is the unbloody Sacrifice of Calvary, and it's the moment of Jesus' death which saved the human race. Yes, His Resurrection is the culmination of His mission here on earth, but it's at the moment of His death that the ransom was paid and where we were redeemed, and it's at this moment of the separate Consecration of the bread and wine that the Real Presence takes occurrence, and the substance of bread and wine changes into the substance of the Body, Blood, Soul, and Divinity of Christ. It's this beautiful reenactment, but not a reenactment like they do in memory of the Civil War. It's an unbloody memorial in the Hebrew Jewish sense, like when they have the Passover Seder meal; they're actually a part of it. This isn't just an act of going through the words and motions. This isn't just people pretending that George Washington crossed the Delaware, which they still reenact every year in his honor. This is an actual participation that, when we go to Mass, takes us to the Upper Room. We are there at the foot of the Cross at Calvary.

Fr. Brighenti: It's unfortunate, but I think a lot of people don't get this.

Fr. Trigilio: People feel like they're just spectators, like they're watching a play or a show. I think it was Kierkegaard who once remarked to a friend of his that at the Mass we are all participants. It's like a dress rehearsal for living out in the world. We're all participating in this divine drama.

Fr. Brighenti: Christ died once and for all on Calvary, but Calvary is then brought to us in the present at the Mass. Jesus doesn't die on the Cross again and again, but His singular death is made present to us here and now. We're invited now to place our lives on the paten and in the chalice, which are then offered up to God, wrapped in the beautiful Sacrifice of the Mass. That is why the priest says at the offertory prayers at the preparation of the gifts: "pray brethren, that my sacrifice *and yours* may be made acceptable to God the Almighty Father." The priest's sacrifice is the bread and wine. The people's sacrifice is their whole being.

18. Receiving Holy Communion

I understand the core of our Church is Christ in the Eucharist, as reception of the Eucharist is our Communion with the Triune God. I recall Christ's admonishment: "Truly, truly, I say to you, unless you eat the flesh of the Son of man and drink his blood, you have no life in you" (John 6:53). He also said, "Man shall not live by bread alone" (Matthew 4:4). Why are we then not required to receive both the Body and Blood of Christ?

Fr. Brighenti: There is a dogma in the Church called the "doctrine of concomitance," and it means that the Body and Blood, Soul and Divinity of Jesus Christ are wholly present in either sacred species; that is, the host or the chalice. If you're coming up to Communion and receiving the host, then you're receiving the Whole Risen Savior. In Jewish thought, death is by separation of the blood from the body, and that's why we have the separate Consecration at the Mass. A small piece of the host is then placed into the chalice, and this symbolizes the Resurrection. Now, some people can only receive from the chalice because they may have celiac disease, or gluten intolerance, or wheat allergy.

Fr. Trigilio: It was Martin Luther who insisted that you had to receive both the Body and Blood as a member of the faithful. The Council of Trent rejected his claim and clarified that the faithful only need receive one. It's only the priest who must receive both to satisfy the Mass, because he is fulfilling the Sacrifice by receiving both elements. Jesus is wholly in either the consecrated bread or the chalice of consecrated wine, because if you kept them separated, you'd have only dead flesh and dead blood, and that's not what we believe. It's the Risen Lord Who is alive. Thus, in one fragment of a host or one drop of the Precious Blood is exactly *both* the Body, Blood, Soul, and Divinity of Jesus Christ. I remember on one occasion we ran out of Precious Blood, so the last five people in the Communion line only received the sacred host whereas the rest were able to take both. One of them came up to me after Mass and complained that he only got half of Communion. I said "No, you are wrong. You received the whole Christ, Body and Blood, even though you only ate the host and were unable to drink from the chalice. Jesus is really, truly, and substantially present in both the consecrated bread and in the consecrated wine."

19. Being Refused Holy Communion

When can a priest refuse to give Holy Communion at Mass? This happened to me once because I was very late. The priest did apologize, but this had a terrible effect on me. I have been at Mass when other people have arrived late but were not refused Communion. I felt like God was refusing me. Although I do agree it was wrong to be late, I did not feel that I was being disrespectful.

Fr. Trigilio: The priest should actually not be denying you Communion only because you're late for Mass, although if you're late for Sunday Mass then you might be guilty of not fulfilling your Sunday obligation. But you can receive Communion as long as you're properly disposed, and only you know if you're in the state of mortal sin or not. Now, if someone is a known public sinner, a mafia-type hitman whose picture has been in the paper, or a notorious politician who is avidly pro-abortion, the priest or deacon or extraordinary minister can then refuse to give Communion. These only apply in cases where the person being refused is well-known, or what we call "infamously known." There's a chance of scandal that might be caused by allowing such a person to receive Communion. In many cases, we obviously don't know what a person's spiritual state is, and some of these people don't even know if they've reconciled themselves or not. But just being late, in and of itself, is not a valid reason for the priest to deny you Communion.

Fr. Brighenti: While the priest was apologizing, that would have been a good time to inquire why he refused you and what his reason was for doing so. Something else to keep in mind is that a priest cannot refuse you Communion if you want to kneel, even if there's no altar rail. I have, however, known some priests in the past who, because they wanted to make a political statement, wouldn't give Communion to those who kneeled. No priest has a right to do that. You have the option to kneel for Communion or genuflect beforehand; both are totally within the guidelines. We priests have to be careful in these situations where people can be scandalized, as we don't want to hurt the prayer life and piety of the faithful. Now, where I was pastor, we were one block from the train station, and that train would go by every twenty minutes. Inevitably, the train would stop traffic, and people would be late for Mass. But I told them that they knew the train schedule by now and that they should plan their morning accordingly. Let's say if Mass is at noon and the train comes by five minutes prior, then you should be getting to church at quarter to twelve so you can park, get in, and prepare yourself for Mass instead of rushing in. And consider staying after Mass to give an act of thanksgiving. Now, in the situation presented by this question, it sounds like being late was not the norm. But in general, everyone should try to get to Mass at least fifteen minutes early to settle in, get into the right state of mind, and detox from the world. As you take the holy water and genuflect before Our Lord in the Blessed Sacrament, you should be spiritually transformed so that you will listen attentively to the readings, receive Our Lord in Holy Communion, and spend some time after Mass.

Fr. Trigilio: I'm glad you mentioned about staying afterward, because I think it's much more disrespectful and much more of a potential sin if somebody leaves Mass for the wrong reasons before it's over. Obviously, if you're sick or the church is on fire, then you've got to get out. But you can't leave Mass early just because you're running a few minutes behind schedule; it's simply disrespectful. If you get to church late, it might be your fault, but at least you tried to get there. Now, I don't want people to think that it's a choice between arriving late or leaving early, but it's definitely a problem when these people leave before the Mass has ended, and the host hasn't even gone down their throats yet.

Fr. Brighenti: People need to plan their day better to make Mass the priority. I know a lot of people like to get to the early bird's special on Saturday at the Vigil Mass. But regardless of whether it's Sunday or Saturday, plan ahead and take your time with the Lord once you arrive. It's practically the only hour we give Him throughout the week. It will be time well spent.

Fr. Trigilio: There's a sign I remember some old monsignor hung at the back of a church once that said, "Remember: Judas was the first one to leave Mass early."

20. Receiving the Precious Blood

What is the benefit of receiving the consecrated wine at Holy Communion? Our parish only offers the Precious Blood on Sundays. Some say it is only for the priests, but it helps me.

Fr. Brighenti: First of all, I'm glad the person asking this question corrected himself. I like to use the proper term "Precious Blood of Jesus." It's in the Consecration of the Mass that the wine becomes the Blood of Christ, but we should always refer to it in its proper title, as "the Precious Blood." Yes, in order for a priest to have a valid Mass and the intention is satisfied, he must receive both the Body and Blood of Christ because he's acting *in persona Christi* (in the Person of Christ) as an *alter Christus* (another Christ). Jesus is both Priest and Victim at every Mass, so there is a mandate. For the rest of those attending Mass, they can choose just to receive the host. They are not required to receive from the chalice, but remember that the sacred host is the Body, Blood, Soul, and Divinity of the Risen Christ, and so is the Precious Blood in the chalice. The separation comes from a Jewish understanding, and that's why we have the separate Consecration at Mass; there's the consecration of the bread and then we have the consecration of the wine, and the genuflection in between denotes the death on the Cross while the mingling of the small piece of host with the chalice denotes the Resurrection. At Mass, you're not receiving the dead Christ but the Risen Savior, and that's why you're receiving the complete package, to borrow on the beautiful terminology of St. Thomas Aquinas in the *Summa Theologica*. There's also a dogma called the "doctrine of concomitance," which teaches us that when people receive the host, they're receiving the Body, Blood, Soul, and Divinity of Christ under the appearance of the host; and from five hundred years since the Council of Trent to just before the present, most Catholics only received Communion in that form. In the Early Church, they received under both species, and this was restored after the Second Vatican Council; Christ said to eat and drink both. "Take, eat; this is my body.... Drink of it, all of you" (Matthew 26:26-27). Now, in Italy and in the Vatican especially, it's interesting to note that when we concelebrate Mass at the Chair of St. Peter, they instruct us priests to dip the host into the chalice and to receive the Body and Blood of Christ in that way to complete the Mass that we're offering. The priest will sometimes do this for the laypeople, as well, for sign value. But receiving the Precious Blood is not required for laypeople, as they're already receiving Christ wholly in the Eucharist.

Fr. Trigilio: I've never actually seen an occasion where they've offered both species in the Vatican, although it's allowed. It's an option, and if you as the communicant want to receive only the host even when they're also offering the chalice, then you don't have to receive from the chalice, as you're already receiving the Whole Christ, His Body, Blood, Soul, and Divinity in the host. A lot of Catholics aren't aware of this fact, especially if they're used to seeing both the chalice and the host distributed at Mass. Like Fr. Brighenti said, the reason why the Second Vatican Council allowed distribution of the Precious Blood was for the sign value, but at that time they were confident that the people would not fall back to the false notion that Christ isn't wholly present in the host, which Martin Luther promoted in the sixteenth century. Many parishes now are going back to only offering the Precious Blood on special occasions, to remind the people that when you receive one, you receive both. If you're consistently distributing both, people might think they're getting half of Communion when they attend a different parish that only distributes the host. But how do you divide God in half?

Fr. Brighenti: It's the Risen, Glorified Savior, and it's a mystery how everyone can receive Him in the host. Something else that happened to me, and probably to you as well, is when a person attempts to take the host and then go to the chalice for intinction, the dipping of the bread into the chalice. Laypeople are *not* allowed to do that.

Fr. Trigilio: Priests alone have permission to practice intinction because we're the celebrants or concelebrants, but a layperson should never do this. First of all, you're not allowed to take the sacred host. You are to receive the host either in the hand or on the tongue in front of the person giving Communion. You are never allowed to take the host over to the chalice for intinction.

Fr. Brighenti: This is a good time to discuss the etiquette of receiving Holy Communion, which seems to be lost in our culture today. At one time, all parishes had the altar rail. The people would kneel at the rail and receive either in the hand or on the tongue, the tongue being the only acceptable method in the Extraordinary Form of the Mass. If you're receiving in the hand, you should make a throne for the Lord with your hands when you receive Him. If you're right-handed, you put your left hand over your right to receive, and then you take the host with your right hand and place it immediately in your mouth. If you're receiving Holy Communion standing up (maybe because there's no altar rail), then you can do either one of these three things: bow your head profoundly beforehand, genuflect while receiving, or make the Sign of the Cross afterward. Certain dioceses choose the gesture. In our diocese, it was bowing before you received Holy Communion. It's an act of reverence before you receive Our Lord.

Fr. Trigilio: The Congregation for Divine Worship and the Discipline of the Sacraments also gives the people the option to choose. I think it was *Redemptionis Sacramentum* that explained that if the common practice is that you stand, you're still allowed to receive Communion kneeling. No one can deny Communion to you. They might say you're going against the standard, but they cannot deny you Communion. They can ask you to please stand, but you're always allowed to kneel or genuflect.

Fr. Brighenti: That's right. Even though bowing was the official method in our diocese, you could still genuflect or make the Sign of the Cross. All of these options are valid.

Fr. Trigilio: At my parish, we put a little kneeler before the altar, just like Pope Benedict used to, so the people have the option to kneel. If they want to stand, then they can stand.

Fr. Brighenti: It's interesting to note at Papal Masses, however, that the people only receive on the tongue from the Holy Father.

Fr. Trigilio: They must kneel for the Holy Father as well. Now, when you go to a Byzantine or Eastern Catholic Church, they always receive by intinction, and you have to open your mouth but keep your tongue in the back. The Body of Christ is in cube form on a spoon in the chalice that contains the Precious Blood. The priest drops it into your mouth without touching your lips or tongue. This is much different from the Latin tradition, where the host is unleavened and you either receive in the hand or on the tongue.

21. Bread Consecrated for Holy Communion

Is the "daily bread" from a bakery? Where do they get it, and does it have to be specially prepared to make it "kosher," so to speak?

Fr. Brighenti: The term "daily bread" comes from the prayer of the Our Father. We ask Our Heavenly Father to "Give us this day our daily bread." In other words, to give us the grace that we need to carry on for the present moment. We pray for our daily sustenance, body and soul. The spiritual food Christ gives us is His very Body and Blood. We eat what appears to be bread, but It is really, truly, and substantially the Body and Blood, Soul and Divinity of Christ. We call this the Real Presence, the Holy Eucharist, the Blessed Sacrament. We're also not so much to be concerned about the future, and the past is past, but as Mother Angelica, quoting an old saying, used to recall, "The present is a present, a gift from God." So, we're asking for the daily nourishment from the Lord, that daily grace and spiritual gift from God to get through our day, to use our talents, and to use the opportunities that are given to us in the best way that we can. We're praying for nothing further than today.

Your question brings up the preparation of bread, so I'm going to cover Holy Communion, too. There are specific guidelines in the Catholic Church for what we call the "sacred hosts" for Mass. There's the bigger, celebrant host for the priest, which is sometimes also broken up for the faithful under certain conditions, and then there are the smaller hosts that are consecrated for the people. All hosts must consist of unleavened bread made from wheat, and they cannot have any other ingredients such as sugar, salt, or flavoring; only flour and water. Normally, they're made by religious sisters, but they don't have to be. The Sisters of the Good Shepherd in Philadelphia are from whom I used to get my hosts for church. On the priest's hosts, these sisters would imprint an image of a chalice, the Holy Spirit, or the Christogram IHS (*Iesus Humilis Societas*, or the Humble Society of Jesus).

Fr. Trigilio: Now, what about in the Byzantine Church? They use leavened bread, so there is yeast in their tradition. But there's also no salt, milk, eggs, honey, raisins, cranberries, or anything else.

Fr. Brighenti: That's because those things would invalidate the matter. All we use is wheat flour and water. No rice cakes, no soy flour.

Fr. Trigilio: To complement this, the wine also has to be grape wine that's naturally fermented. No fortified wine. There must be some alcoholic content to it. Grape juice from the grocery store is invalid matter. Likewise, wine from other sources (rice, for example) is also invalid. Wheat bread and grape wine. Period.

22. Fasting Before Mass

What are the rules for fasting and abstinence? My friend would eat an ice cream cone on the way to Mass because he said it would still be an hour before Communion. What if he is a couple minutes off in his calculations? Is his Communion sacrilegious or invalid? Would he need to confess this?

Fr. Trigilio: When we discuss the obligations of fasting, we need to make some distinctions here. For the Eucharistic fast, you are currently required to abstain from any food or drink (other than water) for one hour prior to receiving Holy Communion. Now, if you attend a parish where the priest or the deacon is a little loquacious, that alone may give you a full hour, and you could actually eat or drink something up until the time Mass begins. But if you're at a parish where the priest or deacon is a bit brief and more succinct and to the point, then you might not have that full hour. In all seriousness, if Sunday Mass is at nine o'clock, I would strongly suggest you fast at least from eight-thirty, since that would give you an hour or more before Holy Communion. You may also fast from eight o'clock if you like, but the minimum is one hour before *receiving* Holy Communion, not necessarily one hour before Mass itself.

However, it's not so much the exact number of minutes and seconds that count, but it's the attitude. You're showing respect by denying yourself some food or drink for a period of time before receiving Our Lord. Now, obviously, if you are under a doctor's care, you're in a nursing home, you're diabetic, you're hypoglycemic, you're pregnant, you need to take food with your medicine, and so on, then you're allowed to have food within a shorter amount of time. After celebrating their first Mass for the day, priests are dispensed from fasting for an hour before any following Masses. When my parents were young and making their First Communion, the requirement at the time was three hours. Before that, our grandparents had to fast from midnight.

Then there's the law of fasting and abstinence that occurs throughout the year, particularly during Lent. Fasting means having one full meal for the day and two smaller meals that, if combined, would not equal that one full meal. This applies to Catholics from the ages of eighteen to fifty-nine inclusively. If you're sixty years old or under the age of eighteen, then you are not obligated to fast.

Abstinence, which means not eating meat, applies to people age fourteen and over, and there's no limit. Sometimes we get senior citizens who say they don't have to worry about Lent, but while they're not obligated to fast anymore, they must still abstain from eating meat. Right now, you only have to abstain from meat on Ash Wednesday and Fridays during Lent, but this doesn't hold true for other parts of the world; England, for example, has gone back to abstinence from meat on all Fridays throughout the whole year. Meat is all beef, poultry, pork, and so on. Basically, meat is any flesh from a warm-blooded animal. Abstinence is therefore not restricted to red meat only. Fish and flesh of cold-blooded creatures are acceptable, though, on Fridays.

Fr. Brighenti: I thought it was interesting that the question mentioned that his friend eats an ice cream cone and tries to calculate the time until Mass. To me, that's portraying minimalism, and minimalism then turns into legalism. What are we trying to convey by this fast? We should be trying to prepare ourselves. Is eating an ice cream cone before Mass the best way to prepare? I would say not. I think recollecting your thoughts spiritually and even reflecting on the Mass readings or getting to church a bit earlier are more effective ways to prepare yourself. Why not get to church a half an hour early, light a candle, and make a visit to the Blessed Sacrament to spend some time in prayer? Why would you only want to be in church for that one hour during Mass? It's a minimalist mentality to be so stingy as to calculate our devotion to God when He is so abundant with His love and grace. While canon law says you have to receive Communion at least once a year during the Easter season, that's only the minimum. We should want to receive Communion more than that.

Fr. Trigilio: It's so surprising when you look at other religions, such as Judaism and Islam. Our bishop once asked the children who were to be confirmed, "When's the time of fasting?" A little girl raised her hand and said, "Ramadan." The bishop said, "Look. I'm here to confirm you in the Catholic Faith, not in Islam." Other religions see the value of fasting and days of penance. For us as Catholic Christians, this is part of our patrimony, and it's so good to die to self. We must decrease so He can increase, to paraphrase St. John the Baptist, and that's the purpose of fasting. It's not that we're bad and need to be punished. It's mortification.

Fr. Brighenti: Now, the Church changed the Eucharistic fast to only an hour because some people are unfortunately minimalists, but we can consider to go beyond that. While in the United

States we are only obligated to abstain from meat on Fridays in Lent, the bishops and canon law say we should make some form of penance or mortification or perform an act of mercy on the rest of the Fridays of the year. Some folks just abstain from meat throughout all the year's Fridays, and that's wonderful.

Fr. Trigilio: You could voluntarily keep the three-hour fast or the fast from midnight onward, especially during Lent, but you are also dispensed if you're in the hospital or under a doctor's care and if you have a condition where you need to eat more regularly, such as diabetes or hypoglycemia. Sometimes, Father or the deacon might get to Mass a little late. If you're already dispensed because of your condition, don't put yourself in a diabetic coma by refusing to eat when your health depends on it. It's those of us who don't have these medical conditions that should be more attentive to following the laws of fasting and abstinence. Pregnant mothers are exempt from fasting and abstinence, too.

Fr. Brighenti: To summarize: Is eating an ice cream cone an hour before Mass wrong? No. But should you? No. Hopefully, you would spend the time you have before Mass in prayer.

23. Receiving the Eucharist and Suffering from Mental Illnesses

I have had schizophrenia for thirteen years and am on disability. I take a lot of medication and am at the doctor's office frequently. Does taking my medication take away from the Eucharist at Mass, and does Jesus make exceptions in blind faith of His Kingdom at Mass? Am I really saved by my faith and Baptism? I'm failing to hold respect and love for my fellow Christians because the medication dominates my life. I can't stop taking my medication, and spiritually I am failing from it. I'm a wreck and I love Jesus with all my heart, but I can't seem to learn and grow in the Church. What should I do if my mental condition is keeping me from being a good Christian? Am I alone?

Fr. Brighenti: There are many people in the Church who are suffering from serious mental illnesses and have to face overwhelming challenges, and I applaud you for staying on your medication. Many of the problems addressed in this question can probably be helped if you continue going to your counselor or psychiatrist to look into these rough edges, and they might have to tweak the medication you're on so it's not so disruptive. I've known several people on medication during the course of their whole lives who have had their medication changed because it didn't work any longer. So, you may be going through a similar moment where your doctor simply needs to change your medication, but you should always stay on it because it will help you. If I understand the question, I think part of it alludes to fasting. You are perfectly fine to take your medication before you go to Mass, or if a priest, deacon, or extraordinary Eucharistic minister is bringing you Communion at your home when you're ill or sick; this is certainly considered an illness. You're dispensed from the hour fast before Mass if you need to take food with your medication, so please do so, as the Church certainly understands and dispenses you from fasting under this condition. Regarding the part of the question which addresses salvation: yes, we are saved through Baptism which remits Original Sin, but after Baptism, we can easily fall into actual sin. If the sins we commit are mortal sins, then we must avail ourselves of the Sacrament of Penance and confess these sins to a priest. So, we do not believe in "once saved, always saved," otherwise Jesus would not have given the power to forgive sins to the apostles and their successors. After Baptism, you and I need to accept and cooperate with God's grace. He gives us sanctifying grace in the sacraments, but also actual grace through the sacramentals and through prayer. This is the supernatural gift that enables us to do good.

Maybe a good thing to pray for is patience in your time of suffering. I also suggest that you read Pope St. John Paul II's encyclical on human suffering called *Salvifici Doloris*. He gave such a wonderful testimony at the end of his life.

Fr. Trigilio: I'm glad you brought up Pope St. John Paul the Great, because you can see the suffering in his later years, particularly with the Parkinson's disease and other complications. In the last few months of his life, he also had to get a tracheotomy, as he was having difficulty breathing. He issued a decree on what's considered the ordinary means of treatment for people, most particularly the dying and the terminally ill. You always have to supply them with at least nutrition if they're able to ingest and assimilate food and water; and then there's normal care, where you give them a blanket if they're cold, clean them up so they're not lying in their own waste, and so on. You care for them with dignity and respect, and you give them pain medication as long as the medication doesn't precipitate or hasten their death. In terms of the condition evident in the question, while it's not life-threatening, it certainly is a difficult thing to bear, and you have to stay on your medication. If the medication prevents you from focusing or keeping your attention, then that's something you need to offer up to the Lord, and He understands. If it's hard for you to concentrate during prayer, remember that you're not obligated to go beyond what you're capable of doing. Because of their meds, some people get a little drowsy, distracted, or even irritable. If it's the medicine or your condition or your ailment that causes this, the Lord understands that, and He wants you to just do the best that you can.

Fr. Brighenti: You should also treat your illness for what it is and take your medication, just like a person who is diabetic has to take their insulin. Treat it in that way, and you will understand it better. Also, a great patron saint for you would be St. Dymphna. She was an Irish saint whose father suffered from a terrible mental illness, and she had to suffer the repercussions from that. She is a great saint to pray to for her intercession to the Lord in your time of trial and crisis.

24. Who Can Receive Holy Communion?

I would like to know who is allowed to receive the Body and Blood of Christ? I would like to receive It during the Mass, but I am not sure that I can.

Fr. Brighenti: I assume that the presenter of this question is not a Catholic but is attending Catholic Mass. These are the requirements to receive Holy Communion: You have to be a baptized Catholic; you have to be at least at the age of reason (if in the Latin Rite; Eastern Rite Catholics receive Holy Communion and Confirmation at Baptism) which the Church deems around seven; you have to have proper catechesis, which means instruction in this Sacrament; and you must receive the Sacrament of Confession before your first time receiving Communion, and if you have any serious sin on your soul after that as well. However, it sounds like this might be a person who's converting to the Catholic Faith, so therefore I would suggest attending the RCIA (Rite of Christian Initiation of Adults) program of catechesis and instruction in the Faith. If you're not baptized, then this program will help you prepare to receive the Sacrament of Baptism at the Easter Vigil, where you will also receive the Eucharist and Confirmation. We call these the three Sacraments of Initiation. If you have received Baptism in the Catholic Church but no other sacraments, or were baptized in a recognizable Protestant church that uses the Trinitarian formula, then you will be received into full communion with the Catholic Church through the celebrations of Communion and Confirmation at the Easter Vigil after the Sacrament of Confession. You should contact your parish priest and inquire about signing up for RCIA.

Fr. Trigilio: A little phrase that I like to use is "One must be in communion to receive Communion." Therefore, we as Catholics, as well as the Eastern Orthodox, don't see Communion as being a means to an end; we see it as the final product, the final result of an already-established unity. As Americans, for example, you and I can vote on Election Day or run for office because we're full-blown citizens, while our ancestors who came to America from Italy, while they could live and work here, weren't able to vote or to run for office until they were full-fledged citizens. For us, to receive Communion is the end result of an already established unity.

Fr. Brighenti: Why don't you mention when the Eastern Orthodox can receive Communion?

Fr. Trigilio: The Catholic Church allows Eastern Orthodox Christians to receive Communion, especially if they're unable to go to their church or if it's not available. Unfortunately, because we're not in full communion with the Eastern Orthodox Church, they don't want their people to receive from us. That said, if an Eastern Orthodox Christian comes to us for Communion, we're allowed to give It to them, but it's a stumbling block since their Church does not allow Catholics to receive. We can go to an Orthodox Church to fulfill our Sunday obligation, but we're not able to receive Communion. Both Churches regard each other as having valid sacraments, however. Due to the break in apostolic succession and defective intention, matter, and form, Protestant "communion" and "orders" are considered invalid sacraments.

25. The Obligation to Attend Mass if Ill

I had two open-heart surgeries performed five weeks apart this Easter. Before the second operation, I was anointed with the oils for the sick. Since I have been home, I've only been able to go to Sunday Mass a few times because the medication I take causes me to get very sick in the morning. I do watch the daily Mass on EWTN and pray the Rosary every day without fail. I worry that since I have trouble getting to church, I may have mortal sins on my soul, and I'm afraid that Jesus will cast me away.

Fr. Trigilio: Well, first off, we want to assure you that we're praying for you and your speedy recovery. Please know that your obligation to go to Mass is conditioned upon your ability to go to Mass. So, whenever there's inclement weather, whether it's six feet of snow or a tornado in the area, your obligation to go to Mass is dispensed. Likewise, if your personal health hinders you or if you're taking care of somebody else with poor health, your obligation to go to Mass is dispensed. Certainly, you go when you can, and when you can't physically attend, you can watch it on television or make a Spiritual Communion. This is the reason why EWTN broadcasts the Mass, because there are so many people we call "shut-ins." These are people who cannot get out of the house or the nursing home. Sometimes, they may be sick. They're not necessarily all elderly people, but they could be people who are temporarily homebound, like someone who had a hip replacement for example. When my dad was alive, he was dying of leukemia, and the day he died he was watching the Mass on EWTN. It was the feast of Our Lady of Lourdes, and within half an hour of the Mass being over, he passed away. I know that when I and many other priests bring Communion to the sick on First Fridays, the people will often be watching the Mass on TV. So, please do not think that you're committing a mortal sin. It's only a mortal sin if you're physically able to get to church, in terms of your health or weather conditions, and you don't go. What if there's no Catholic parish in your town? Obviously, you don't have to drive fifty or one hundred miles. But if it's only a few blocks away, and it's a bright sunny day, and you're in good health, then you've got to go.

Fr. Brighenti: When I was pastor and bringing Communion on First Fridays, I would sometimes run across that person who was originally sick and in the hospital but had recuperated and was now out shopping and running errands, yet still staying home for First Friday Communion calls and not going to Mass. That's where the problem lies. If you can go to the mall, if you can go shopping, and if you can go to the dentist, then you can definitely go to Mass as well. So, we had a little "come to Jesus" moment as I had to explain this to them. In fact, when I was bringing Communion to that person, no one was home. She was actually late getting into the driveway and out of the car, and I was kind of surprised because I didn't know she was that well and getting better. So I said, "I guess you can start coming to Mass on Sunday." But also, when people are home and receiving Communion, they are dispensed from the fast, especially if they have to take pills or they're diabetic. And even if they are going to church but are diabetic and have to eat at a certain time, then they should go ahead and do so.

Fr. Trigilio: If you're on dialysis, if you're hypoglycemic, or you're getting chemo or radiation and so on, then you're dispensed. A pregnant woman or a nursing mother is also dispensed.

Fr. Brighenti: There's also a proper etiquette for the home when we're bringing you Communion. Please have a candle, a crucifix, and a nice linen that you only use to place the Blessed Sacrament on. These little things are very devotional and beautiful to have in your home. There used to be these neat little sick-call kits that looked like a crucifix, and when you opened it up there would be two candles and a little holy water. You sometimes see these in antique stores. There's a real beautiful one I saw recently where the crucifix was on top of a box, and when you opened the box it had a little religious scene inside, and there were all the candles and devotional items as well. Regardless of what you use, a nice linen, a candle, and a crucifix would be appropriate to greet the priest for Communion.

Fr. Trigilio: I must also strongly emphasize that when the priest or deacon or extraordinary minister of Holy Communion arrives, please turn off the television. I can't tell you how many times we would come to bring Communion to the sick and *Wheel of Fortune* or the news is on in the background. If the TV is on, we are then in competition with the television as we're trying to get this person to say the Our Father or an Act of Contrition while there are commercials playing in the background. It's fine for you to watch television up to the point we arrive, but it would be even better if you were quietly preparing in advance to receive Our Lord. If Father is coming at ten o'clock, then consider turning off the TV at a quarter to ten so the priest can help you get into prayer mode, as opposed to leaving the television or radio on. I've seen more attention given to the plumber and the cableman than when the priest brings Communion.

Fr. Brighenti: And don't feel offended if the priest can't stay long, as he is carrying the Blessed Sacrament. He can't stop for coffee or hang around to socialize. He has to go on to the next call, and he might have quite a few on the list, and depending where they are, he might have a long day of travel ahead of him. It's really not respectful for him to stay with the Blessed Sacrament for coffee or for lunch.

Fr. Trigilio: It's not that the priest isn't being friendly, but when he's got fifty more stops to make (some priests have up to one hundred people to bring Communion to on a First Friday), it's simply impossible to stay longer. It's not the right opportunity, either. It's like in the confessional: you're not there for spiritual direction, but you're there for Confession. If you need counseling, then you should make an appointment. This same concept applies on the First Friday visits or anytime the priest comes to anoint the sick. Now, if you want to schedule something separately, ask Father to come over on a certain day to talk and schedule that as a separate appointment. This way, you both do each other justice. And whenever needed, you can go to the priest for the Sacrament of Confession just before he anoints you and gives you Holy Communion.

26. The Purpose of Tabernacles

What is the significance of tabernacles, and why do Catholic churches display religious shrines on top of the altar?

Fr. Brighenti: The significance revolves around the Sacrament of the Holy Eucharist. We place the consecrated host, which is the Body, Blood, Soul, and Divinity of Jesus Christ under the appearance of bread, for exposition in the monstrance (also known as an ostensorium) that comes from the Latin word for "to show." A monstrance generally looks like a sunburst. We place it on the altar for a period of time for adoration, concluding with the liturgical celebration of Benediction, which is derived from the Latin word for "blessing." The priest then puts on a humeral veil, which is this long garment that also covers his hands, and this shows that Christ in the Blessed Sacrament is giving the blessing and not the priest himself. The tabernacle is a place of reservation of the consecrated host. After Communion, where the host is distributed to the people at the Mass, the remnants of the hosts are placed in the tabernacle. Those hosts are used to bring Communion to the shut-ins or the sick in the hospital and for private Adoration of the Blessed Sacrament, but not necessarily for exposition in the monstrance. When people come to church, you'll see a red sanctuary lamp hanging near the tabernacle to signify that Jesus is present in the Blessed Sacrament. We never reserve the Precious Blood of Christ under the appearance of wine; it's only the species of the sacred hosts that are stored in the tabernacle. There is a warm presence when you see that sanctuary lamp. It's St. Elizabeth Ann Seton who often looked at that lamp when she was an Episcopalian, and its warm glow led her to inquire about our doctrine and our belief in the real presence of Jesus.

Fr. Trigilio: I think this was when she was visiting the Filicchi family in Italy while her husband was under quarantine for tuberculosis. You wouldn't typically find a tabernacle or a monstrance in a non-Catholic Christian church, because these churches do not have a definitive profession of faith in the Real Presence in the Blessed Sacrament, nor do they have the reservation of the Sacrament as we do in the Catholic and Eastern Orthodox tradition to bring Communion to the sick. But this particular idea of Adoration is so important. When people see it in practice, they realize it's because we believe the Blessed Sacrament literally is the Body, Blood, Soul, and Divinity of Christ, that it's the Real, True, Substantial Jesus. If we believe that the Blessed Sacrament is Jesus, then we have to adore Him in the same way as we read in the Gospels where people fell at His feet and adored Him, just like the Magi did at the Epiphany.

Fr. Brighenti: Just think of that beautiful scene in the Garden of Gethsemane when Our Lord asked the apostles to keep vigil with Him. Adoration is our chance to keep vigil with the Lord, to take up the fruits of the Mass, and to further expound upon these things in our thoughts and meditations. Plus, the chief purpose of why we were created is to give God worship, adoration, and thanks, and we have the opportunity to do so by making private visits to chapels, oratories, and our parish sanctuaries. Unfortunately, some of the parishes following Vatican II misrepresent or misinterpret the doctrine, and the Blessed Sacrament was moved from the center of the sanctuary to a little side chapel or separate room or building. This was not the intention of the Second Vatican Council. Now, if we're talking about a public building, like St. Patrick's Cathedral in New York City, where due reverence is not always given, then a private Blessed Sacrament chapel is appropriate. But for a regular parish, the Blessed Sacrament should be in the main body of the church. Since the new Missal of 2000, thankfully we see lots of churches restoring the Blessed Sacrament to the center of the church in the sanctuary. If you look at it, this concept has biblical roots. It comes from the temple of the Holy of Holies, where the sanctuary was directly behind where the congregation would gather in the center. So, a proper place for the Blessed Sacrament would be in the center of the church, behind the altar, and viewed by everyone to venerate and make reverence.

Fr. Trigilio: When Mother Angelica was having her Shrine to the Most Blessed Sacrament consecrated, the night before I actually got to the top and saw the seven-foot monstrance up there. I teased her, saying, "Mother, how is a priest going to do Benediction picking that thing up?" She said, "Father, no one's going to touch that." Normally, the ones you see in church are able to be picked up by a priest or deacon so they can give Benediction.

Fr. Brighenti: That was a special monstrance, too, a personal gift to Mother Angelica from Pope St. John Paul the Great. I also want to remind our audience that the tabernacle that contains the Holy Eucharist often is designed to look like the Ark of the Covenant, which had contained the Ten Commandments. Those were the words of God written in stone on Mount Sinai. The tabernacles used in Catholic churches today contain the Word made flesh, that is, the Incarnate Word, Jesus Christ.

27. Christ Is Fully Present in the Eucharist

My mother is a new Catholic, full of both zeal and questions. One of the many things she is wondering about is why we are not required to take Holy Communion in both the accidents of bread and wine. I've always understood that the Lord is fully present in either one, yet she says that the Lord is fully present only in both together, and she insists that He commanded that we eat His Body and drink His Blood. She feels that by only taking the host that she is receiving only half the grace of Communion. She suspects that the Church instituted a "partial communion" as a way to save time during Mass and feels that this is an abuse. Is she correct in her thinking? I've noticed that anytime an "optional route" is given to a sacrament, most people tend to take what they perceive as the easiest path.

Fr. Trigilio: The Council of Trent made it very clear in the sixteenth century (in response to Martin Luther's assertion) that the Whole Christ, His Body, Blood, Soul, and Divinity, is fully present in either one of the sacred species. So, whether you take a sip of the Precious Blood from the chalice or receive the host on the tongue or in the hand, you're receiving all of Jesus. You cannot divide Him. The separation of body and blood is death, and we're receiving the Risen Lord, not a dead lord. Even though there's a separate Consecration at the Mass, when the mystery of faith is proclaimed we're saying that Jesus is Risen. We then receive His Body and Blood. Now, it's true that for a while both forms were given more frequently, but this changed following abuses where people were spilling the Precious Blood, and there were also risks of contagion, such as the Black Death, which alone killed one-third of Europe. In any event, the practice started to go into decline. When the Protestant reformers insisted that you had to receive both the Body and the Blood, the Church in turn declared that you don't, and to ensure that the people knew this, it stopped offering both at the Mass. Only a priest is obligated by Canon Law and by liturgical law to receive both the consecrated host and the Precious Blood. Since the Second Vatican Council, receiving both has been encouraged on a number of occasions, but in many places this practice is still not the norm because we want people to know that they are receiving both in one. I performed a little experiment at my parish. When I first got there, we were offering the Precious Blood all the time, and I decided we'd offer it only once a month. When people came to me, complaining that they were only receiving half of Communion, I got to explain to them that they are receiving both in one. There is no way you can quantify something spiritual. This is the Body, Blood, Soul, and Divinity of Jesus Christ, the Son of God. How can you divide Him up? You can't. You can divide up the species, such as breaking the host into tiny, little pieces, but you can't quantify something that's unquantifiable. To make the point, we have Communion under both forms once a month, and we also have to make sure there are present either deacons, who are the ordinary ministers of Communion with the priest, or extraordinary ministers of Holy Communion, which are those laypeople who have been delegated by the bishop. There's a real necessity to using them. You are receiving all of Jesus. You have no need to worry, and receiving only the host makes receiving the Precious Blood even more special when it's offered on special occasions, such as Christmas, Easter, Corpus Christi, Father's anniversary of ordination, a priest's first Mass, and so on.

Fr. Brighenti: Also, if there are concelebrants, they must take from the host and chalice that were consecrated at that Mass and not from the tabernacle. They are to receive Communion from that present Mass, and this completes their sacrifice, for the mandate to "Take and eat, take and drink" was given to the apostles. You'll often see the priest at Mass very scrupulously clean the corporal, which is a cloth beneath the paten that contains the hosts. He also purifies the chalice after consuming any remaining Precious Blood, and this is done out of reverence and respect for the presence of Our Lord in the Eucharist.

Fr. Trigilio: That act alone is a wonderful testimony to our belief in the Real Presence.

28. The Accidents of the Precious Blood

My husband has a dilemma: He is a recovering alcoholic and has been questioned as to why he does not receive the Blood of Christ at Holy Communion. People have argued with him that it is no longer wine, which is true. However, he has a brother who is a priest and has refused to use non-alcoholic wine at Mass, and this brother is struggling with alcohol addiction as well.

Fr. Trigilio: We'll start at the end of this question and work our way backward, as it will be a little easier for me with regard to this particular topic. A priest, even if he's an alcoholic, still has the obligation to consume the Precious Blood in order to complete the Sacrifice of the Mass. Whereas, as a layperson, you have no obligation to receive from the chalice, since you receive the Body, Blood, Soul, and Divinity of Christ in the host. Your husband has no need to be embarrassed, and people should really mind their own business.

Fr. Brighenti: In addition, there are plenty of people who don't receive from the chalice.

Fr. Trigilio: The reasons vary, too. You could have an allergy to grape wine, you could have an addiction to alcohol, you might have a cold and not want to get others sick, or you're used to the Extraordinary Form of the Mass where you typically only receive the host. You can simply tell anyone who asks that it's your personal preference not to receive from the chalice. But the priest has to receive both, because he's offering up the sacrifice. That being said, the priest has to use mustum, which is available from winemakers. It's the first pressing of the grapes; it is not wine, but it does contain a negligible percentage of alcohol, and if you let it sit long enough, it will eventually become wine, but it's used long before that takes effect. A priest cannot use the typical grape juice you'd find at the store for Mass.

Fr. Brighenti: It would be invalid matter, and all those Masses would go unsatisfied.

Fr. Trigilio: That's right, so that option is clearly off the table. The priest must use the mustum. Evidently, the husband's brother went the wrong direction and started using the regular wine, but regardless, the husband doesn't have to receive it. Now, what can conversely happen is someone who has celiac disease or a gluten allergy and maybe can't receive the host. There are low-gluten hosts which you can get from certain religious sisters that a priest can consecrate and give to people. In fact, I did this recently when I was offering a Mass. But if this option isn't available, then people can talk to the priest before Mass. Just tell him that you have an allergy, and receive from the chalice.

Fr. Brighenti: Yes, grab the priest ahead of time, and he can make this arrangement. Now, if it's someone's first time in the parish and the priest doesn't have those low-gluten hosts, then that person can choose to receive from the chalice until the priest orders the hosts. I've done this many times, including for a seminarian and for religious sisters at the convent. It's not an uncommon practice to do anymore.

Fr. Trigilio: The last thing I would like to add is that even though the wine is consecrated and becomes the Precious Blood of Christ, it still appears under the accidents of wine, and if you drink too much, you can still get inebriated. I know this from personal experience, as it happened to me in Hanceville where they had this huge chalice that nobody else drank from. I had to consume the equivalent of a bottle of wine. It was consecrated. It was the Blood of Christ. But the accidents were certainly there and I felt them all right.

29. Incense

What is the significance and purpose of incense used at certain Masses?

Fr. Brighenti: Smells and bells are some of my favorite things. Incense has been used in liturgy going as far back as the Jewish temple sacrifice. In fact, one of the Psalms says, "Let my prayer be counted as incense before thee" (141:2). Obviously incense rises, and it's just like when a person lights a candle and asks that their prayers continue for as long as that candle burns in honor of the Lord or a certain saint from whom they're seeking intercession. Incense has that same type of character of your prayers rising to the Lord. Remember that Catholic liturgy reflects its theology. We are an incarnational people, and so our liturgy is very incarnational as well. We praise God not only with our intellect but also with our body. All five of our senses praise the Lord. When we think of sight, we think of our beautiful churches with stained-glass windows, artwork, statues, the beautiful vestments and liturgical colors, and the altar appointments, all by which we give God praise through our eyes. Our ears give praise to God not just through sermons and prayers but in the hymns, the beautiful singing, and the organ, the king of instruments. We praise God through touch, which would be genuflection, making the Sign of the Cross, kneeling, and the Sign of Peace. We praise God through taste through our reception of Holy Communion; as another Psalm says, "O taste and see that the Lord is good!" (34:8). Finally, we praise God through the sense of smell. I love going into Catholic churches where they have real candles that can be lit for a certain saint. The pleasant smell of those candles alone just reminds you of church. Well, incense is another way we praise God through the sense of smell. A thurible is used to incense the sanctuary, and one of the largest ones that can be found is at the Shrine of St. James in Santiago de Compostela, Spain. It's so large that it's on a pulley and swings from one side of the church to the other.

Fr. Trigilio: When the pope was there, it took five guys to throw this thing so it could sway back and forth like a pendulum. You mentioned the use of incense goes back to Jewish times in the temple. Not only is this practice consistent with the ancient worship of God, but we can also see that the Church is the new temple. It's more than just a building. The temple in Jerusalem had the Shekinah, the glory of God made manifest, because both God and the Ark of the Covenant dwelled within. Because of the Real Presence in the tabernacle at our churches, we've also got the dwelling of God. So, just like in the Hebrew times, we burn incense, which was always a sign of divinity. Remember, one of the three kings brought incense to Jesus, as well as gold for being a king and myrrh for being a man. Incense and divinity are always closely connected, and even the pagans burned incense in their temples. The use of smell in church affirms the divinity of God. I'd also like to point out that at funerals we incense the body and the casket, because the body was a temple of the Holy Spirit while it was alive on earth, and that body is also going to be resurrected on the last day. Many people don't realize that the use of incense at funerals is to affirm the sanctity and dignity of that body, which we firmly believe will be raised up.

Fr. Brighenti: This is an excellent point, as incense is often used to highlight the importance behind certain concepts. For example, the altar is incensed during liturgy because it symbolizes Christ.

During the liturgy, the Book of the Gospels is incensed just before the Proclamation of the Gospel. At the Offertory, the gifts that will become the Body and Blood of Christ are incensed, the priest is incensed because he is the presence of Christ, and then the people are incensed because of their Baptism. If a bishop is present, then when the host and the chalice are elevated at the Consecration, you'll hear the bells ring and see the incense of each to denote the Real Presence of Our Lord. There are other objects that are incensed in church as well, such as the crucifix during the liturgy and the Paschal candle during Easter or in the funeral liturgy.

Fr. Trigilio: In the Eastern Church, they use ten times as much incense as we do, because they incense every icon, and it's to promote the sense of mystery, as the cloud of smoke makes it seem like you're on the very brink of Heaven. It's an awesome experience.

30. Jesus' Baptism

Why did Jesus undergo Baptism? What did He mean by His response to John when He said, "Let it be so now; for thus it is fitting for us to fulfil all righteousness" (Matthew 3:15)?

Fr. Trigilio: The Baptism offered by St. John the Baptist was purely symbolic; it was not a sacrament. But once Jesus went down into the Jordan River, He transformed Baptism into a sacrament, not because of who was doing the baptizing, but because of *Who* was being baptized. At the moment of Jesus' Baptism in the river, a loud voice came from Heaven saying, "This is my beloved Son" (Matthew 3:17), and a dove was seen coming down. Jesus was anointed not with oil but with the Holy Spirit, and this fulfilled the prophesies of the Old Testament that had foretold Jesus' role as the High Priest. A high priest had to be anointed, and in the Old Testament he was anointed with oil.

Jesus was going to be anointed, too, but not with oil, because His high priesthood is eternal, and so He was anointed with the Holy Spirit. The Baptism was symbolic, because the ritual washings were necessary in the Old Testament. Because Jesus is the Son of God and because of the virtue of the Immaculate Conception where no Original Sin was transmitted from Mary to Jesus, He was in no need of any sacramental Baptism, and John's Baptism wasn't going to wash away Original Sin anyway.

Fr. Brighenti: John also alluded to this fact when he said, "I baptize you with water; but he who is mightier than I is coming, the thong of whose sandals I am not worthy to untie; he will baptize you with the Holy Spirit and with fire" (Luke 3:16). Even he realized that the Baptism he practiced was only a prelude to what the real sacrament was going to be. Now when we baptize, we do so in the name of the Father and of the Son and of the Holy Spirit. It's not us performing the Baptism; it's Our Blessed Savior.

Fr. Trigilio: When you speak the words of the Trinitarian formula, all three Persons are expressed in that image. There's Jesus standing in the Jordan, the Holy Spirit flying down in the form of a dove, and God the Father speaking directly from Heaven. The entire Trinity is alluded to at that very moment.

Fr. Brighenti: It's the fulfillment of the Old Covenant and the initiation of the New Covenant.

31. Baptism for the Dead

My teenage son had a discussion with a Mormon classmate who said that in 1 Corinthians 15:29, St. Paul commanded Baptism for the dead so that those who have died would inherit salvation. I have never read this, but sure enough, it was right there in our Catholic Bible. Now we are both very confused. We tried to look up explanations in a biblical reference, which gave no answer. We asked my son's catechist, who was just as surprised as we were. Can you help us better understand what St. Paul was talking about?

Fr. Trigilio: It is true that in the Mormon religion, they have this belief that you can baptize the dead. That means if someone dies unbaptized, you can compensate for that by having them baptized later by going to the cemetery and saying some prayers. We as Catholics don't believe that's what St. Paul was talking about. When you read the text itself, it speaks of Baptism for the dead, but remember that St. Paul is talking about those who are dead in sin. They were dead in the Law, because they thought the Law was going to save them. He also is talking about the resurrection of the body, which the Corinthians were having trouble believing. In talking about Baptism for the dead, he's talking about the Baptism of the living who are dead in sin, and that Baptism not only washes away Original Sin but also brings sanctifying grace—life—to the soul. The soul is alive, metaphysically, but it's not alive with grace until that person is baptized. St. Paul is not talking about the *ex post facto* Baptism of somebody who's in the ground. He's talking about the Baptism of someone who's dead in sin, which all of us are when we come into this world until we are baptized.

Fr. Brighenti: In addition to this, if we commit a mortal sin, which is a grave matter that we know is wrong yet choose to do anyway, that also deadens the soul, because sanctifying grace—the Triune God—is removed at that instance. We must be careful never to commit mortal sin and definitely not die with mortal sin on our soul, unrepentant. If we do commit a mortal sin, then we must go to the Sacrament of Confession to restore the sanctifying grace and supernatural life in our soul that has been lost by that serious sin. As far as the dead are concerned, we should always say prayers for the faithful departed. Unfortunately, in the last fifty or sixty years, people have grown forgetful to pray for the dead or offer a Mass for the repose of their souls in case they're in Purgatory and waiting to enter Heaven. At certain times of the year, my family goes to the cemetery to remember our departed loved ones. We not only do this during the month of November, which is devoted to the Holy Souls in Purgatory, but at Christmastime we place an evergreen "Christmas blanket" over the graves to honor our faithful departed. We then pray, and we also like to bring the braided palm cross on Easter or Palm Sunday. If there were veterans in the family, we also visit them on Veterans Day or Memorial Day. We've always had a wonderful and healthy devotion to pray for the faithful departed in our family, but I also encourage people to pray for the faithful departed in general, because some of them might have no one else praying for them. A departed priest could have been all but forgotten.

Fr. Trigilio: Having Masses said for the faithful departed is the single greatest thing you can do for the Holy Souls in Purgatory. So many times, people assume their loved ones are in Heaven and that they don't need a Mass said for them, but you simply don't know if they're in Heaven yet. If they're in Purgatory, a Mass can be of infinite benefit to them, and it's so many times better than the flowers you throw on the casket that are going to be disposed of later that same day. I remember when I was newly ordained, they would have an abundance of Mass cards that we would take back to the parish. Nowadays, you might only get five or six of them, if that many. Sometimes, even in my own parish, we don't get enough people asking for Masses for the dead, yet offering a Mass for those in Purgatory is the best thing you can do for them, and for the living, too. If you have personal intentions for yourself or for the repose of a soul, the Mass is the most powerful tool available to you.

32. Blessed Salt

What is the history of blessed salt, and how may it be used?

Fr. Brighenti: Salt is an ancient commodity, and it was certainly more valuable in times before refrigeration. It was the element that preserved food. At times, it was also used as money and given as wages to the Romans.

Fr. Trigilio: "Salary" comes from the Latin word *salarium*, which means salt. Roman soldiers were given a wage of salt as well as gold.

Fr. Brighenti: There's also an old famous road called the Via Salaria, which means "the way of the salt," and it leads out of Rome through the Catacombs of Pricilla and up into the northern regions. This road was a major trade route, and since salt was a leading commodity for many years, whoever owned the roads by which salt was transported wielded tremendous power. That's the secular story behind it. The spiritual side of salt is that it's one of the elements that can be blessed in conjunction with holy water and added to it. In the sacramentary, it was used in the blessing of the water at Sunday liturgies, and you can then add the salt to the water, or you could even do this when blessing holy water in general to provide for the fonts or for a holy water tank.

Fr. Trigilio: While it's not required, blessed salt was a preferred ingredient for making holy water.

Fr. Brighenti: One of the reasons blessed salt was mixed with holy water is that, when a devil is cast out of a person, it enters into a lower created thing, like the swine when Christ cast out the devil from the man who resided in the tombs. The swine then rushed into the water and drowned (Mark 5:1-20). The idea of water being blessed and exorcised along with salt was one of the reasons why they were combined.

Fr. Trigilio: There's a nice distinction there that before the water is blessed, the water is exorcised, and that's not to say all water is possessed. However, the fact that some water can have evil spirits within it is very intriguing. In the Rite of Baptism, there used to be the custom of placing salt even on the baby. We don't do this anymore, but the baby was sometimes given a little salt as an exorcism was said over the baby. It wasn't that the baby was possessed, but that the baby was under the reign of the devil through Original Sin, and the exorcism would occur just before the Baptism, because Baptism is what makes that baby a child of God and pulls him out from under the jurisdiction of the evil one.

33. Infant Baptism

A non-Catholic recently asked me why Catholics baptize infants. He said that you had to be old enough to accept Jesus in order to be baptized. I tried to explain that it was the sacrament that conferred the grace, so why does it matter how old you are or what your understanding is when you receive it? He then said that Baptism isn't a sacrament and that it doesn't confer anything. If Baptism doesn't do anything, I wonder why he cares when you receive it or whether you receive it at all? Can you shed any light on this debate?

Fr. Brighenti: Some Protestant denominations, namely those in the Baptist, Evangelical, or Pentecostal circles, don't baptize someone until they become able to "accept Jesus into their heart as their personal Lord and Savior." However, there's nothing in Scripture that says you can't baptize a baby, and there's nothing in Scripture that says in order to be baptized you must accept Jesus into your heart. That being said, Baptism can be given to a baby or an adult. Adult converts attend RCIA (Rite of Christian Initiation of Adults), which is a program that goes through the year and ends with special liturgical functions during the Lenten season for the converts to receive Baptism, Confirmation, and First Communion, collectively known as the Easter Sacraments. For babies, the reason why Baptism is encouraged is because it confers sanctifying grace and is therefore the key sacrament that unlocks the door to all the others. The non-Catholic in the question who said Baptism is not a sacrament is wrong, because Christ instituted it Himself when He declared to "Go therefore and make disciples of all nations, baptizing them in the name of the Father and of the Son and of the Holy Spirit" (Matthew 28:19).

Fr. Trigilio: Even though Jesus didn't use the word "sacrament," He still instructed the disciples to *go and baptize*. The New Testament also affirms that *whole households* were baptized, so not just adults, but children as well, when pagan Greeks and Romans converted to Christianity. Later, Christian parents had their infants baptized soon after birth.

Fr. Brighenti: There are a lot of words that we use, like "Bible" itself, which are not found in the Bible. "Trinity" is not in the Bible, yet we believe in the Trinity. So, no, you won't find the word "sacrament," but it's explicitly described in the teachings of Jesus Christ.

Fr. Trigilio: And while Scripture doesn't say explicitly to "Go and baptize infants," it does imply that children were included with the whole families and entire households that were baptized.

Fr. Brighenti: Christ had a special fondness for children. When His disciples tried to stop the children from reaching Him, He said, "Let the children come to me" (Matthew 19:14). He also gave a teaching on the simplicity of a childlike faith—not a childish one—but a childlike faith, which means simplicity and innocence. Our Lord was giving us references to the importance of this sacrament to be administered as quickly as possible. Now, a Catholic doesn't have to say that they're "born again" when they accept Jesus as their personal Lord and Savior. You accepted Jesus as your personal Lord and Savior when you were baptized, and you're living that throughout your whole life. It's renewed daily, and it's specifically renewed at the Easter Vigil or on Easter Sunday where all Catholics renew their baptismal promises. In lieu of the Creed, the priest reads the Rite of Baptism: "Do you renounce Satan and all his works and empty promises?" The people respond, "I do." The priest then goes through the Creed and the questions, just like you do at an actual baptismal ceremony.

Fr. Trigilio: People who profess that they're born-again Christians will often give you the exact day and time of when they accepted Jesus, and it's a wonderful thing to be proud of, because they've accepted Christ as their Lord. But in the Catholic tradition, remembering when you've been born again, even if it occurs as an infant, is not any more important than remembering you were born naturally; what's important is that you were born again and you now have citizenship in God's kingdom, just as you would have U.S. citizenship if you were born here in America. The point though is that you become a citizen the day you're born. You would not want your parents going to the government and saying, "I don't want my child to be considered a citizen until they can choose for themselves at age eighteen." Instead, you enjoy the benefits and privileges of being a citizen right away. If you want to renounce your citizenship when you're eighteen, then you can do that. But in the meantime, it's part of your identity, and it's a protection for you. It helps you. Likewise, as a baptized Christian, you are now a child of God. It's part of your identity. You're receiving the grace, and if you want to, God forbid, you can repudiate that when you're old enough to decide for yourself, or you can continue in the Faith. Confirmation is a very important time in our tradition, because the children who were baptized as babies are now young adults and can, in one sense, renew being born again in Christ, although we don't ascribe it to a particular time and place. It's not about an individual moment where someone accepts Jesus as their personal Lord and Savior, because He's also the Lord and Savior of the whole world. Salvation is in the context of His Church, His Mystical Body, as opposed to a private moment by oneself where someone accepts Jesus. We believe that a person is born again as an infant within the context of the family of faith, just like a baby isn't born by itself. A baby is born through the mother and father; it's from the family that one receives natural life. Likewise, it's through the spiritual family that we obtain spiritual life.

Fr. Brighenti: It's a key sacrament. You cannot receive any other sacrament unless you start with Baptism. Why deny a baby grace? Why deny a baby the indwelling of the Blessed Trinity? For us, we don't have to be adults to receive Our Lord and Savior. We can receive Him right from the start when we're little through Baptism and through our prayers. Every day is a conversion from ourselves toward God. It shouldn't have to wait until you're older.

You could start immediately as an infant and continue all the way into your old age. The abundance of grace should not be hindered.

34. Baptism in the Catholic Church

I was baptized at twelve years old when my sister had taken me to her church. I didn't know I was being baptized, and my parents weren't even there. The preacher did not say, "I baptize you in the name of the Father and of the Son and of the Holy Spirit." I was simply dunked into this pool of water, and I didn't even know what was going on. I never went to church again until 1984, when I started attending Masses in a Catholic church. I have been going there for many years now, and I am truly happy with this religion. I want to get baptized in the Catholic Church, but I understand you can only be baptized once, and I do not know if my baptism at twelve years old was valid or not.

Fr. Brighenti: Yes, you can only be validly baptized once. The Catholic Church recognizes all valid baptisms, but not all baptisms are *de facto* valid. If someone is validly baptized in the Anglican, Episcopalian, Lutheran, Presbyterian, Methodist, Congregational, Baptist, or other similar churches, then we do not "rebaptize" them when they convert, or more accurately, come into full communion with the Catholic religion.

Yes, you can get baptized in the Catholic Church. There is a required matter, form, and intent to make a sacrament valid, and the matter of water was present at your baptism at your sister's church, but the form and intent were not, as the preacher did not include the necessary Trinitarian formula, "I baptize you in the name of the Father and of the Son and of the Holy Spirit." He would have then poured water on you or dunked you in water at the mention of each Person of the Holy Trinity. Also, at twelve years old, you were above the age of reason, yet you didn't know what was happening, and what happened was possibly against your will. But first and foremost, there was no form or intent involved, which means the baptism was invalid. After proper instruction in the Catholic Church through the RCIA (Rite of Christian Initiation for Adults) program you will not only receive Baptism at the Easter Vigil but also First Communion and Confirmation. We call these the Easter Sacraments. If you fall into sin, you will then have access to the Sacrament of Confession to seek forgiveness from God through absolution. Part of your instruction in RCIA will give you knowledge of these sacraments. By all means, contact the priest of your parish and enlist in the RCIA program. Once you receive the Sacrament of Baptism, that will be registered in the book, and your baptismal church will be a point of reference for the rest of your life. For example, if you move away and you're going to marry or join the Holy Orders, they always refer back to your "church of baptism," because that's where you received the key sacrament to all the other sacraments. You cannot receive any other sacrament until you first receive the Sacrament of Baptism.

Fr. Trigilio: Now hypothetically, what if someone doesn't remember if the Trinitarian formula was used at his previous baptism or not? What if he isn't sure if he was dunked or sprinkled or not? When there's a matter of doubt, what happens then?

Fr. Brighenti: We then administer a conditional Baptism. This applies when a person may have been baptized but has no record or witnesses to prove it. The person in question would then be conditionally baptized, where the priest would say, "If you are not yet baptized, I baptize you in the name of the Father and of the Son and of the Holy Spirit." In regard to the question, however, it seems they didn't use the Trinitarian formula, and that's easily verified. A lot of mainstream Protestant religions though are becoming more New Age, and they're dismissing the Trinitarian formula altogether, even though their registers might have it. Instead, they're using phrases like, "In the name of the Creator and of the Redeemer and of the Sanctifier." That is not the proper form given to us by Jesus Christ. Unfortunately, there was even an incident in a religious community in Boston that baptized under this invalid form, and they had to contact all two thousand babies who were thought to have been properly baptized, and they had to each be validly baptized with the correct form. However, conditional Baptism isn't the case in regard to the question.

Fr. Trigilio: I only bring it up in case somebody is in the RCIA program, and the priest or deacon says they're going to conditionally baptize you. It's not insinuating that you weren't baptized; it's just in case you weren't or cannot prove it; they're using this as an absolute guarantee.

Fr. Brighenti: Baptism is a one-time sacrament that leaves an indelible mark on your soul; you can't undo it. It's just like Confirmation and Holy Orders, which are one-time sacraments. There are then sacraments you may receive multiple times throughout your life, such as the Holy Eucharist and the Sacrament of Confession when you need it, and if your spouse dies you can receive the Sacrament of Marriage again. You can also receive the Anointing of the Sick as many times as you need if you're in grave danger of illness or before surgeries and anesthesia. Those are sacraments that are received more than once, whereas those that leave an indelible mark on your soul, meaning they're recognizable after death, would be Baptism, Confirmation, and Holy Orders.

35. Catholic Burial and Cremation

My niece recently asked me why Catholics have their own section in two cemeteries where both Catholic and non-Catholic family members are buried. Why is this? Also, is it okay to cremate and have ashes scattered? My uncle did this with a relative, but the ashes blew back in his face, and he got the chills.

Fr. Trigilio: At one time, it was absolutely mandatory and obligatory that you only be buried in what we call hallowed ground, and it's still highly encouraged today. There were Catholic cemeteries, and if not, then part of a public cemetery was portioned off where the bishop would come and bless that particular piece of earth. It wasn't that the other people buried there weren't going to Heaven, but this practice conveyed to the people, particularly to the Catholic faithful, that the resurrection of the body is a crucial doctrine of our Faith. To reemphasize this, it was important to ensure that you were interred until the end of time, not just anywhere, but in hallowed ground. Like I said, every town or parish either had its own cemetery, or a portion of the public cemetery was allotted to it. Nowadays, you can get buried almost anywhere. A lot of people who are in the military, for instance, can be buried at the Arlington National Cemetery. We have Indiantown Gap in my diocese in Pennsylvania, and when a Catholic is buried there, the priest or deacon will bless the ground in general rather than blessing a whole section, because of the way they shuffle things around these days.

It's important to know that the cremation of the remains is permitted by the Catholic Church, though at one time the 1917 Code absolutely forbade cremation because the Church was concerned people would lose their belief in the resurrection. Actually, from the very beginning Christians buried their dead, even during the time of the Roman Persecutions (during the first three centuries A.D.) and you can visit them in the ancient catacombs. The pagans burned the bodies of their dead while the Christians buried them, since they believed in the resurrection of the dead by Christ at the end of time.

But although cremation is now tolerated, what you may do with the ashes is very limited, as you must bury them in their entirety in a container in the ground or at sea; they are not to be scattered. It's okay to have the person cremated if it's for financial reasons or in terms of contagion, as sometimes there's a plague and they don't have time to bury all the bodies. But those ashes need to be treated with respect, because they are going to be resurrected one day, just the same as the bodies that are buried intact. You are not allowed to open up the container and let the wind blow the ashes around, which unfortunately happened to some political figures not too long ago, and the cardinal of that area intervened, as scattering ashes or putting them on a mantle dishonors the resurrection. Worse yet, I've seen in funeral parlor brochures where you can place a teaspoon of someone's ashes in a little vial and wear it around your neck, or as earrings, or on your dog's collar.

Fr. Brighenti: Practices have gotten extremely pagan today. Families are literally dividing up their loved ones so each relative can have a portion of the ashes. It's disrespectful to the human body, which was a temple of the Most Holy Trinity through Baptism. With that embedded dignity, the body needs to be interred in a proper place with a proper ritual and prayer. Now, there are times when people or ashes are buried at sea due to disease or for military purposes, but they're supposed to be intact, not scattered in the wind. This is because we believe in the doctrine of the resurrection of the body; we do not believe in reincarnation. Replacing the proper burial of the body with pagan practices and wearing the remains of people like jewelry is extremely disrespectful to the human body that's been created in the image of God. The body contained a soul, and it was a temple of the Holy Trinity.

36. The Merits of Sacrifice

I can't understand why sacrifice is pleasing to God. What father would yearn to see his son suffer? A father would only want the best for his son.

Fr. Brighenti: Without a doubt, our modern generation does not like the word "sacrifice." Just like commitment, it carries a distasteful connotation in our jargon today. My father, who was a World War II veteran, understood what sacrifice was all about while fighting for his country. Soldiers in his day went to the trenches in Europe and suffered all sorts of things: weather, bombing, and horrible conditions. Indeed, even American service men and women today in the Middle-Eastern deserts suffer similar elements as well. In marriage, spouses are expected to make sacrifices, and perhaps a reason why there are so many divorces in our world today is that people don't understand marriage involves sacrificing their wants, their will, and their desires for the sake of their spouse, and that when both spouses are doing this, their marriage will be far better off, as it will be purged of selfishness. Christ is the ultimate Sacrifice, and He sacrificed His life for all of us so that we may have eternal life. We bring our sacrifices to the Lord, uniting them on the Cross, and in a mysterious way our crown of thorns is transformed into a crown of victory through grace as we participate in the Passion of Our Lord. There is a beautiful part in the Offertory of the Mass where the bread and wine are offered by the priest, who is in the name of Christ making this offering. The people in attendance place themselves on that paten and in that chalice, and they bring their families, their joys, their happiness, as well as their sorrows and sufferings. They offer their lives to the Lord as a pure oblation to God, in which they hold nothing back from Him. Nothing is too sacred in our lives for God; we offer Him everything. There are beautiful devotional prayers where you consecrate your senses and whole being to the Lord so that you may be His instrument in the world. It is in this freedom of giving ourselves to the Lord that we find an abundance of grace and a deep intimacy in relationship with the Lord Jesus Christ.

Fr. Trigilio: Not only is "sacrifice" a dirty word in modern society, but it is an incomprehensible concept to the many people who have become so receptive to the idea of giving until it feels good or to only do so in order to gain an advantage in some way. But Jesus said that there is no greater love than to lay down one's life for a friend, and God so loved the world that He gave His Only Begotten Son. Pope Benedict put it so beautifully in *Deus Caritas Est* that God is love, and love is both sacrificial and possessive. It's a give-and-take relationship, and it's not that a father wants to see his children suffer, but that he knows sacrifice is worthwhile because of the fruit that comes from it. For instance, it was worth it to our fathers to put their lives on the line in World War II, not for the sake of sacrifice itself, but for the purpose of defending their country. Another example would be taking a second job and working late hours, not for the fun of it, but for your family, to put a roof over their heads, and to send your kids to college. I think that's where our society misses the point, as it only sees sacrifice in the act itself, and that's why they pamper and overcompensate, giving little Johnny or Susie whatever they want so they don't ever cry. As I tell young parents, it's good for your child to cry and to learn that their cry is not going to get a response, because sometimes the answer is no or that they have to wait. As an adult, we don't like that answer either, because we live in a culture and society that conditions us differently. In the material world, if you make enough noise, someone's eventually going to placate you. In the spiritual realm, it's just the opposite.

Fr. Brighenti: Sacrifice also entails discipline, and this is where Lent helps to invoke discipline in our lives. During Lent, we're encouraged to sacrifice things that we enjoy for the greater good, and this is just a small nudge in the right direction of how our whole lives should be. Lent teaches us that we should be making sacrifices for the rest of our earthly lives and not just during those six weeks of penance. Being sacrificial means being selfless like Christ Our Savior. It's the act of modeling our lives after Him.

Fr. Trigilio: You can see this effect even in marriages, and this is why many marriages and families break up, because people say, "Oh, why should I be a doormat? Why should I let other people walk over me?" They're unwilling to make the sacrifice, or people are not appreciative of the sacrifices being made in that marriage or family.

Fr. Brighenti: The key to success is to give and take. Receptive giving is a two-way street, and this would be something to teach our young people who are preparing for Matrimony, that not only is marriage a permanent commitment, but it's one of perpetual sacrifice. To recapture the essence of what our Holy Father wrote in his encyclical concerning love, sacrifice is absolutely critical for a successful marriage.

Fr. Trigilio: Don't forget, a loving father allows his son or daughter to learn a lesson even if it involves some suffering so that a greater good can be achieved. That's why my dad allowed me to fall off my bike so I could learn to ride better and on my own. If he prevented me from falling off, I would never learn to do it myself. Like gold tested in fire, often our aches and pains, if not of our own doing, are not *per se* penitential but medicinal. Athletes know well the axiom, "no pain, no gain." If God prevented us from all suffering, we would not long for Heaven where there is only joy and happiness. C.S. Lewis said that darkness helps us appreciate the light; sickness, health; pain, laughter; death, life.[10] We learn from our mistakes and we are strengthened by overcoming trials and tribulations. Collin Raye sings a song in which he says: "I prayed for strength / and I got pain that made me strong / I prayed for courage and got fear to overcome ... I don't always get what I want / I get what I need."[11]

37. The Necessity of the Sacraments

Does everyone need the Sacraments of Baptism, Confession, Communion, and Confirmation? I can see the need for Baptism and receiving the Eucharist, but what happens if I don't want to be confirmed? Am I prevented from "graduating" in some way so that I'm not a full-fledged member of the Church? What if I receive Communion every Sunday but have my reservations about Confession and don't go because it makes me scrupulous about everything I do?

[10] C.S. Lewis, *Mere Christianity*.
[11] Collin Raye, "What I Need," written by Jason Blume and Karen Taylor Good; Epic Records, track 4 on *Can't Back Down* (2001).

Fr. Trigilio: I know you mean well, but I think your outlook on the sacraments is too materialistic in the wrong sense that they're just tradition. The sacraments are outward signs instituted by Christ to give grace to the people, and they're sacred celebrations in the Church; they're not private events. I tell people it's not their Baptism they're receiving, and it's not my Mass I'm celebrating. These belong to Christ and to His Church, and therefore they're always public celebrations. Even though your confession is between you and the priest, it's still a public action that's taking place in the Church. That said, it is true that until you receive all three Sacraments of Initiation, as spelled out in the Code of Canon Law and in the *Catechism of the Catholic Church*, you're not fully initiated into the Church.

Fr. Brighenti: I dislike when people use the term "graduating." That word is never used in the text, but people feel like they've finished eighth grade and they're getting confirmed now, and once they've graduated, they're done. That's not how this works.

Fr. Trigilio: Also, the pastor can sometimes be tempted to put Confirmation off until high school, because that way the children have to attend CCD (Confraternity of Christian Doctrine) or religious education. The concern is that after they've been confirmed, they won't want to go. However, the problem with putting off Confirmation is that doing so is a form of bribery, and the pastor is treating the Sacrament as a tool. In reality, you should want the kids to desire Confirmation, because just as in the Jewish tradition, it's an honor for the boy or girl to get bar and bat mitzvah. Sometimes kids do things only because their family is putting pressure on them; the same thing can happen in the Catholic Faith. The point is that you want them to desire the sacraments which confer grace, and the beauty of

Confirmation is that it gives them the grace to be an adult in the Faith: that they're going to fight the good fight, be a disciple of Christ, and endure even in times of persecution. Back when we were confirmed under the old rite, the bishop would actually slap us lightly on the face to symbolize Jesus being slapped in the presence of Pontius Pilate. This was a reminder that you are going to suffer indignities, and that you're going to suffer for the sake of the name of Jesus Christ.

Fr. Brighenti: Also, you have to remember that it is Our Lord Who's absolving us in the Sacrament of Confession. When we hear the words, "I absolve you of your sins," it's in the first-person tense. Concerning scrupulosity, I suspect there are some underlying issues beyond what the question includes. There are two extremes: the lax perspective, which doesn't see any sin, and the scrupulous one that sees sin in everything. You're aiming for a balanced view in your spiritual life. If you're not going to Confession, then you're missing out on an opportunity to receive grace from Our Lord to heal, to build up, and to strengthen you against further temptation. A good habit to get into is to pray the Daily Examen, which was instituted by St. Ignatius of Loyola. It's usually done around noontime and again in the evening. It only takes a minute to reflect upon all the wonderful opportunities you had throughout your morning and to thank God for those opportunities, or to see where you actively did something wrong. Add a minute of quiet time in which you allow the Lord to inspire and instruct you, followed with a conscious decision to be more attentive to God throughout your day, and ending with a devotion, either the Angelus prayer or a litany. In the evening, the examination of conscience of your whole day helps to prepare you for the Sacrament of Confession. It keeps you alert. It also helps you prevent yourself from sinning again, because you're more aware of these things. I wonder if the person asking the question is struggling to put his confession into words? There are little booklets you can find with the examination of conscience that will help you with this process.

Fr. Trigilio: It's very typical for people to develop a mechanical idea of Confession. When we were growing up, everyone took it for granted and went every Saturday, followed by Communion on Sunday. Confession lines were long. They emphasized the fact that you only needed to go if you're conscious of mortal sin, but we encourage people to go on a regular basis. Once that custom of going every single Saturday faded away, we saw the repercussions. People went from going to Confession on Saturdays only to not going at all. I tell people that if they're going to take their car in for an oil change every three months, then they should also get their oil changed spiritually every three months. I call this "Jiffy Lube spirituality." Plan Confession like you would an appointment for your car or if you were going to go to the dentist or to the eye doctor. Mark it on your calendar or smart device: "Confession this weekend." If you don't take it that seriously, then it won't be a part of your life.

Fr. Brighenti: Our Lord gave us the sacraments as tools to help us work out our salvation. A wonderful way of preparing to receive the Holy Eucharist is going to Confession and searching your soul. Ask yourself how you want the Lord to be the light in those areas of your life that need to be uprooted, such as those pet sins that you have domesticated in your life or the fond memories of those pet sins, so that you can grow spiritually in the Lord. Confession shouldn't be seen as something negative, but rather something positive. We have an encounter with grace in all of the sacraments, and Confession and Communion go hand in hand.

Fr. Trigilio: Look at them as opportunities as opposed to obligations. They are there to help you. Never worry about going to Confession. Scrupulosity would be if someone felt they had to go to Confession every day confessing the exact same previous sins, over and over again, thinking the first absolution did not work. This is different from committing the same sin over and over again, in which case it is necessary to confess before Holy Communion if a mortal sin, and it is allowed to be confessed if a venial sin to get the grace of the sacrament. Avoid both extremes of a too-lax conscience that is blind to sin and an overly-scrupulous conscience that sees sin where it is not.

38. Common Mortal Sins

I am curious if you could direct me to a complete list of common mortal sins. I want to receive Communion correctly and understand that most people aren't aware of the requirements. I want to know, so I can inform my family that there are standards for receiving Our Lord.

Fr. Brighenti: We need to first look at the Ten Commandments, which are our guiding principles. The first three deal with our relationship with God, while the other seven concern our relationship with one another, so there are various levels at which we can violate these Commandments. Let's also look at the seven deadly sins, the root of all sin being pride, followed by greed, wrath, envy, lust, gluttony, and sloth. Scepter Publishers prints a handy little manual[12] pertaining to the Sacrament of Confession, which would walk you through the Ten Commandments, as well as the Six Commandments of the Church. Fr.

---

[12] Dónal Cuilleanáin, *A Guidebook for Confession: The Sacrament of Reconciliation* (Princeton, NJ: Scepter Publishers, 1996).

Frederick Miller also wrote a beautiful pamphlet on Confession, *A Primer for Confession*, and this is available from Casa Maria (that is, the Sister Servants of the Eternal Word in Irondale, Alabama).

Fr. Trigilio: It can be helpful to keep a mental list of sins you must avoid. The seven deadly or capital sins can kill the life of grace if committed with full intention. There are three requirements for this criteria: the sin has to be a grave matter, which any of the seven deadly sins or violation of the Ten Commandments would already be; you would have to know what you're doing is wrong; and then you have to choose freely to commit the act anyway. If someone is under the influence of drugs or alcohol or enormous stress, this doesn't vitiate or completely remove their culpability, but it can reduce or lessen it to the point where they may be objectively guilty of mortal sin, but not subjectively. This is an area where going to a priest for Confession or to your spiritual director can help you determine the gravity of your sins, just as a doctor would analyze what's ailing a sick patient. I'll admit that many people take mortal sins far too trivially. It's bad enough that we treat venial sins so lightly, yet a mortal sin is like a malignant tumor: it's deadly, and it's going to kill you.

Fr. Brighenti: A sad reality is that the loneliest time for a priest is often in the confessional. We're sitting in there, waiting for customers, so to speak. Every time I hear the door to the church open, I hope that someone's going to climb inside the confessional. I won't believe that everyone is a saint right now and in no need of Confession. We're all sinners in the process of becoming saints, and I myself go to Confession frequently. An older priest once told me, "Boy, as we get older, we really see the need for Confession more and more." I said, "Yes, because we see our time is limited here more and more." When priests go to Confession, it's an example for the people to also go. Confession and Communion go hand in hand, and a good way of keeping yourself in check is to do an examination of conscience at the end of the day, where you take a brief moment to review all the things that you did which were good and in cooperation with God's grace, then all the things where you either didn't cooperate with God's grace or actively did something wrong, and then you ask for forgiveness at that moment. This is followed by a period of quiet reflection and ends with the Act of Contrition. If you do this every day, it will help prepare you for your next confession, and hopefully you go frequently. A little examination of conscience at the end of the day is so important to your spiritual growth. All it takes is some time to go over your day and see how you did. Maybe there was a person you ditched in the parking lot, or perhaps you cursed at someone on the highway after they cut you off, or you might've become impatient with someone. These may not be grave matters, but the more we examine our conscience, the more we become aware of sin, and then the more we want to go to Confession to cleanse ourselves. Confession will never hurt you. The more you go, the more you will find help through God's grace.

Fr. Trigilio: You and I are old enough to remember that when we were kids, there used to be a long line of people going to Confession every Saturday, because everyone actually wanted to go to Confession. It wasn't that they were more sinful in the fifties and sixties than they are today; it's actually quite the opposite. Back then, people wanted to be properly disposed to receive Communion. It was a beautiful custom; I remember my parents taking my brothers and me, and my mother would remind us on the way over that we had misbehaved the previous week or disobeyed our father. It was actually quite edifying that our parents went to Confession. It was wonderful to go as a family every Saturday, although my brothers and I got nervous as kids, because our parents would go to Confession before us, and we would wonder if they were tipping off the priest.

Fr. Brighenti: Here's a callout to all priests: you need to make Confession more available in your parish. When I was pastor, I held devotions in the parish during the week and would offer Confession before or after the devotion, and I would catch a lot of the school moms picking up their kids or some of the older people who wouldn't necessarily come to Confession on Saturday. A couple times a week before the morning Mass, I would get there at six-thirty in the morning and wait in the confessional, because you never know when a commuter might want to go to Confession or what have you. You should offer Confession more times throughout the week than just before the Saturday Vigil Mass, which might be inconvenient for a lot of people who could be working or going to Sunday Mass. If the priest can offer the Sacrament of Confession during the week, then publish it in the bulletin so people will know.

Fr. Trigilio: When I was stationed at the cathedral in Harrisburg, Pennsylvania, one of the blessings we had was Mass and Confession every day at lunch hour, because all these people who worked for the government had only half of their lunch break to spend either going to Mass or to Confession. It was so inspiring to see their commitment. Another great idea is to offer Confession after a wedding rehearsal, so that those who need to confess serious sins can receive Communion the next day. Also, I think it was the Archdiocese of Hartford, Connecticut, where the bishop had asked every single parish to make the Sacrament of Confession available from six to seven-thirty either every Tuesday or Thursday night.

Fr. Brighenti: Yes, this occurred during the Lenten season.

Fr. Trigilio: People can always suggest this to their pastors as well.

Fr. Brighenti: The pastors should preach about Confession, too, how it personally enlightens us, guides us to Communion, and gives us the grace to avoid future sin. The more we preach about Confession and make it available, the more people will take advantage of this indispensable sacrament.

39. Making a Good Confession

I have not been to Confession in forty years. With the recent death of my wife, I feel a calling back to my faith and to the Church. How can I count my sins and recall all I have done wrong over such a long period of time? Can you help me start the process of going back to Confession?

Fr. Brighenti: Thank God you're beginning to accept the Lord's invitation back to this great sacrament. I really don't understand why people are so afraid of it. We priests go quite frequently, because as we get older and are closer to being called home ourselves, we find more necessity in examining our consciences daily and going to Confession. Even if we don't have mortal sin on our souls, a good devotional Confession is beneficial to the soul. In this case of having not been to Confession in forty years, you're not going to remember every specific detail or event, but you're going to want to go over an examination of conscience, which includes the Ten Commandments and the Six Commandments of the Church, as best you can. There are also some terrific confessional guides available online at the EWTN bookstore that you can order. I would suggest checking out our catalogue first to find an examination of conscience, and it will include the Act of Contrition, in case you've forgotten how to recite this prayer. Once you have this material before you, go over those Commandments prayerfully, maybe in a Holy Hour before the Blessed Sacrament, and try your hardest to remember where you might have failed in each of these areas. Also, know that Confession is not a one-time deal. You need to get in the habit of going frequently, and you're only accountable for what you can remember. Unlike American law, where you're held accountable regardless of whether you knew what you did was a violation, God is so much more merciful. He will still forgive us if we've truly forgotten our sin, but not if we're simply too embarrassed to say what we've done. The good sisters had taught us in Catholic school to end our list of sins in the confessional with the words, "I confess these sins and all the ones that I've forgotten since my last confession."

Fr. Trigilio: It's so important to remember that you want to confess and root out the venial sins in your life as well, and not just the mortal sins. That's why devotional confession is critical. I make the analogy with going to the dentist; you'll certainly go when you've got a cavity, because there's the chance that it could become abscessed and need to be pulled or filled in, but even when you go for a regular checkup, your teeth might still need some cleaning with the metal toothpick and power brush. This may be because you haven't been brushing as well as you should, even though it's not as urgent as a cavity. However, if you let this habit continue, then you could very well end up with a cavity, and a cavity can become an abscess, and it could lead to blood poisoning. People have died from this situation. Now, if this snowball effect is true in the medical realm, physiologically, it's also true in the spiritual. When you become too comfortable in your venial sin, it becomes easier to fall into mortal sin, and therefore you should always be aware of the little things: your weaknesses, faults, and failures; and you need to work constantly on them. You're never going to get to the point where you don't have any more weaknesses, because there's always going to be something upon which you could do better, and you should always try to do so.

Fr. Brighenti: As we progress in our spiritual lives from the purgative to the illuminative to the unitive levels, we become more and more aware of our imperfections as the Lord reveals them to us the closer we bring ourselves to Him. Eventually, even our fond memories of sin will be revealed to us, and we can detach ourselves from them. We want to let those pet sins and the memory of them go, and Confession will help you do this, because you'll become actively conscious of these faults. Welcome back to the Church after forty years. The sacraments are here for you. Don't be embarrassed to use Confession much more frequently. Get the spiritual tools that you need to make a good confession and move on from there.

Fr. Trigilio: Don't ever be afraid to go to Confession. The priest will never yell at you and ask why you did something or get on your case why it's been so long since your last confession. The priest is there to help you. First of all, going to Confession costs you nothing, and the priest cannot tell anyone your sins.

Fr. Brighenti: Under the sacred seal of Confession, a priest can never reveal anything that he has heard in the confessional.

40. The Necessity of Confession

As part of the Introductory Rite of Holy Mass, we are called to bring our sins to mind, and the priest says, "May Almighty God have mercy on us, forgive us our sins, and bring us to everlasting life." This prayer is preceded in the Daily Roman Missal with the instruction: "The absolution by the priest follows." If the priest gives us absolution during the Mass, then why is it necessary to go to Confession?

Fr. Trigilio: I'm glad you asked this question, because I get this from people who are even sometimes cradle Catholics. When we use the term "Penitential Rite," people automatically assume that it's a general absolution and thus have made their confession. This is not the Sacrament of Confession. You have not gone to Confession individually. It's a corporate expression, a communal celebration of the fact that we are all in need of God's mercy, and so we're all repenting. There are four different types of prayer, and one of them is the prayer of contrition (along with adoration, thanksgiving, and petition). In this case, we're being contrite to offer the perfect sacrifice of God the Son to God the Father, yet we are imperfect and have to own up to our own sinfulness. We're not being absolved of any mortal sins, although we are being remitted of any venial sins. The gesture of making the Sign of the Cross is not to be made. People may do that in the Extraordinary Form of the Mass, but in the Ordinary Form or the Novus Ordo that we commonly have today, the only gesture that's made is you beating your breast at each of the three instances of the phrase, *mea culpa*, which means "my fault." We say, "through my fault, through my fault, through my most grievous fault." When the priest says the Absolution, it's not a sacramental absolution; therefore, you don't make the Sign of the Cross because you're not having your sins remitted, as only happens when you go to Confession and the priest gives you absolution.

Fr. Brighenti: During the Absolution at Mass, you don't hear the words, "I absolve you of your sins."

Fr. Trigilio: Instead, we hear, "May Almighty God have mercy on us, forgive us our sins, and bring us to everlasting life." It's a communal affirmation that we're in need of forgiveness and need to repent.

Fr. Brighenti: This might be a good time to explain mortal and venial sin. There are three requisites in order to have mortal sin on your soul: the sin must be a grave matter, you must know it's a grave matter, and you must commit it willingly. If one or more of those requirements are absent, then it becomes a venial sin.

Fr. Trigilio: Any venial sins you may have committed do get remitted at the Absolution, but let's say you deliberately missed Mass even though the weather was fine and you weren't ill or taking care of someone who was, then you're guilty of a mortal sin. You knew it was Sunday, you knew you had to go to Mass, but you chose not to. You now need to go to Confession. If, however, it's a holy day of obligation that snuck up on you and you forgot, weren't aware of it, or didn't know if it fell on Wednesday, Friday, or Saturday or to whichever day it got moved to in your diocese, then missing Mass may be a venial sin in this case.

Fr. Brighenti: On certain years, the Feast of the Immaculate Conception is supposed to be a holy day of obligation in our country since it's the patronal feast of America, but when it falls on a Sunday and gets transferred to Monday, the obligation is removed. This can be confusing for most people.

Fr. Trigilio: Even I get confused when I head down south and Ascension Thursday has been moved to Sunday. Up north, it's still on Thursday. This is a perfect example where you may have missed Mass but were not aware that you were obliged to attend. In these cases, you would not be culpable of a mortal sin. But if you knew it was obligatory, had the opportunity, and freely chose not to go, then you would have mortal sin on your soul.

Fr. Brighenti: A good practice is to perform a daily examination of conscience. Start by ordering yourself an examination guide. St. Ignatius of Loyola often preached about doing a daily examination, usually at noontime, maybe in the evening around six o'clock, and then a shorter one before you go to bed at night. I specifically like the noon hour, because I take a minute to see how my morning went and all the opportunities in which I was able to cooperate with God's grace. I then take another minute and look at all the opportunities where maybe I didn't cooperate with God's grace or where I might have actively fell into sin. Then I take yet another minute to say how I would like to work the rest of my afternoon with God's grace in the opportunities that fall before me. Finally, I say the Act of Contrition followed by a minute of silence to let the Lord speak to me. I then end with a devotion, like the Angelus or the Litany of Saints. It's a beautiful way of practicing the examination of conscience. It takes all of five minutes, either before or after lunch. By doing this on a daily basis, it helps keep in mind our faults and our failures, and it's material to take with us to Confession. A lot of people will tell me they don't know what to say at Confession. Well, are you doing a daily examination of conscience?

Fr. Trigilio: If you're up to date with your sins, you'll know what to say. One of the beautiful parts of the Night Prayer from the

Liturgy of the Hours has the Act of Contrition, and while it's not a sacrament like going to Confession, it can still remit venial sins. It's like examining yourself so that when you go to the doctor, you can tell him what you noticed about your health. If you don't keep an eye on that, you won't know what to say to the doctor.

41. Penance for Sins

Please explain the concept of doing penance for the sins which have already been forgiven by Christ. If Christ paid the price for our sins, why should we do penance after confession? Is there anywhere in the New Testament where this is spoken of?

Fr. Trigilio: It's true that Jesus paid the price for our sins. He paid it with His life. He atoned for all of us. Therefore, we do not pay the penalty for our sins through penance. Penance and mortification are similar in this regard. Mortification is self-denial, where you prepare and strengthen yourself for future temptations. Penance, on the other hand, is a voluntary act of remorse for past sins, so that you're showing your love of God in cultivating within yourself this regret that you made a mistake. To give you an analogy, it'd be as if your parents told you not to monkey around the house in case you break something. Well, you do it anyway, and you end up smashing an expensive statue. There's no way you're ever going to afford a replacement for that statue on your own, so your parents will have to pay the price for a new one, but they are also going to make you appreciate that you did wrong and either ground you or ask you to do some extra chores around the house. You're not doing this so that you can pay them back; you're doing this to express regret and to learn to obey your parents. Many times, we think of penance as a penal juridical activity, but it's more medicinal. Sometimes medicine tastes bad, and sometimes it's even painful, but it's only so because of the good that it's going to achieve as opposed to you paying your fine, like running a red light and paying the ticket. We need to shift away from this juridical mentality and move into the medicinal perspective in order to appreciate penance for what it truly is. For instance, if you go to Confession and say, "Father, I missed Mass a couple of times," maybe he'll give you a penance of saying ten Hail Marys. Those Hail Marys are not your punishment. You're not atoning for your sin. Jesus atoned for your sin. Also, penance is not always given in the form of prayer. Sometimes, it can be through works of charity. If someone confesses abortion, for example, a confessor might ask them to donate one day a month at the local soup kitchen or to the hospital as an auxiliary volunteer and so forth. Again, this is not done as punishment but to express that you made a mistake and give you the opportunity to show your love of God by trying to make up for what you've done.

Fr. Brighenti: In addition, your penance never takes away the insult that you have committed against God. It's a symbolic gesture, and that's why the Church asks us to live our whole lives in a penitential way. During the Lenten season, we're reminded of the certain disciplines and sacrifices and mortifications that we should offer up. By doing so, we're then preparing ourselves for Heaven as we become less attached to material things and more attached to the spiritual ones, these being the things of Heaven and of Our Lord. It's a way of disciplining ourselves and our lives. It should also be mentioned that sometimes after Confession we can obtain a plenary indulgence in certain times and circumstances, like during the Year of Faith. You can only receive a plenary indulgence if you're in the state of grace, thus it's not granted as forgiveness to sins but to sins that are already forgiven. This is a special treasury of merit that Christ has won for us on the Cross and can be bestowed upon us by doing a spiritual work or a pilgrimage or a recognition to remove any temporal punishment due to already-forgiven sins. This alludes to the fact that your penances don't pay the price for your sins.

Fr. Trigilio: An indulgence is greatly misunderstood by a lot of people today. It's not a freebie or a "get out of jail free" card, but it's applying the infinite merits of Christ and the superabundant merits of Mary and the saints toward our temporal punishment due to sin. An act of penance, again, is not something to be taken as penal, but akin to this is the biblical concept of salvific suffering. St. Paul writes in Colossians 1:24, "Now I rejoice in my sufferings for your sake, and in my flesh I complete what is lacking in Christ's afflictions for the sake of his body, that is, the church." It's not that Jesus did not suffer enough for our salvation, but He purposely left a little space so that you and I could offer up our sufferings and unite ourselves with Jesus' act of obedience on the Cross.

42. How Often Do We Need Confession?

What is the longest time that one may go without Confession and Communion and not lose one's right to receive Communion? I am concerned for my son who started college but does not desire to go to Mass, though the chapel is just down the road from his dorm room. He brought a couple of small statues with him along with his St. Benedict crucifix, so I have a measure of hope.

Fr. Brighenti: One of the precepts of the Church is that we go to Confession at least once a year. If we are guilty and cognizant of any mortal sins, then we need to confess them and receive absolution from a priest before going to Holy Communion. But this is the minimalist approach to faith, seeking to do the bare minimum. Around Lent, we often hear about our Easter duty (another precept of the Church), which is to receive Communion usually between Ash Wednesday and up until about Corpus Christi Sunday or Trinity Sunday. However, you must go to Confession if you have mortal sin on your soul, even outside the Easter season. If you're missing Mass, then you're breaking one of the Ten Commandments. This would result in mortal sin, and you wouldn't be properly disposed to receive Communion. We are glad that your son at least has some statues and the St. Benedict cross. Obviously, you really are a good Catholic parent, since you're so concerned about his soul and his spiritual welfare. If your son's not at a Catholic campus, try to see if there's a Newman Center nearby, which is a Catholic chaplain association that can be found at these colleges. Usually, a priest is assigned to it.

Fr. Trigilio: You will want to check it out for yourself, because some of these places may say they're Catholic but sometimes are not.

Fr. Brighenti: Indeed, but most are truly Catholic. In fact, many of our vocations coming into our seminary now are from these Newman Centers because of their many good priests. There's also a great organization of lay young people called FOCUS (Fellowship of Catholic University Students). They give two years of their life after college to work on campus with the chaplain. They'll hold Bible studies and read the *Catechism*. This ministry really livens the whole Catholic institution. If a campus's Newman Center has a FOCUS missionary group available, you know that the center is on the right track.

Fr. Trigilio: If there is no FOCUS or Newman Center, there could be an Opus Dei Center, like at Princeton. They always have something near a college or university that you could avail yourself of. If that's not available, then you could look for a local parish, which in this case it sounds like there's one right down the road from the dormitory. I'd like to also address the minimalist requirements: as a parent, would you want your kid on life support? Of course not, because that's the bare minimum where they're lying there with an IV hooked up to them, and they're unable to help themselves. Instead, you would want them to be able to get out of bed, eat their own food, be able to walk around, and to live life to its fullest. Spiritually, it's the same thing. Don't be content with the bare minimum of just making sure they get Communion once a year, but see to it that they're getting Communion as often as they can, and at least by going to Mass every week and on holy days of obligation. You want them to have a healthy, vigorous spiritual life, just like you would want them to have a healthy, vigorous physical life.

Fr. Brighenti: I would assume that this was the case in this family's home, and now this is the first time that the son is out on his own, as it was mentioned he had brought some statues with him. It sounds like Catholicism is important to this family. But for those families in which it may not be, it's never too late to start practices and customs in your home to instill the Catholic Faith in your children. Go to Mass together. When you're visiting your son at the campus, go to Mass with him.

Fr. Trigilio: Exactly. Make that part of your visit. Tell him you're going to Mass together and then you're going to dinner.

Fr. Brighenti: Introduce your son to Father at the Mass, and maybe there's an organization he can get involved with, such as the Knights of Columbus. Sometimes that little introduction to the parish priest can open up doors and avenues so children don't feel so threatened as they go out on their own for the first time.

Fr. Trigilio: Unlike Fr. Brighenti and I, who had the benefit of going to minor seminary, a lot of vocations today are coming from people who aren't attending seminary school but are from either Catholic or non-Catholic universities. The college atmosphere is still conducive to vocations, and that's why I tell parents that it's important to go with their sons or daughters to visit colleges and look at all the alternatives and opportunities for their spiritual welfare. A college may have the best computer program in the world, but if there's no one there within a twenty-mile radius who's going to provide spiritual support and an orthodox teaching on the Faith, then you're wasting your money and jeopardizing their soul. Fortunately, as we've stated, there are many of these Newman Centers, and there's the Cardinal Newman Foundation that evaluates these colleges and provides you with a criteria. There are then some wonderful colleges like Ave Maria in Florida, Thomas Aquinas in California, Christendom in Virginia, and the Franciscan University of Steubenville in Ohio. There are so many options today, so you don't have to relegate to the Ivy League anymore.

Fr. Brighenti: There is a Newman list for colleges and universities. When the list comes out, there's certain Catholic criteria that a school has to meet in order to be recommended. That's a good place to start when you are picking out colleges and institutions for your son or daughter.

Fr. Trigilio: It is an important part of their formation, and it's part of your responsibility as a parent.

43. Settling Conflict

My ex-husband and I have been divorced for eight years, but he continues to harass me and make rude comments in front of my daughters. There are times, however, when he is more tranquil and demonstrates that he wants to be a good dad, and that is why I allow him to see my daughters. What prayers do you recommend for my daughters and me to pray for him? My daughters feel saddened by his behavior, and I need recommendations on how to handle this delicate situation.

Fr. Trigilio: I highly recommend that you develop a devotion to St. Monica. She is the mother of St. Augustine, and she had to endure a lot throughout her life. Not only was her son a no-good bum and a hedonist for a part of his life, but her husband was an abusive alcoholic. She had to suffer through an unpleasant marriage until her husband finally converted before his death, and St. Augustine converted, too, as a young man. She's a wonderful saint to read about and to go to for prayer and inspiration. I would also suggest calling your parish, which can contact your diocese to see if Catholic Charities might have someone who could offer counseling. Obviously, when your husband is behaving himself, it's a good opportunity for him to spend some quality time with your daughters. But as soon as he becomes belligerent, have your daughters call you on the cell phone so you can pick them up, and don't waste a second. Here's the rule: if he behaves himself, then he can spend time with the kids, but if he acts like a bully or an animal, then the visitation ends right there.

Fr. Brighenti: When I first read the question, it sounded like maybe the ex-husband had a bipolar issue. Perhaps praying to St. Dymphna would be appropriate, as she is the patron saint of mental illnesses. St. Rita of Cascia is another one that blessed marriage, and she's also the patron saint of impossible cases.

Now, we know that the saints are only intercessors, and it's God Who works the miracles, but St. Rita also had a husband who was not very kind to her. She always wanted to be a nun, but her parents wanted her to get married. She did marry and brought forth two sons, but her husband was a bear of a person, and a lot of people held vendettas against him. St. Rita prayed fervently for his conversion, and he did convert toward the end of his life, but it was a bit too late for the vendettas though. He made an untimely debt. Eventually, St. Rita did enter the convent and became an Augustinian nun, but the point is that she's a patron saint of impossible cases. Her feast day is May 22, and her life might be worth the study along with St. Monica's. St. Margaret of Scotland also had a very difficult husband for whom she offered prayers and mortifications, and her holy example and good will led him to accept God's grace and eventually to convert.

In addition to the prayers and devotions, it would be good to sit down with your daughters every time they come back, as they might be upset about their father and how this has been playing out, as they may even feel like they're walking on eggshells. They may be wondering if their father is going to be in a good mood or not every single week. It's good that you let the father see his daughters, because after all he is their father, but tell your daughters to pray for him, because there are obviously some issues he needs to deal with, and maybe he doesn't have the courage to do so. This is why these devotions are so helpful.

Fr. Trigilio: Serious verbal or emotional abuse, just like physical abuse, is something you do not have to put up with, especially if it becomes harmful to you or the children's well-being. If your ex-husband refuses to seek counseling, then a temporary cessation of visits may be the only alternative.

44. The Difference Between a Religious and a Diocesan Priest

What is the difference between a religious and a diocesan priest?

Fr. Brighenti: For starters, to say a priest is not a religious certainly doesn't mean that a diocesan priest isn't religious in the sense that he doesn't have a spiritual life. We're talking about a canonical distinction between two roles in the Church, religious communities as opposed to diocesan men, who are attached to a diocese that is attached to a certain bishop. There are cloistered orders, like the Benedictines, Trappists, and Cistercians, and the priest here would be called a religious. There are the mendicant orders, such as the Dominicans and Franciscans, who go out and preach but still live a semi-monastic life by praying together and living together. There are the post-Reformation communities and congregations, such as the Society of Jesus, better known as the Jesuits, and also the Redemptorists. Later on, we get the Congregation of the Mission, commonly known as the Vincentians, and the Oblates of St. Francis de Sales, who were considered religious because of the order they belonged to, and they would typically take vows of poverty, chastity and obedience. Now, the diocesan priests live in what we call the simplicity of life, obedience to the bishop and to the Church, and a vow of chastity and celibacy. They're not on the same level of the vows the Franciscans take, but we are still called to live a life of poverty, chastity, and obedience; a simplistic life. We're not supposed to be materialistic or live above the means of our people; and we must be obedient to Holy Mother Church and to our bishop, which we pledge to do at Ordination; and finally, we take the vow of celibacy. The vocation to the priesthood is both one of priesthood and celibacy at the same time, and chaste celibacy at that, and so a diocesan priest is formed and educated in those three aspects of their life, but their attachment is to the bishop of a particular diocese. Now, a diocesan priest, as well as a religious priest, can be commissioned outside their diocese or religious community to serve in a different institution, and many of them are sent to Rome, the Eternal City, to work in the offices or in the missions.

45. Marriage Between One Man and One Woman

I am having a very difficult time explaining to my daughter why same-sex "marriage" was not the intention of God from the beginning. She insists that if two people love each other, why would God be against it, since God is Love? She also relates this to the love of two females being best friends and who identify as the same gender. Please help me explain why marriage should only be between one man and one woman!

Fr. Trigilio: Unfortunately, this is not an uncommon question today. Many people are having to explain what for centuries didn't have to be explained. Society had taken for granted the truth that marriage is a natural institution founded by God between one man and one woman. Today, it's not a given anymore. People are asking why, which is a valid question, but the problem is that people are confusing terminology, and we always want to be precise with our nomenclature. Marriage is more than just a friendship. It may start out as a friendship between a boy and a girl, but marriage is much more than just an elaborate friendship. You can obviously have more than one friend, and we want people to have many friends, and maybe you have one best friend, but marriage is a very special relationship. It's a covenant for the rest of your life, and there's this complementariness between the husband and wife, the bride and groom, that mirrors the relationship of God and His people. This is personified in the Old Testament when God kept being faithful no matter how many times the Israelites were unfaithful. In the New Testament, St. Paul uses the imagery of Jesus being the Bridegroom and the Church being His Bride. When people today claim that a homosexual couple are just two people that love each other, we know that friends can love each other, but the love of a husband and wife is very special, because that love needs to be permanent, faithful, and fruitful so that it's open to the possibility of new life, of children and offspring. Same-sex unions don't offer that possibility. Also, just because two people love each other, this does not mean that they're eligible for marriage. What if two people who love each other are not just two men or two women, but are a brother and a sister? It's against both natural law and civil law for a brother and sister to get married, and it's illegal and unnatural for a parent to marry their child, even if there's a genuine love between those persons. Marriage transcends that love, and it is very unique and sacred. We also exclude polygamy, the practice of having multiple spouses at once. If you redefine marriage to include two people of the same gender, eventually you will be redefining it to include three or more people, and it could be a brother and a sister or parents and their children. You would have people marrying in all different scenarios. It's not that we're trying to show prejudice or discrimination against people by saying that the Church is upholding this moral law, but it comes from God Himself. We see in the Book of Genesis when Adam encountered Eve for the very first time and the text specifically says the word "wife" with regard to Eve's relationship to and with Adam (2:25). Now, you may ask when they got married, but that's a ceremonial question. The point is, at the natural level, Adam and Eve were husband and wife, male and female, as we're told in Sacred Scripture.

Fr. Brighenti: And God told them to "be fruitful and multiply" (Genesis 1:28). The thing to look at here is the terminology. In regard to the second part of the question, it seems that the daughter isn't so much questioning same-sex marriage but is rather having a hard time understanding the love that we've just explained. Pope Benedict XVI came out with an encyclical called *Deus Caritas Est*, which means "God is Love." He explained the different levels of love, as certainly there is a love between friends, and there's fraternal love as well. Our Holy Father of fond memory, Pope St. Paul VI, summarized those three points in his encyclical *Humanae Vitae* with the two ends of marriage, the unitive and procreative. Even if a couple is beyond the procreation state, they would still have to remain open to life. Here's another instance in which the state has no right to interfere in an institution that God created. When we have these debates about same-sex marriage, there is an opportunity to say that God instituted the Sacrament of Marriage. For centuries, this was never questioned, and it's only a modern invention now for the state to allow such things to take place, even though doing so is not within its authority. I would have to say that the media, television shows, movies, and Hollywood certainly confuse these issues. But if you go straight to the *Catechism*, it explains so beautifully what marriage is, along with the different levels of love. This is another area that is being distorted in our society, but the Church has the clear teaching on it.

Fr. Trigilio: People often make the mistake of reducing this matter to an issue of pure sentimentality. They'll say, "Well, they're a nice couple. They love each other. So, why not just leave them alone?" Well, while it's perfectly fine for you to have friends of either gender, the institution of marriage designed by God has specific purposes. If you redefine one element, you redefine all the elements. Like I said, if you allow for same-sex union, you will then later have to allow for polygamy, incestuous marriage, and so on, based on the same thought process that these people love each other, regardless if they're brother and sister, and it's sad to say that some people do have those disordered inclinations. There are people who would want to marry their brother or sister, if it wasn't for the fact that the state presently won't allow it. It's not that you just allow people to do what they want; you have to allow people to do the right thing for the right reason.

Fr. Brighenti: God created the gift of human sexuality and said, "Be fruitful and multiply." That's one of the ends of human sexuality. Any misuse of that gift would be a sin, and there are many sins one could commit in this regard, including same-sex activity. If a person is suffering from same-sex attraction, then they need to live a chaste life of celibacy. There is a wonderful Catholic organization called Courage that can help people to live a chaste lifestyle, which they would necessarily have to do since God designed the gift of human sexuality to be performed only between one man and one woman as a husband and wife for the sake of their marriage and procreativity.

Fr. Trigilio: That's why it makes perfect sense for the Church to say that fornication is wrong, because sexuality with the opposite sex, whether it's adultery or premarital sex or even any unchaste act upon yourself, is equally as immoral as homosexual activity, because these things would be taking place outside of marriage. If you're having contraceptive sex, then you're frustrating the idea of love and life, of unity and procreation within the context of the covenant of marriage, which is the only place where human sexuality is acceptable. In the *Theology of the Body*, Pope St. John Paul the Great elaborated on the fact that the body is designed in such a way that it symbolizes an invisible reality. The complementariness of the male and female, husband and wife, isn't just by happenstance or by accident. It's by design.

Fr. Brighenti: In the aberrations of these sexual acts, whether it's an abuse that you do to yourself or fornication, adultery, or same-sex activity, it is an act of selfishness. It's self-gratification. It's using yourself or the other person as an object. It's only in the context of marriage between a husband and wife where there's the possibility and opportunity of being a selfless gift of oneself to another. Even if a married couple is practicing artificial contraception, the marital act would be reduced to selfishness as well. That's why the Church teaches that artificial contraception is wrong.

Fr. Trigilio: There's consistency and an integration so that these are not separate issues. They're all woven together as a fine fabric.

46. Venial Sins and Informing Others of Actual Sin

Are venial sins forgiven in the Mass? And if I know that my friend's spouse is committing a mortal sin, should I say something? I don't think her spouse is aware that he is participating in serious sin and seems to receive the Eucharist joyfully every week. Should this be left between him and God in hopes that God will reveal it in his heart?

Fr. Trigilio: As we see in Scripture, you're encouraged to discreetly confront the person who's guilty of the sin, and this is called fraternal correction. If that doesn't work, then bring someone along, and if that doesn't help, then bring it to the Church. Now, to circumvent that and go directly to the spouse is a risky move. If the person is in serious danger or is involved in something horrible like terrorist activities and their life is in danger, then you've got to say to your friend, "Hey, I don't know if you're aware of this, but your husband is dealing with Al-Qaeda." Now, if the husband is cheating on her or if he's misbehaving, you don't want to get involved directly unless you're a close confidant and you two already share some confidentialities, and only then would you discreetly ask your friend if she knows what her husband is up to. The problem is that, if you become a wedge between them, people can be defensive, and your friend may take it the wrong way and think you're attacking her husband, even though what you're telling her is true. This is a very delicate matter, and that's why we advise people to pray about these things, and if you don't feel comfortable saying something directly to the husband, then you need to evaluate this and talk it over with your spiritual director or your confessor. Now, concerning the forgiveness of venial sins at Mass, any sacramental remits venial sins, whether it's making the Sign of the Cross with holy water or reciting the Penitential Act during the Mass. Receiving Communion also remits venial sins; mortal sins, however, can be remitted only through the Sacrament of Confession.

Fr. Brighenti: The way I was reading the question, I thought she was referring to her spouse. If that's the case, we need to remember that married couples are there to help each other on the way to salvation. If it was her spouse, and it's a matter of practicing artificial contraception, then she can gently inform him that what he's doing is sinful and is not what the Church intends.

Fr. Trigilio: If this is between the spouses themselves, they need to have dialogue, but if you're a friend of someone and you know that their spouse is doing something wrong, then you need to be careful how you go about informing them.

Fr. Brighenti: In that case, the information you share with your friend could be either calumny (false statements) or detraction (the revelation of another's sins without valid reason). You must apply caution while informing people of another's sins.

Fr. Trigilio: You can do things discreetly without being too blunt, and you can certainly do this with compassion.

47. Man's Role in Pursuing Marriage

I am interested in a man at my church, and I think he may be interested in me as well, but he has not tried to talk to me yet. My Protestant friends say that it is the man's role to initiate and pursue. He seems natural and reserved, but they told me to do nothing but pray that God will give him the courage to approach me, if it is His will. They told me not to approach him or even start a conversation with him, because God gave the role of pursuer to the man. Is this the right thing to do?

Fr. Brighenti: Well, if you don't do anything about it, you may as well enter the convent! Some men are very shy, and you might have to initiate the conversation with kindness or a simple "hello." Prayer is important, though. It's crucial that you ask the Lord to send the right spouse that He wants you to have in your life, and that's if you're called to the married life in the first place. People today have this idea of dating without marriage in mind, and it's really a shame, because they're only doing it for fun, and it becomes a waste of time. Sometimes they end up in marriage and find that they've married the wrong person, and this is because they didn't take the time to pray and ask the Lord if this is the right spouse for them. You should always pray to the Lord for this and date with a view of marriage. What does that mean? It means that you want to know your potential spouse politically, emotionally, and spiritually. It means you want to know his family. Dating is a time of communication to learn all these important matters which later on could be very problematic if you don't know about them ahead of time. I think that's why we have such a high divorce rate right now, because people are not getting to know each other when they're supposed to during the dating period. But in regard to who initiates the conversation, there is no problem for a woman to spark the conversation with a kind word or gesture.

Fr. Trigilio: Social conventions change over time, and so in the old days people had arranged marriages, and for our grandparents there was the idea that the man had to be the pursuer, the one who would initiate the conversation. But then I remember my mother telling me that when she first met my dad, he was very shy. She's the one who said to him, "Are you going to ask me out on a date?" If she hadn't said that, I might not be here today. So, it's a prudential judgment, as far as who speaks up first. It is true, however, that once they're married, the husband is the head of the household. It doesn't mean he's the despot or the tyrant, but as one priest told couples who were getting married, the husband has fifty-one percent of the vote; the wife has forty-nine percent. Sometimes, there are big decisions to be made, and if the vote is split fifty-fifty, there's going to be a deadlock.

Fr. Brighenti: My mother has a great expression about that. She says, "Yes, your father is the head of the house, but I'm the neck that turns the head."

48. Being Invited to Same-Sex Weddings, Part 1

Earlier this year, we were invited to a same-sex wedding involving our nephew and his partner. Because of our Catholic Faith and the sanctity of marriage between a man and a woman, we chose not to attend. At the reception, our nephew's mother wrongly accused us of condemning their family to Hell. We definitely never said this, much less thought it. We did not attend the ceremony because we did not support the union. Were we wrong in our decision not to attend?

Fr. Brighenti: Unfortunately, because of the legal system in our country that is allowing this, more and more families are going to be faced with these types of issues. I would like to mention that this is not considered a valid marriage in the sacramental sense that the Church would consider a marriage, which is a union between one man and one woman in the holy bonds of Matrimony. God instituted the Sacrament of Marriage, and the civil state (which has no competence in the area of the sacraments) is attempting to change it, and it's highly insulting that they are trying to do this. From the Catholic perspective, we don't consider a same-sex union to be a marriage; we consider it a farce, and I suppose that the mother of the nephew is probably experiencing a little guilt in her faith. She sees that this is not right. Considering that she made her accusation when you didn't say anything negative, she's feeling guilty about this and knows that it's wrong. To be honest, I would not have even gone to the reception or sent a gift, because doing so can send mixed signals. This is such a blatant offense to the Sacrament of Holy Matrimony, the way that God intended it to be, and any type of celebration to the contrary is extremely grievous.

Fr. Trigilio: Plus, Catholics shouldn't even be attending invalid marriages, whether it's two men or a divorced man and woman without proper dispensations. We don't want to cause scandal. We want people to be edified. And sometimes that act of tough love or fraternal correction, while it's certainly needed, is not always welcomed. If a parent or sibling has genuine and credible fear that their close relative will never speak to them again, I would only advise going under duress, not attend the party, and give no gift. Explain that you cannot condone and affirm something that violates your religion and your conscience. Acting as if this were a normal event can and will cause grave scandal.

49. Being Invited to Same-Sex Weddings, Part 2

I am a faithful Catholic. If I am invited to a same-sex wedding, should I go or gracefully say no?

Fr. Brighenti: Unfortunately, because the modern state is tampering with the definition of marriage, we are receiving more questions of this nature. From the time of creation, society has taken for granted the way God created marriage in the natural state between one man and one woman, and our Blessed Savior then elevated this to a Sacrament. Today, we see these issues coming up in civil law, and of course you should decline to attend. It's against our belief, it's an offense to the sanctity of marriage between one man and one woman, and it's giving credence to a lifestyle that's totally opposite of what we believe as Catholics. It is very important for us to make a statement, and it's going to take courage to stand up against this, just as it is for us prolifers. There are several Catholic and devout Protestant business owners in the wedding industry who are refusing to supply flowers or endorse these same-sex unions, and they're being sued in court now, which will cost them a large sum of money. But these are Christians making a righteous stand for the Faith, for what they believe, and for what is right and true and good and holy. When you do say no to the people who invited you, however, I would definitely put it in a nice letter and explain why you're not attending. Maybe add that your prayers are always with them or that you'll pray for them before the Blessed Sacrament that they'll come to realize that their way of life is a harmful one, and consider having a Mass said for their conversion.

Fr. Trigilio: We also need to see some consistency. If you're going to boycott a same-sex wedding ceremony, then you should also boycott an invalid marriage, such as a divorced Catholic getting married outside the Church with no dispensation. Now, if a non-Catholic couple is getting married for the first time, it is obviously a valid union. Now, if you've got somebody who's been divorced and remarried but didn't receive an annulment, then it's an invalid union. You should not attend any of those weddings, but you should explain to the couple why. The reason why you can't have same-sex marriages is the same reason why you can't marry a close relative (say, for example, your brother or sister) because it's against God's design. Marriage was designed to be between only one man and one woman who are not too closely related, and there are parameters. If the state can change or redefine marriage at one level, then it can and will redefine it at all levels. We've heard the crazy reports of some lady marrying her dog, and on another occasion one woman married herself. I really don't know how that's going to work, but I guess she'll put the ring on the other finger, and maybe she'll end up with mutual visitation rights. The point is that marriage was designed by God, and if we are consistent, just like we are regarding our pro-life activities and being against both abortion and euthanasia, then we must remain consistent in our sexual ethics as well. If you only boycott one kind of wedding and not the other, then people will rightly call you a hypocrite.

Fr. Brighenti: Also, when you inform someone that what they are doing is a sin, don't be condescending. Don't be judgmental. Just state the facts and show that you have a concern for them and that you will be actively praying for them, and maybe even offer up a mortification for them so that they will open their hearts and see the light. In other words, be prudent about how you write this letter or however you're going to communicate. It's important to show that we are going to stand up for the Faith and what we believe in, but it's also just as important to explain it in a pastoral way so that they understand why we have such a genuine concern for them. Many times, organizations like Courage have helped people struggling with sins of this nature really to see the light of Christ and encourage them to live a chaste lifestyle and to walk away from sexual perversion. With God, there's always hope and possibility.

50. Marriage and Annulment, Part 1

My wife had been previously married in the Catholic Church. She attempted to receive an annulment in New York, but her ex-husband refused to cooperate, and as a result she was never able to get her marriage annulled. Her ex-husband refused to have children, which I believe is a valid reason to annul their marriage. Is the hope for an annulment gone forever because my wife's ex-husband refuses to cooperate? We now live in Connecticut. Can my wife apply for an annulment twenty-three years later?

Fr. Trigilio: I worked in two tribunals for a spell, and it's true that under the old 1917 Code of Canon Law you were sort of limited as to where you could petition the case for a decree of nullity, and you as the petitioner also needed permission from the respondent, the person you were married to. Since the 1983 Code of Canon Law, along with some revisions made by Pope St. John Paul the Great and later by Pope Benedict XVI, you're now allowed to petition the case where you live as well as where the ex-spouse lives, or where the original wedding took place. Obviously, what they call the court of first instance would be where the marriage took place or where the respondent lives. If your ex now lives in a new location, then that would be the appropriate place for jurisdiction in this matter. It is true that an intention not to have children from the very beginning of the marriage would be grounds for an annulment or decree of nullity. This evil intention is called *contra bonum prolis*. St. Augustine wrote that there were three goods of marriage: procreation, permanence, and fidelity. These are referred to as traditional grounds. If you can show that either the bride and or the groom had the intention of not having children, or the intention of not being faithful, or the intention to later break this permanent union, then any one, two, or all three of those reasons would render that bond invalid, and therefore the decree for nullity could be granted. Canon Law also says that for a valid marriage, both the bride and groom must have due competence and due discretion. That means they must have been capable of fulfilling the obligations and responsibilities of Christian marriage and that they both were capable of making such a permanent commitment. Now, you don't need the respondent's permission, but the tribunal does have to contact him, because what applies to you also applies to him. If the wife gets the marriage annulled, then that would mean that the husband is also then allowed to remarry.

Fr. Brighenti: Another important aspect is your witnesses. Now that it's getting to be twenty-three years later, you might not want to wait too much longer, because your witnesses might be dead by the time you petition for an annulment. The witnesses can be people who knew you from before and at the time of marital consent, or at least someone who knew both of you while you were still civilly married.

Fr. Trigilio: You can't use somebody that you just met.

Fr. Brighenti: Exactly, because they will be testifying that an impediment existed before the consent—the "I do." But I would say that you have a very good chance of getting this marriage in question annulled by the tribunal. Start by making an appointment with your parish priest. He'll begin the paperwork, and the diocese will take it from there.

Fr. Trigilio: I'm glad you mentioned the witnesses, because it's so important that you don't exclude anyone. Some people might know something, or they might not know anything. You'd be surprised by how many relatives there are who tell you, "Father, I knew there was something wrong, but I didn't want to say anything." This is often because the marriage in question involved a friend or a relative.

Fr. Brighenti: Love is blind.

Fr. Trigilio: Precisely. They may have had reservations but neglected to express them. Family members are always the first people to approach as witnesses. They don't even have to be Catholic or even convert to Catholicism, and they don't even have to believe in the annulment process in order to give testimony, because all the tribunal is trying to do is ascertain if this was a valid sacramental marriage. It doesn't mean that any children you had were illegitimate either, as that's a civil matter. As long as you were civilly married in the eyes of the state, your children are civilly considered legitimate. The Church got out of that whole business of determining who's legitimate and who's not a long time ago, because back in the Middle Ages that would determine if you were the king's heir and would become the new head of state or not. In the Catholic Church's current status, legitimacy is not a concern. If your kids are legitimate from the day they were born, they stay that way. This is about the Sacrament, whether you're bound to death to this one person or can now marry another person. An annulment is not the equivalent of a divorce, either. It's never a "Catholic divorce." Jesus said that Moses only allowed divorce back under the Old Testament because of the stubbornness in the hearts of the Israelites. What God has joined together, let no one separate. Christ is the one who elevated the expectations for marriage, and we must always respect it.

Fr. Brighenti: Yes, and seek an annulment right away, because right now you can't receive the Eucharist at Mass or be a sponsor for Baptism or Confirmation, and so I highly encourage you to see if it's possible for an annulment to be granted. You are never guaranteed when you start the process.

Fr. Trigilio: That's right. You need to wait and be patient.

51. Marriage and Annulment, Part 2

My husband recently converted to Catholicism and is able to receive the Eucharist, while I am not, due to my annulment taking so much time to be approved by the tribunal. If he is able to receive, why am I not? We were married ten years ago in his former church.

Fr. Trigilio: First of all, your husband should not be receiving Communion, because his marriage to you needs to be both recognized and rectified (that is, convalidated). Even though he may not have needed an annulment for him to marry you, you are still in need of an annulment. This means that this union between you two needs to be reconciled, since both of you are married outside the Church. We tell people in the RCIA (Rite of Christian Initiation for Adults) process that we must take care of their marital situations first. If you or your current spouse is in need of an annulment, that has to be resolved. Once the marriage is convalidated or "blessed," you're then able to be brought into the Church and receive the sacraments. It would make no sense to give someone Baptism and Confirmation only to then refuse them Holy Communion, so the annulment comes first. Whoever handled your husband's initiation into the Church seems to have dropped the ball concerning this, and while I don't want to sound inconsiderate here, pastorally speaking, both of you shouldn't be receiving the Holy Eucharist until this is resolved. Now, having worked on the tribunal a few times myself, I suggest you simply call and ask them what the status of the annulment is. You're not being a pest—unless you're calling every day, of course—but call at least once a month and find out what the status is. Let them know you're interested. Some cases just take longer than others. Make sure your witnesses all are expeditious in this regard. Also, what applies to your husband applies to you, and it also applies to your former husband. If the annulment is granted, then he is allowed to remarry in the Church as well.

Fr. Brighenti: My advice is to be patient. Both of you need to refrain from the Sacrament of the Eucharist and persevere. Hopefully, the process will continue so that your marriage can be blessed in the Church, and then the two of you can go back to receiving the Holy Eucharist at Mass, following a good confession.

Fr. Trigilio: Just think how meaningful that's going to be when they can both receive Communion at the same time. That would make it so much more special for them.

Fr. Brighenti: I would also add that they should be practicing chastity right now since they're not really in the vows of marriage yet.

Fr. Trigilio: This is true, as they're not yet validly married. They're living as husband and wife legally, but if they can, I suggest living their marriage as a brother and sister type of relationship.

Fr. Brighenti: The only incident I could think of where receiving Communion would be permitted is with the Sacrament of the Anointing of the Sick in the danger of death.

Fr. Trigilio: It's called *in periculo mortis* in the Latin. You have a wide latitude regarding this. People who are in need of dispensations or who have impediments or who are invalidly married may receive the Eucharist in this situation.

Fr. Brighenti: Now, if they get better, then the obligation is still there. If they're conscious, I always make sure I make them aware of their obligation. I've had a similar situation happen with a heart patient in very bad condition who was expected to die, and I gave him Communion, but he then recovered and was able to continue to work on his annulment afterward.

Fr. Trigilio: Another thing we want to remind our followers is that when a priest anoints people, say at the hospital or in an accident, he doesn't ask the people what their status is. We go right ahead and anoint, because we presume that these people may be in danger of death. We're not going to ask people for their Church membership cards or baptismal certificates. Now, if you want to be a sponsor for Confirmation or Baptism, then you have to prove your credentials, so to speak.

52. The Purpose of Marriage

What is the purpose of marriage for humanity?

Fr. Trigilio: Marriage has a very practical purpose, as it continues the human race through procreation. Marriage is the foundation of society, whether it's secular society, which we sometimes call the state, and not as in one of the fifty states, but as secular government in general. Marriage is also a foundation for the Church, and this is why the Church is so concerned about the sanctity of marriage, which was created by God, not by government. Adam referred to Eve as his wife, although there was not a wedding ceremony. She didn't walk down the aisle, there wasn't some flower girl throwing petals all over the place, and there wasn't a rehearsal dinner or bachelor party. In Genesis, we have from antiquity the existence of marriage, and there's a practical aspect along with a spiritual: the mutual sanctification of husband and wife. We see this particularly since the time of Jesus. He elevated marriage from a natural state to a supernatural one, making it a sacrament, and this is why the priest or deacon is important to the celebration of this sacrament. The couple marries each other, and the ordained ministers witness this sacred union on behalf of Holy Mother Church.

Fr. Brighenti: Pope St. Paul VI wrote, in his 1968 encyclical *Humanae Vitae*, that marriage is for the couple to build up their love for each other and also to bring forth children, which implies that marriage is a stable environment to bring forth children. We've all seen the results when this isn't the case, with divorce and the separation of families ravaging society and wreaking havoc even on members in the Church. It is a fundamental building block in the Church and in society. It's a very important sacrament to be upheld and supported, and with the recent synod on marriage, we're really seeing that the Church is stepping up in teaching and preparing its future candidates the necessity of stability in marriage.

Fr. Trigilio: Yes, and we remind people that marriage is of divine origin. We can't change it. The state can't change it any more than we can change the need for water at Baptism or that you must be a baptized male in order to be ordained a priest. This is why traditional marriage is more than just a nostalgic concept of the past. It's an ontological reality. You have to have one man and one woman in this special bond which mirrors the relationship of God in the Old Testament with His chosen people, and this is reflected most intimately in Jesus, Who, as St. Paul says, loves the Church as a groom loves his bride. From this standpoint, marriage is the center of the spiritual life.

Fr. Brighenti: Marriage is also a breeding ground for vocations. We're wondering why vocations are in such decline today, and the instability of married life is one of the key factors. The family plants the seeds of vocations to the priesthood and religious life. That's why it's so important to support married couples not only in society, but in the Church, with the various programs we have available to keep them together so that they can be the leaven in our Church.

Fr. Trigilio: St. Augustine talked about the three goods of marriage: the openness to children through procreation, permanence in that the bond lasts until death, and fidelity, that you're not going to cheat on one another, just like God has always been faithful no matter how many times the Israelites were unfaithful toward Him.

53. Raising Children Catholic

My daughter married an agnostic four years ago, and I've been praying for them ever since. Presently, she is six months pregnant and wants to have her baby baptized, but she does not want to be required to raise the baby Catholic unless the child wants to. She hasn't abandoned the Faith entirely, as there is still a flicker of the Holy Spirit within her, and my wife and I continue to be loving parents as we pray for them. Why do these things happen? My daughter and her husband are educated people with master's degrees but have little to no religion. However, I have another daughter who is single, ten years younger, and keeps the Faith, and she even counsels my oldest daughter about attending Mass. What more can I do?

Fr. Brighenti: Unfortunately, I get the picture quite well. This has become the norm and is very troubling in our society today. It's the passive notion to let the children decide what to believe when they get older. Well, if that's the case in regard to religion, then to be consistent, we shouldn't dictate what the children know or how they should function in any other area of life. Yet we still send them to school so they can learn to read and write and do arithmetic. We also teach them how to bathe and dress themselves and how to brush their teeth. The fact is that we can't wait until they get older to teach them how to do these things properly, and the same applies to religion, which also encompasses morality and what is right and wrong. Just like with their education and physical well-being, a Christian parent must tend to the children's spiritual well-being as well and raise them up in the Catholic Faith. Pertaining to the question at hand, there are a couple of questions that came to mind. First of all, did your daughter and her husband get married in the Catholic Church, and was there a proper dispensation to marry? I would assume the agnostic husband is not baptized, or is he baptized but doesn't believe anymore? As a priest, these are questions I would be asking as I began to prepare this couple for Matrimony. It's one thing when you're preparing to marry a Catholic with a baptized non-Catholic, such as a Protestant or Orthodox, but in this scenario where you're not dealing with two believers, then the burden falls on the Catholic spouse-to-be. Is the non-believer wearing down the Catholic? In this case, it seems like the married daughter comes from a stable Catholic home, and the younger daughter is practicing her Faith. I'm wondering what kind of influence the agnostic husband has. I suspect that it's something more than just letting the children decide for themselves later on, but regardless, the obligation for the Catholic spouse in this marriage is to not only baptize any and all children she has but to also raise them up in the Catholic Faith.

Fr. Trigilio: If they were married in the Catholic Church, this requirement would have been asked of the couple at Pre-Cana and during the ceremony: "Will you accept children lovingly and raise them up according to God's laws?" I fear that this is one of those concepts that people take far too casually today. Raising the children in the Church is part of your marital commitment.

Fr. Brighenti: Also, Baptism is not just some Christian superstition; it's so much more than that. What I would like to see is the younger daughter seize more influence in trying to get her sister back into the Faith. The couple has master's degrees, so I'd assume that they are rational and reasonable people. We have a whole history of wonderful literature, not only on theology, but also in our spiritual theology, and in our fictional writings such as *The Chronicles of Narnia* by C. S. Lewis and *The Lord of the Rings* trilogy by J. R. R. Tolkien, both of which teach good Catholic and Christian principles. If your married daughter reads, then consider introducing her to these titles. We also have the great spiritual writers, including saints who wrote on theological treatises. If your daughter and her husband have their master's degrees, then they should be able to handle the more complicated pieces of fuller explanations of the Faith. This may take a bit of digging, but on the surface it seems as though there are many underlying issues at play, and maybe even the non-Catholic spouse is indirectly persecuting the Catholic one, as this could be the reason why she wants to have the Baptism but is afraid to go any further than that.

Fr. Trigilio: Now in regard to postponing Baptism, as we never outright deny this Sacrament, I've run into a number of occasions where one of the parents is Catholic and the other either is not or isn't practicing. If we have moral certitude or assurance that someone is going to raise that kid Catholic, whether it's one of the parents, a grandparent, or an aunt or uncle who lives nearby who can assure us this will happen, then we can go ahead and baptize the child. But if there's not any reasonable hope that this kid is going to continue in the Faith, then you're not doing them any service by getting them baptized. It's like getting a child inoculated against all these terrible diseases but then not ensuring that they get good nutrition, that they bathe, that they have a roof over their head, or a set of clothes on their back. Their health is more than just an inoculation. It's a whole lifestyle and a process, and so it is with their spiritual life.

Fr. Brighenti: The younger daughter would probably be an excellent godmother, but again, the parent would have to allow that child to go to church.

Fr. Trigilio: You must have their cooperation, and what happens many times is if the parents are lukewarm but there is an aunt or uncle or a grandparent who takes the child to church, when the child makes their first Communion, it usually serves as an inspiration for the parents to clean up their act and one day receive Communion themselves.

Fr. Brighenti: It's part of my duty in the seminary to assign seminarians to teach in Catholic schools. One of the seminarians mentioned that it is through these children who are going to school that the Faith is then brought into the home. If this child becomes a practicing Catholic, maybe through the godmother or the grandparents, then he may be able to bring at least the mother back into more active participation in the Church. There is hope.

Fr. Trigilio: That's why we're always hopeful. Like I said, we never deny Baptism, though we may postpone it until you can find a suitable godparent.

54. Marriage Outside of the Church

I am married to a man with whom I am not in love. Our marriage was performed through the state. I feel so guilty that I did this, and I am not sure how to feel better about this situation. I am not planning on divorcing my husband. Do you have any suggestions?

Fr. Trigilio: It's sad, because we hope and pray that people get married for love, and as a Christian you always want to get married with the possibility and desire that this be a sacrament as well, because then you're going to get God's grace to help you along your journey. If it's just a natural union, where this is the first marriage for either one of you and you're getting married by a Justice of the Peace or the captain of a ship, then without it being a sacrament you're not going to tap into that reservoir of grace or have the spiritual resources to fall upon. One of the things that could be quite helpful to you is to think about getting this marriage convalidated in the Church. This is where a priest or deacon prepares you just as if you were getting married for the first time, and you and your civilly-married husband take your vows before the priest or deacon with two witnesses, and that would then be the day of your sacramental marriage. It's not a renewal of your vows, because your vows are being made for the first time in the presence of God. However, if you truly don't love this person to whom you're legally married, then ask yourself if you're willing to commit yourself to a faithful, a permanent, and God-willing, a fruitful union for the rest of your life, because that's what the Sacrament of Marriage is about: total commitment of oneself for the rest of your natural life. It's not just something you do until you and your spouse get sick of each other, so now is the time really to discern. If you don't love this person, then you need to ask yourself why you are even in this relationship. Now, the question at hand didn't mention anything about children being involved, but obviously children deserve that their parents optimally be husband and wife and provide a stable family environment. This doesn't just mean that they have the roof over their heads, clothes on their back, food on their plates, and a place to go to school, but that the family situation that's built upon the rock of marriage stands firm so that the children can develop properly in terms of spirituality, just as is expected in every other regard.

Fr. Brighenti: For Catholics who are struggling with marriage, there are some great programs available in the Catholic Church. One of them is called Retrouvaille, which is a retreat that couples go on to try sincerely to get back to the nature of their vows, where they promised to be faithful in good times and bad, in sickness and health, until death do them part. There are other programs in the Church as well, one being Marriage Encounter. Again, this program helps revive their marriage vows together in a wonderful spiritual retreat. If you're going to have your marriage convalidated in the Catholic Church, then I suggest calling your parish priest to find Catholic counseling, which can be set up through the local branch of Catholic Charities in your diocese. They are Catholic counselors who share the same morals that we have in regard to marriage, and there are family counselors, too, in the event you do have children who are suffering from a poor marital situation. I also want to mention that the parents of St. Thérèse of Lisieux were just beatified, and part of their relics were given to the Carmel in Philadelphia. We both went to the installation of these relics, and Fr. Fred Miller of Immaculate Conception Seminary (in Seton Hall, New Jersey) gave a wonderful talk, and he's also written a book on the sufferings of St. Thérèse. He's very devoted to the Little Flower and to her parents, who were in the likeness of St. Anne and St. Joachim, the grandparents of Our Blessed Savior and the parents of Mary. They are patrons of good Christian and Catholic marriages, so I may also suggest to pray through their intercession. Carmel also has a booklet of devotions and a litany for St. Thérèse's parents. You can certainly ask for their intercession as you discover and seek these things out, because I hear in the question that you want to make this union into a permanent Catholic marriage.

Fr. Trigilio: I think you should also discern the reason why you don't love your spouse. Is it just that you don't have that warm and fuzzy feeling anymore, or is it that you don't have the same physical intimacy or level of attraction? Over time, those things come and go, and after many, many years, it's not going to be the same experiences as when you were newlyweds. But as Pope Benedict XVI said in his encyclical *Deus Caritas Est*, that ablative and possessive love is the willingness to give and take, that you're willing to do anything to preserve the marriage and that you're willing to do anything for your spouse. It's a permanent bond. Your physical appearances change over time, your temperament or moods, too, but your love for each other only grows. Ask yourself: do you really love this person? Is it that you don't love him anymore or that your emotions or affectivity for him has changed? This is going to take some discernment, and you may need to find a good spiritual director to help you with this.

Fr. Brighenti: I don't know if you're aware, but because you are in an invalid marriage right now, you're currently prohibited from receiving Communion until you get this rectified.

Fr. Trigilio: Make a spiritual Communion, but do not make a Sacramental Communion.

Fr. Brighenti: Both you and your spouse will need to sit down with a priest if you're going to have your marriage convalidated. I would suspect, if that's going to be the commitment, a lot of things will come out. The counseling will be helpful, your prayer life will be helpful, and the priest in your parish is going to be helpful as well. Maybe things will improve and move in a positive direction.

55. Marriage and Annulment, Part 3

It is my understanding that when a marriage is annulled, it is deemed that the marriage never took place. Does an annulment affect the legitimacy of children born of that marriage?

Fr. Brighenti: There are so many erroneous statements that have been made regarding annulments throughout the years, and this particular misunderstanding is why some people have not petitioned for an annulment. Another is the concern of paying an exorbitant price. First of all, the Church doesn't charge an exorbitant price when it comes to an annulment; it requests an offering to help offset the expenses at the tribunal, which is the place where annulments are worked upon. There are laypeople who work there and receive health benefits, but if the person petitioning for an annulment is poor, then the parish usually comes in and helps the parishioner in need of funds for this process. Another common concern would be the effect of the validity of children. You have to remember that marriage is both a civil institution and a sacrament. When the Church grants an annulment, it's not saying that the marriage in question never took place in the civil aspect; it's only sacramentally that for one reason or another, the husband or the wife or both were not free to consent to the marriage vows. There was something impeding the ability to say "I do," such as a drug or alcohol impairment. When we receive an annulment, the external witnesses that knew the couple from the time before their vows to afterward confirm whether certain conditions did indeed exist and if they would have impeded the consent of that marriage, and the Church will then decide if the sacrament took place or not. It has nothing to do with civil law. If the marriage was performed in accordance with the state, then the legitimacy of the children is not in question, as that is solely a matter for civil law.

Fr. Trigilio: Exactly. The legitimacy of a child is a civil matter determined by the state, and as long as the parents have a valid civil license, then the children are legitimate. Here in the United States, the priest represents the state in the sense that we witness the marriage and sign the documentation. But if the couple doesn't get the marriage license, then we're not allowed to marry them civilly. At one time, we used to have secret marriages, where a priest would celebrate the Sacrament of Marriage without civil authorization. An annulment only focuses on the sacramentality of the marriage, whereas back in the Middle Ages, there was a question about whether a particular king and queen were validly married, because there was no such thing as divorce until King Henry VIII came along, and if the monarchs in question were not validly married, then their illegitimate child wouldn't become the next ruler. That's why this idea trickled down into our own age where we tell people that if your children are legitimately recognized by the secular government, then that's how the Church recognizes them as well.

56. Confirmation

Why be confirmed? Is this sacrament like Baptism in Protestant churches, done willingly in late teen years by a conscious decision to accept Jesus Christ into your life and to live in His ways?

Fr. Brighenti: The Sacrament of Confirmation doesn't have to take place in the teen years. In fact, the present Archbishop of Denver, Colorado, back when he was the Bishop of Fargo, had written in his *ad limina* report a defense of Confirmation for children in the second or third grade. Canon Law really leaves it open for when exactly you can receive it. That said, Confirmation can be received at various ages, but let's say it is in the teenage years. There is a beautiful philosophy and theology behind it, as when you receive Confirmation, you're becoming a "soldier of Christ." It's a renewal of our baptismal promises and when we receive the gifts of the Holy Spirit, which confirm and strengthen us in our Faith to go out and defend Christ in the world, because that's what we're called to do. Confirmation is also one of the three Sacraments of Initiation, which begin with Baptism, are followed by First Communion, and end with Confirmation. The Eastern Catholic Church or Orthodox Church, on the other hand, gives these Sacraments to the baby all at once—Baptism, Communion, and Confirmation (called Chrismation). In these Sacraments of Initiation, you renew the gifts of the Holy Spirit, which are Knowledge, Counsel, Wisdom, Piety, Fear or Reverence of the Lord, Courage, and Understanding to help you be a Catholic in our world that is growing dimmer and dimmer in sin. Confirmation is a beautiful sacrament that may need to be theologically explained better to the faithful so that they can see the importance of it in their lives.

Fr. Trigilio: As a pastor, my encounter with Confirmation is twofold. We've got the young people being confirmed by the bishop on a regular basis every year, usually in eighth grade or high school, though some dioceses like Denver are a bit younger, and then we have adult converts who were baptized in another Christian faith tradition but are now being brought into full communion when they're confirmed at the Easter vigil. It's a powerful witness for people to see adults getting confirmed. It's such a beautiful testimony to the affirmation of taking baptismal promises seriously and getting confirmed in the Holy Spirit, just as the apostles were emboldened by the chrism of the Holy Spirit in the Upper Room to go out and preach the Gospel without fear.

Fr. Brighenti: It's interesting that our bishop is giving permission in our diocese for pastors to confirm adult Catholics who have never received this Sacrament at times other than the Easter Vigil. I always choose the Feast of Pentecost, which is the Feast of the Holy Spirit, where the tongues of fire came down upon the apostles and the Blessed Virgin Mary, and they were filled with these wonderful gifts. It's a springboard to teach the whole community the Faith and to renew them in their baptismal promises and as a witness to these adults receiving Confirmation at the Feast of Pentecost.

57. Wearing a Veil at Mass

After much prayer and loving surrender — all by God's grace — the Lord, our Spouse, led me to wear a veil at Mass. I cannot express in words the spousal love that God has placed within me by inspiring me to do so! It has been an enormous blessing, almost like a sacramental. It is also a precious reminder that I belong to Christ and that He is truly my Bridegroom. This has led me to be more reverent and focused on Christ while celebrating Mass. Would you add your blessed knowledge and wisdom in commenting on the veil?

Fr. Brighenti: Before I finished reading the question, I thought that maybe she was a nun who was returning back to the habit and the veil, which we rejoice in, because it's an outward sign of a nun's vows of chastity, poverty, and obedience.

Fr. Trigilio: Today, wearing a veil or a hat to Mass is optional, but it used to be mandatory for women under the 1917 code, just like in other cultures and traditions, such as the Jewish men wearing yarmulkes or the Islamic women required to wear hijabs or burkas.

Fr. Brighenti: It's pretty sad actually, because we went from one extreme to the other. My sister once told me that if she went to Mass at school and didn't have her chapel veil with her, one of the sisters would put a little tissue on her head. Today, people dress like slobs, and while we are happy that they're at least attending Mass, it should really be so much more than that. We're going to the Eucharistic banquet of Christ Our King.

Fr. Trigilio: It's the wedding garment motif. It's not about how much you paid for it, and it's not only about the veil, which I've seen some of my parishioners wear devoutly. It's just like the biretta that the priest can wear. While women are no longer obligated to wear a veil, they still have the option to put in a little extra effort.

Fr. Brighenti: This is the reason why Catholic schools have uniforms, because it's been proven that the sharper you dress, the more sophisticated your etiquette tends to be. Yes, we're happy that you're going to Mass, but now put in the extra effort. We're in a society where you can afford nice clothes, and most people probably have a closet full of them. This is a little pet peeve of mine, because the way you dress is an outward sign of respect for the Lord. I was at a funeral recently where the funeral director had to remove the hat off of a fellow who was about to put a cross on his grandmother's casket. Since the late 1960s, it seems like etiquette and other related concepts have been falling apart.

Fr. Trigilio: It's more than just being casual and informal, and there are a lot of young people today who don't even realize that it's impolite to wear your hat in a public building, and even more so when you're in God's church. I remember a sister renting out a chapel veil for five cents if one of the girls didn't bring one. My mother would always have a head covering, and to this day she still wears a hat. Again, it was the idea of putting on Christ. While it's not mandatory, it's highly recommended that women cover their heads when they go to the Papal Masses in Rome, and particularly if they're going to have the honor of meeting the Holy Father. The greatest honor a human being could have is going to Mass, where we join in the worship of God with all the angels and saints. It's not about wearing costly attire, and it's not just a throwback to the days gone by, but it's an extra, voluntary effort to show your reverence for God.

Fr. Brighenti: Like you said, it's not mandatory anymore, even if you went to the Extraordinary Form of the Mass, because we're in the new code now. But we need to have a balance. We went from too extreme to too casual in the way we dress.

Fr. Trigilio: Some people only do things because they have to, and I have great respect for these women who wear the veil, because it's optional yet they wear it anyway. That said, I certainly don't give a dirty look to those who don't want to wear it; it's just like with the biretta. There are priests who wear it, and there are priests who don't. This does not make you a better priest.

Fr. Brighenti: I did notice that if you go into the Shrine of the Blessed Sacrament in Hanceville or in Rome, there is a dress code. You can't wear shorts or sleeveless shirts, for example, and we do try to enforce these rules in our own parishes. We don't refuse people to come in, but we try to put our dress code in the bulletin or on the doors in the summer months, because other people are also going to church, and they don't necessarily want to see you at Mass in your beach clothes.

Fr. Trigilio: When you think of the Parable of the Great Banquet (Luke 14:15-24), the man who was not dressed properly was reduced to complete silence. Some people would say it's not fair, that he was invited at the last minute, but the point is that everybody had a wedding garment, and it didn't matter how much you paid for it. It showed respect to the person who invited you and to the event you were going to. It was disrespectful to not show up in a wedding garment. Even when I was helping out in Erie, New York with Fr. Levis and Fr. Krause, at some of the poorest parishes in town, mostly Hispanic and African American, the people were still dressed to the nines every Sunday, and the ladies wore these spectacular hats.

Fr. Brighenti: When we were growing up, my mother had church clothes for us that we would wear only for church, and we would change into something else as soon as we got home. Twice a year, for Christmas and Easter, our parents would go out and get us new suits just for Mass. We were certainly not very wealthy when we were growing up; we were middle class and barely making it, but we always had clothes set aside for Mass. I think we've really lost our etiquette and respect for the Lord today.

Chapter 3

Morality

1. Grace

What is grace, why do we need it, and how do we get it? Do we need it all the time, or can we survive without grace until it becomes essential? St. Paul had written to pray without ceasing, but does that mean we are in constant need of grace? What level of urgency are we to maintain, like the crew of an aircraft carrier in a war zone? Or does this depend on our calling?

Fr. Brighenti: Our calling from Baptism is to be saints, of course. We should always be vigilant in our fight against evil. Grace is always necessary. St. Thomas Aquinas so eloquently explained that grace builds on our nature, but it doesn't negate the fact that we indeed require grace.[13] Grace is a supernatural gift that God gives to us; His very life breathed within us. We call this sanctifying grace, and we receive it through the sacraments, beginning with Baptism in which we are infused with the Triune God and where Original Sin is removed, but especially in the Holy Eucharist. Every time we encounter the Lord's Body, Blood, Soul, and Divinity, we are encountering grace. But we can lose

---

[13] *Summa Theologica*, I, q. 1, art. 8.

this grace through mortal sin. To commit a mortal sin, it has to be a grave matter; you have to know that it's a grave matter; and you have to choose to do it anyway. If you do commit a mortal sin, then you can lose this supernatural gift of sanctifying grace. The only way you can restore it is by going through the Sacrament of Confession. I like the analogy of an aircraft carrier in a war zone, because there is a possibility of losing our grace. We have to be vigilant in avoiding all occasions of sin.

Fr. Trigilio: St. Thomas Aquinas said in his *Summa Theologica,* "*Gratia non tollit naturam, sed perficit*; Grace does not destroy nature, but perfects it."[14] I think one of the key distinctions between Catholic and Protestant theology in terms of grace is that we both definitely believe in grace, yet Martin Luther had this idea of grace that *covered* over our sins. He said in his own words that grace covers over us and the repugnance of sin like snow would cover a mound of something that the pooch left behind. But we are more than just sin, and it's not human nature that is repugnant to God, but the sin itself; our human nature is only wounded by sin. Grace doesn't cover us over, but it heals and perfects us. It's like how medicine helps the body heal itself and restore it back to a robust condition. On the spiritual level, we're mortally wounded by sin, but then grace heals us. It's a blast of life support that revives the body and makes the wound from sin disappear. At this stage, a person is able to operate at the level they were initially meant to. However, because of the Original Sin we inherited from the fall of man in the Garden of Eden, we're still very much susceptible to sin, but Baptism is a fountain of grace that helps us stay the course. Consider when a baby is

14 Ibid.

born; it's not born with many diseases but with the vulnerability to infections and viruses like the chicken pox, measles, and so forth. So, what do the parents do? They take their baby to the pediatrician for an inoculation, and that shot gives the baby the ability to fight off the diseases to which it previously had vulnerability. So, too, in Baptism, that sanctifying grace removes Original Sin and now helps the soul fight the temptations that lurk along life's path.

Fr. Brighenti: The more we increase in sanctifying grace and the more we increase in God's life within us, the closer we grow to Him and the more repugnant sin becomes. Its fond memories become repellent to us, even the venial sins which are sins that are less serious. God is not only healing us, but He's also building His life within us as we cooperate with Him, and that's the key: we have to cooperate with His abundant gifts.

Fr. Trigilio: As the sisters taught us so well when we were in Catholic school, God doesn't give you grace. He *offers* it. If we accept it and work with it, then it can increase. The more grace you receive, the more capacity you have for grace. It's like a balloon; the more you blow into it, the larger it becomes and the more capacity it has for air. It's a process that you never want to be stingy with. God offers a plenitude of grace, and we need to take advantage of every ounce of it.

2. Taking the Lord's Name in Vain

The Second Commandment says, "You shall not take the name of the Lord your God in vain." What does that mean?

Fr. Brighenti: Obviously, it means that we don't curse with Our Lord's name or use it in any sacrilegious manner. There should be respect for God's name. In the Old Testament, the Israelites were afraid even to utter the proper name of the Lord. It was so revered back then, and unfortunately today, too many people take it for granted. But you know, we should not only express reverence to God, but also to the holy things that are related to God, such as sacramentals, the sacraments themselves, and the Church. Anything that violates this code could be considered sacrilegious. Finally, we don't take any false oaths; when we place our right hand on the Bible at court and swear to tell the truth, the whole truth, and nothing but the truth, we are swearing an oath before Almighty God.

Fr. Trigilio: A lot of people tend to think that the Second Commandment simply prohibits taking the Lord's name in vain, which we are forbidden ever to do, but as stated, there's also sacrilege in showing a disdain for holy things, whether it's a rosary, a crucifix, a saint, or even a person, like a nun or a priest. Anything that comes across as anti-religion is sacrilege, and therefore blasphemy, and these all fall under the umbrella of the Second Commandment.

Fr. Brighenti: When people confess that they struggle with using Our Lord's name in an irreverent manner, I always tell them that a good remedy is to pray the Divine Praises, which are like a little litany that comes after the Benediction: "Blessed be God. Blessed be His Holy Name. Blessed be Jesus Christ, True God and True Man." Try to say that every time you misuse the Lord's name or do something wrong with a sacramental. This helps to restore the reverence of God and the holy things that are due to Him.

Fr. Trigilio: I think it was an Irish priest who started the Holy Name Society, where men took an oath not to use the Lord's name in vain, though unfortunately they've since gone by the wayside. It's ironic today that you'll hear actors use the Lord's name in vain on television and in movies, yet they'll bleep out four-letter words which aren't blasphemous but are vulgar, though we shouldn't use either.

Fr. Brighenti: It is truly a shame that our society has been losing reverence for everything that we hold dear. If you don't have a Holy Name Society in your parish, it would be a good idea to start one. It's a national organization, and you just need a few men from your parish and a commitment. I really came to appreciate it, because on Holy Thursday they kept Vigil at the Holy Sepulcher, and they had different devotional prayers that they said on the hour until we put the Blessed Sacrament away for the evening. It was a beautiful devotion that they maintained, and they did plenty of other notable things in the parish, too. Overall, it's a great men's organization; they just need to have good chaplains and priests or deacons to inspire them. You could also start a junior Holy Name Society for the youngsters.

3. Did Jesus Suffer for Venial Sins?

Since venial sins do not keep us out of Heaven, did Jesus only suffer for Original Sin and mortal sins?

Fr. Brighenti: Just to review, a mortal sin is committed whenever it's a grave matter, and whoever is committing a mortal sin knows it is a grave matter and willingly chooses to commit it anyway. It would be classified as a venial sin if one or more of those factors were not present. However, a venial sin is still an offense against God, no matter how small or insignificant we think it may be, and still has ramifications in the world. Even our private sins will eventually spill out into the public sphere and influence others in a ripple effect. We should never try to rationalize away our venial sins simply because they're "smaller" than mortal sins. When you grow closer to God, you begin in the purgative stage where you expel the mortal sins from your life, very much like a sculpture who's carving a beautiful statue, and hefty chunks of marble are being cut out. You then move into the illuminative stage, where you're refined as all the venial sins are chiseled out. After that is the unitive stage, where you undergo all the polishing and buffing and come out as that beautiful statue. At that point, we become so detached from our sin that even the very thought of it becomes repulsive to us. If we're at the level of venial sins, we still need the Sacrament of Confession, as well as all the other spiritual tools available to us in this warfare so that we don't regress into mortal sin.

Fr. Trigilio: At the seminary, I remember Fr. Sullivan, who was our dogma professor, reminding us that even one measly venial sin is still repugnant to the infinite truth and goodness of God, and we must be careful not to take venial sins too lightly. I tell people that if you went to the doctor and had some unsightly growth on your face that turned out to be benign, you would still ask him to cut it off. Even though it's benign, it still doesn't belong there. Likewise, while venial sins are not malignant, meaning they're not deadly to our souls, they are still ugly in the sight of God, and we need to get rid of them.

Fr. Brighenti: It's important to do so, because maintaining a tolerance for venial sins can easily encourage mortal sins, which would then cut us off from God completely.

4. Venerating Saints

Why do Catholics put so much emphasis on the saints? Isn't this considered idolatry?

Fr. Brighenti: The saints are real, living examples to help us follow Christ. They were sinners who cooperated with God's grace and had a profound conversion experience, and the memory of them serves as a model for the rest of us. We don't worship the saints, but we honor them. We only give worship to God, but we also honor His handiwork, in this case the saints, who have made it to Heaven before us. Take a look at our secular world and its culture. Here in the United States, we honor our forefathers: George Washington, Thomas Jefferson, Abraham Lincoln, and so on. We're not worshipping these men but are instead honoring them for what they've done for our country, and we even erect images of them in their memory, such as Mount Rushmore. The same applies to the saints. In theology, we call this *dulia*, and the Blessed Virgin Mary is due the highest honor: *hyperdulia*. Only God receives our worship, and that's called *latria*. It sometimes bothers people that the saints were sinners, but we can name a few, like St. Augustine, who had a great conversion. St. Jerome, for example, struggled with a short temper that he had to work on, and with God's grace he and the other saints were able to overcome their flaws and change for the better. They've become wonderful examples for the rest of us, and not only do they intercede for us with their prayers, but we can learn much from their personal lives as well.

Fr. Trigilio: I think a reason why some people are uncertain about the saints today is that a lot of contemporary heroes in modern society, be they football stars or celebrities, fall short when their weaknesses come into the spotlight and they drop from their pedestals. When we look at the saints, we're not denying that they had weaknesses of their own, but we're saying that, by God's grace, they overcame those weaknesses. They are heroes and role models—not in a perfect sense, as only God is perfect—but because of their perseverance in Christ. One thing I always mention to our non-Catholic friends is that plenty of Protestants have a high regard for St. Paul, and with good reason. They consider his strong faith, his perseverance, and all the trials and tribulations he went through during his various missionary journeys. That's exactly what we see in the saints, including St. Paul. We honor his strength and courage, which he received from God alone, and that he persevered in his faith. We're not pushing Jesus out of the way by honoring St. Paul, any more than the Corinthians or the Romans, to whom he had written letters, did when they honored him.

Fr. Brighenti: The Scriptures also highlight his remarkable conversion. The Bible says St. Paul fell to the ground while on his way to Damascus. Caravaggio, a well-known painter, captures this scene of St. Paul by depicting him falling off his horse at his moment of conversion. It may be artistic license, since Scripture does not mention any animal, but in any event, the sacred text does say he fell to the ground before Jesus spoke to him. This is a terrific conversion for us to model our lives after. Our own conversions may not be as momentous as St. Paul's, but they happen daily where people turn away from the lesser things of this world and embrace God.

Fr. Trigilio: If there is anything wrong with honoring St. Paul, then by no means should you ever mention him outside of reading his epistles, nor would you ever name a church after him. Yet we see many non-Catholic churches named after St. Paul, and St. Peter as well.

Fr. Brighenti: Consider that St. Peter denied Christ three times. But he then sought the Lord's forgiveness; that's the key, and that's why we honor him with images and feast days. Again, it's not about the saint himself. The Second Vatican Council reminds us that our devotions must all be Christocentric. These saints lead us back to Christ, Who saved them all.

Fr. Trigilio: As Americans, we love parades, like when the troops come home from the war, and it's a wonderful thing to have in honor of our brave men and women. Well, processions are essentially a spiritual parade where we honor the soldiers for Christ who fought the good fight. By no means are we taking any glory away from Jesus, but we're honoring these foot soldiers, so to speak, in the spiritual battlefield. We're all on the same side, working for Christ and with Christ, but just like when the troops come home, we're simply saying thank you and we're honoring the courage and valor of these saints who inspire us to be more like Christ.

Fr. Brighenti: Even more beautiful are the Feast of Corpus Christi processions, in which the Blessed Sacraments Themselves, Our Lord in His Body and Blood, are brought through the streets under an extravagant canopy. We used to practice this in my parish where I was pastor, and at the First Holy Communion class we would drop rose petals before the Blessed Sacrament. This devotion to Our Lord in the Most Blessed Sacrament enlivens the sensitivity of the people, and the festivity encourages them to grow deeper in their love for the Lord in the Eucharist.

Fr. Trigilio: There was a document not too long ago that reminded us that processions and pilgrimages are of the same genre; they're manifestations of a spiritual reality that we're all pilgrim people on a journey from this world to Heaven, as stated in Vatican II. Think of a procession as a mini-pilgrimage. Processions and pilgrimages themselves are abbreviations of your whole spiritual life from your Baptism to burial, and it reminds us to keep our eye on the destination: Heaven.

Fr. Brighenti: Pilgrimages were a pious medieval practice that are being rediscovered, and one of the most famous pilgrimages is the one to the Shrine of St. James in Santiago de Compostela, Spain. There is an old pilgrim trail that weaves through various towns and villages and all the way into France. Tons of people are doing it for several reasons, and hopefully it's to fuel their faith in Christ. Perhaps they don't start out that way in the beginning, but they may have a sense of conversion by the time they reach the Basilica of St. James. In *The Canterbury Tales* by Geoffrey Chaucer, he wrote about these types of pilgrimages and the things that happened along the way, as Catholic England had many great pilgrimages down to the Canterbury Cathedral where St. Thomas Becket was martyred. Pilgrimages have been a part of our spiritual life forever, and they've been encouraged to the Holy Land or to the four main basilicas in Rome, which would be the Basilicas of St. Peter, St. Mary Major, St. John Lateran, and St. Paul Outside the Walls. Pilgrimages to these basilicas serve as an extension of our faith, and they mirror our lives, as we are constantly on a pilgrimage to the next life. A pilgrimage is different than a journey, because a pilgrimage has both a beginning and an end, while on a journey you're simply wandering. We are certainly on a pilgrimage in this life and hopefully toward Heaven.

Fr. Trigilio: Pilgrimages also reaffirm a core teaching of our Catholic Christianity: that we are a body and a soul. Just like with bowing, genuflecting, processions, and making the Sign of the Cross, our body gets involved with the soul on these pilgrimages.

Fr. Brighenti: Yes, we worship through our five senses.

Fr. Trigilio: When you march through the church at a forty-hour procession, when the priest moves around the sanctuary for the Stations of the Cross, or when you're at a Corpus Christi procession, you are physically on a pilgrimage with the cooperation of your body and soul, because that's how God created us. After the Incarnation, we now have a wonderful union of divinity and humanity, the spiritual and material worlds combined. We're not just otherworldly; we're of this world, too.

5. Burying a Statue of St. Joseph

Is it superstitious to bury a statue of St. Joseph upside down in your yard when you are trying to sell your house?

Fr. Brighenti: Yes, it is superstition, and I simply cannot stand it when I go into Catholic bookstores and see these St. Joseph kits, which come with instructions explaining the procedure of burying the statue, followed by the prayer that you say. If you need to sell your house, then all you really should do is say the prayer. You can also venerate the statue of St. Joseph in your home, as he is the patron of the universal Church as well as the provider of jobs and income. There's a devotion to St. Joseph on March 19 which includes the blessing of food such as bread, because there was once a devastating drought in Sicily and the people prayed to Almighty God through the intercession of St. Joseph, saying that if rain would come, they would always provide a table for the poor. God answered their prayers, and to this day, St. Joseph's Table is honored, and not only in Sicily but in many places, including the United States where Italian parishes have settled. It's not just a time for families and friends to celebrate, but to also provide for the poor. There are so many excellent devotions to St. Joseph, and you can also pray a novena, which is nine days of prayer in honor of a particular saint from whom you're requesting intercession on your behalf to Almighty God. These examples are all perfectly fine to practice, but to bury a statue upside down reeks of superstition and should not be done.

Fr. Trigilio: The root of the problem is this false idea that the statue itself is going to sell the house. When we were researching for our *Saints For Dummies* book, I remember reading that this practice goes back to a religious brother in Canada who had placed St. Joseph medals on a piece of property that the monastery wanted to acquire, and within a few days they obtained it. The difference is that this was an act of piety that was tied into prayer, and it wasn't the medals themselves that achieved it; it was the prayer and the faith of the brother and the intercession of the Saint. If people think that the statue itself has supernatural powers, then that becomes superstition.

Fr. Brighenti: Plus, if I were St. Joseph, I wouldn't want to be buried upside down in the ground.

6. Mass Obligation

Is it still true that, according to the Third Commandment, missing Mass is a sin?

Fr. Trigilio: Missing Mass is considered a sin when you do it deliberately and for no acceptable reason. Now, if the weather is bad, like when they had seven feet of snow in Buffalo, New York, or you're terribly ill, or you're taking care of someone who's ill, or something unavoidable prevents you from attending Mass, then it's not a sin. During the COVID-19 pandemic, bishops around the world dispensed the faithful from the Sunday obligation, so missing Mass was not a sin. Once the epidemic is over, the obligation resumes. So, serious health issues, serious inclement weather, and burdensome traveling distance automatically exempt you. However, if you're going to spend your day going anywhere else, like the beauty parlor, the mall, or the grocery store, then you clearly have the time and means to get to Mass, and skipping it would then be a sin. Missing Mass because you forgot it's Sunday is also not good enough, especially today with all of the electronic connections we have. You can very easily set your phone to remind you to get to church or that it's a holy day of obligation. In olden times, everybody in town knew when it was time to go to church because the bells would ring. Today, people are on different schedules, they go to different places, and they belong to different denominations. Nonetheless, we know things so instantly today. We know immediately when the president or the pope hiccups. Yet people will say, "Oh, geez! I didn't know today was a holy day." Well, the information is out there. You just have to look for it.

Fr. Brighenti: It's about making our Faith a priority. Sometimes we make the mistake of approaching it with such a minimalist perspective. How late can I come to Mass and not break the third Commandment? What's the minimum number of times I must receive Holy Communion or go to Confession annually? How many days must I fast and abstain in Lent? We should always be doing the maximum because we want to be doing these things; because we want to know, love, and serve God in this life and to prepare ourselves to be with Him for the next. If we only straightened our focus and knew that what we want to be doing with our lives is drawing closer to God, then why wouldn't we want to be going to Mass? Why wouldn't we want to be receiving Our Lord in Holy Communion? It was St. Thomas Aquinas who wrote in a beautiful prayer for Corpus Christi Sunday, "Communion is the foretaste of Heaven,"[15] which means that what we're receiving in Communion, the intimacy with the Lord, we will receive in its fullness with the Lord in Heaven. We should be wanting to do this more instead of only performing the bare minimum of what the Church instructs us to do.

Fr. Trigilio: If you're talking to God every day through daily prayer, which every single person, man, woman, and child, is expected to do, then going to Mass once a week isn't just an obligation; it's a privilege. This is just like how you would text or tell somebody on the phone that you'll see them on Sunday, because you want that personal encounter with them. It's the same thing with God.

Fr. Brighenti: Pope St. John Paul II wrote a beautiful letter regarding the Sunday Mass entitled *Dies Domini* which said that Sunday should be an event, the pinnacle and highlight of our whole week, because it's the honor of the Resurrection, and the primer to elevate Sunday is by attending and worshipping at the Mass, followed not by useless, menial work, but by spending time with family. When I was growing up, Sundays were sacrosanct, and no stores were open. On Sundays, everybody in the family would come over, and my parents, in their old age, still maintain this wholesome practice today. Every Sunday, the family knows dinner's ready, although my parents never know who's going to be coming over. It's an extension of that Sunday which we should give to the Lord to recharge our spiritual batteries, and to recharge our human batteries by being with our families. Give

---

[15] *Summa Theologica*, III, q. 73, art. 4.

Sunday to the Lord and give Sunday to your family. You can always go shopping another day.

7. When Work Interferes with Going to Mass

What if I am unable to attend Mass on weekends because of my job?
Is it sufficient to attend Mass on a weekday instead?

Fr. Brighenti: For this situation, you need to look at every possibility. Many employers, for other denominations, allow their employees to attend their worship services before they have to come into work. In certain states, it's actually a requirement for employers to give their employees that opportunity. The employee might make up for that hour or so that they're going to be at that service, and it may mean that you're going to have to get up a bit earlier. You might need to make the seven o'clock morning Mass or the late Vigil Mass on Saturday evening, so if you work an early shift then you will certainly be off in time. That's why the Vigil Mass came about, because of the workers. It wasn't meant to replace Sunday, but it provided a chance to attend Mass for those who have jobs that require them to be on duty on Sundays. Besides the early morning Mass, you can often find a Sunday evening Mass in your area. Sometimes that Sunday evening Mass might be in a different language, but it's still the same Sacrifice of the Mass. These are all the options that you should exercise first. Maybe start with going to your employer and tell him you need to attend Mass, or if you have an unusual type of schedule, look into the Vigil Mass on Saturday night or try to see if there is an evening Mass on Sundays that you can attend. Now, if you've exercised all those options and nothing fits your work schedule, then contact your pastor and see if he could commute your obligation to a weekday Mass, but this is a last resort.

Fr. Trigilio: When I was an assistant pastor, I had people who ran pizza parlors that had to be opened on Sundays, and they worked late on Saturdays, too. There was no way they could physically be at Mass, so the pastor dispensed them, and that meant these people had to attend one of the weekday Masses. So, if on Monday the restaurant was closed, then they came to the Mass on Monday morning, and that fulfilled their Sunday obligation. If something happens where you just are unable to get there and it's not your fault, like you're called into work because you're a doctor or a nurse, then you obviously don't need any permission; you're dispensed automatically. This also applies if you're a caregiver or if you're a parent and your child is sick, then you have to stay home, obviously, and you don't need the pastor to dispense you. But if it's for a reason that's not a serious health issue or other emergency or obstacle, such as seven feet of snow like they have in Buffalo, New York, then you may need to look into it further and exercise prudence.

Fr. Brighenti: Many times when there is inclement weather, the diocese will send out a message on the community radio or the news or a Flocknote to your cell phone. If there are dangerous roads or there is a state of emergency, the bishops will even encourage you to stay home, because you could be a danger to yourself and others. At that point, then, you can watch the Mass on EWTN if you have cable television, say your devotional prayers, and partake in spiritual Communion.

8. Sunday as the Sabbath

I am a Catholic, tried and true. However, about two years ago, God tugged at my heart about whether Saturday or Sunday is His blessed, holy, sacred day of worship. I study more and more, trying to align my reasoning with the Church, but my study keeps leading me back to the original day of Saturday.

Fr. Brighenti: This sounds like a question from a Seventh-day Adventist.

Fr. Trigilio: I'm glad you mentioned that, because that's exactly what their position is, that Saturday is the Sabbath, and therefore it is the only day you can worship God. It's the seventh day when you look at the calendar, the current one we all use being the Gregorian calendar instituted by Pope Gregory, and it's the one we go by in the Christian world. Sunday is the first day of the week, Saturday is the last day of the week. In fact, Saturday in Italian is *Sabato*. So, why is it that we worship God on Sunday and not the Sabbath? Because the Saturday Sabbath day worship was commanded by God in the Old Testament. In the New Testament, because Jesus rose from the dead on Easter *Sunday*, the very first Christians would meet on Sunday. They performed their religious duties on Saturday as faithful Jews, but, as Christians, they got together on Sunday for the breaking of the bread, which is the most ancient biblical reference for what we now call "the Mass" or the "Eucharistic liturgy." We do today what the early Christians did back then. Now, why don't we worship exclusively on Saturday anymore? Because we're no longer under that older dispensation of the Old Covenant, the Old Testament. We're now in the New Testament times. Some people may point out that we have a Mass on Saturday night, and that's because when the sun goes down, we consider the Saturday evening as part of Sunday, as the Jewish computation of time was that it was the next day as soon as the sun set. Because there were so many working people who were unable to attend Mass on Sunday, the Church granted a dispensation

Web of Faith

so that you can attend the Saturday Vigil Mass to fulfill your Sunday obligation.

Fr. Brighenti: If you go to the Vatican website, you can read for free Pope St. John Paul II's letter about Sunday called *Dies Domini* where he shines some light on the Lord's Day, the Resurrection, and its divine relevance for us as Christians. It's like a mini-Easter every Sunday, and this carries on after Mass in regard to what we do as a family. We shouldn't be performing menial labor or shopping, but we should spend quality time with our loved ones. Sunday is time to rest and recharge ourselves for the week ahead. I think we've lost that sense of Sunday's importance because it's been taken over by what we call the weekend. I always get a good chuckle when in the television show, *Downton Abbey*, the Dowager Countess (played by Dame Maggie Smith) had never heard that term.[16] In reality, it is a fairly new concept from the twentieth century. Before, people worked all the way through Saturday, and Sunday was the only day of rest. So, it was really a special day to recharge their batteries. But the stores stay open now on Sunday. In the United States, we used to have the "blue laws" that required stores to stay closed on Sunday, but these laws have been repealed, and people now work on Sunday, otherwise they'd lose their jobs. Being stuck working on Sunday breaks up the family, and it breaks up God's family, too, as Mass is our primary duty on Sunday, followed by recharging our physical bodies and being around the table with our loved ones.

Fr. Trigilio: Now, we know people are busy and that their time is limited because they work a lot and there's so much activity

---

[16] *Downton Abbey*, season 1, episode 1, directed by Brian Percival, written by Julian Fellowes, aired January 9, 2011, PBS.

going on. We understand that it may be difficult to go as a family to Mass on Sunday or to have a family meal together. But the pope made it very clear that it's worth the effort. You should at least try. I recommend the family try it first one Sunday a month by all going to the same Mass, followed by a family meal. Then hopefully step it up to twice a month and then to every Sunday. Start gradually and work toward it, and you'll find it so marvelous that you'll want to keep it forever.

Fr. Brighenti: At the seminary, too, I always love being there on Sunday afternoons, because they do something very traditional that all parishes should do: sung Vespers. Maybe fifty years ago, something that parishes always had on Sunday was Benediction of the Blessed Sacrament and Vespers, the Evening Prayer from the Liturgy of the Hours, and then the hymns with a beautiful one to Our Lady at the end. It's such a pleasant way of closing up Sunday, finished with a good supper.

Fr. Trigilio: I believe the Anglicans still do this, too. It's a tradition that spans between Catholic and non-Catholic Christians.

9. Holy Days of Obligation

Can you explain in detail about the holy days of obligation that are in the year? What are they, and what's their purpose? Are they always obligatory?

Fr. Brighenti: I'm going to give the whole list, but keep in mind the episcopal conference of the United States Catholic Bishops (USCCB) can choose from this list which holy days are of obligation to the people, after approval from Rome.

Fr. Trigilio: There's a standard number, but we can be dispensed from that.

Fr. Brighenti: That's right. So, on January 1 we celebrate the Solemnity of Mary, Mother of God, and this feast centers on the maternity of Mary. She is the Mother of God, or *Theotokos* as we say in Greek, as she gave human flesh to the Second Person of the Blessed Trinity. In the Second Person, we have divine nature and human nature, and we call this the "hypostatic union." Mary is the Mother of God because of this union. January 6 is then the Feast of the Epiphany, which commemorates the three kings, or wise men, who visited Christ in Bethlehem and brought the gifts of gold, frankincense, and myrrh. In the United States, this holy day has been transferred to the Sunday closest to January 6, but in Italy and some Latin American countries, January 6 is still the day for the Epiphany, so it could be during the week and that would be both a holiday and holy day for them. The next feast would be the Solemnity of St. Joseph, who is the patron of the universal Church. Pope St. John XXIII inserted his name into the Roman Canon and Pope Francis added it to the other three Eucharistic prayers. In the United States, this feast day falls on March 19. It's not a holy day of obligation for us, but I believe it is in Canada. It's also interesting to note that St. Joseph's Day in Italy is actually Father's Day, because he is the foster father of Our Blessed Savior. Forty days after Easter is then Ascension Thursday, upon which Christ ascended into Heaven, and this is also the Second Glorious Mystery of the Rosary. In most of the United States, this holy day has been transferred to a Sunday. In the Northeast, as well as some dioceses in the West and Midwest, it's been retained on that Thursday, and it always baffles me why they change it, because forty days after Easter is scriptural. Thursdays are important, as we have Corpus Christi, the Last Supper, Holy Thursday, and Ascension Thursday, yet for whatever reason this holy day has been transferred to the seventh Sunday in many areas. So, when there's Mass being taped at EWTN on a Northeasterner's Ascension Thursday, it would be celebrated on a Sunday.

Fr. Trigilio: It depends on where you're located geographically.

Fr. Brighenti: Next would be the Feast of Corpus Christi. Now, Corpus Christi is the Feast of the Body and Blood of Christ, and in Rome this feast is celebrated on the Thursday after the Solemnity of the Blessed Trinity, which is on a Sunday. In the United States and many other areas, this feast has been transferred to the Sunday after. There are then the Feasts of Saints Peter and Paul, which are on June 29. Saints Peter and Paul are both patrons of Rome and the Pillars of the Church, Peter as the first pope and Paul as the prime evangelist. In the United States, these feasts are left on that day, but it's not a holy day of obligation. We then go to the Assumption of Mary, which is August 15, and it's also the Fourth Glorious Mystery of the Rosary. Now, in the United States, if this solemnity falls either on a Saturday or a Monday, then there is no obligation to attend Mass. But if it's from Tuesday to Friday, it would then count as a holy day of obligation.

Fr. Trigilio: So, you've got to keep your calendar handy to see what day these feasts fall on.

Fr. Brighenti: Yes, and you really have to pay attention to the bulletin and announcements at your parish. Next is All Saints' Day on November 1. Again, in the United States, if this day falls on a Monday or a Saturday, the obligation to attend Mass does not apply. This feast honors those who are in Heaven but are not officially canonized and recognized on the calendar. Next up is the Feast of the Immaculate Conception on December 8, which is the Immaculate Conception of Mary in the womb of St. Anne, where Mary was preserved from Original Sin. This is a holy day of obligation in the United States, even if it falls on a Saturday or a Monday, because it's the patronal feast here in the United States. Finally, we have Christmas on December 25, commemorating the Birth of Christ, the Third Joyful Mystery of the Rosary, and that is always a holy day of obligation.

Fr. Trigilio: So, to recap: in the United States, we have typically six holy days of obligation, depending on your region in the country. We have the Solemnity of Mary, Mother of God; Ascension Thursday; the Feast of Mary's Assumption; All Saints' Day; the Feast of the Immaculate Conception; and Christmas. This can be confusing, because I think, for example, that in Hawaii there's only two holy days that must be observed, those being the Feast of the Immaculate Conception and Christmas. Originally, the intent was to make it easier for people, because they found it a little burdensome to go to Mass when it was too close to Sunday. I can also see that when you're in Alaska, getting to church might be difficult because of the snow, and I couldn't say how difficult it is on the Hawaiian Islands, but keep a calendar nearby and check your parish bulletin.

Fr. Brighenti: All of this information and more is available in our book *Catholicism For Dummies*.

10. Mass Obligation, Part 2

The substitute priest we had at Mass this past weekend said that there are no holy days of obligation, and if you don't feel like going to Mass for All Saints' Day on November 1, then don't go. He then said that no one would go to Hell if they missed Mass. I felt that this was the wrong message to give, especially since I know plenty of Catholics

*who do not attend Mass on a regular basis. Shouldn't the priest tell
the people what is right and wrong? This was very confusing to me.*

Fr. Trigilio: That is one priest you don't want covering for you.

Fr. Brighenti: Quite right. A priest should tell you what is right
and what is wrong. Obviously, there's some confusion regarding
the holy days of obligation, but we know that the Code of Canon
Law set aside certain days with solemnities that are required to
be attended. The episcopal conferences throughout the world
can choose from this list. Canada's list is a little bit different
than ours here in the United States, and there have been some
changes in the schedule for holy days of obligation. It sounds
confusing, but it really isn't. Unfortunately, the substitute priest
should know this.

Fr. Trigilio: It's one thing for a layperson to be confused, but
Father should never be confused when it comes to the laws of
the Church.

Fr. Brighenti: In the seminary, we have a Priestly Integration
Assessment for our fourth-year deacons, and one of the questions is: "Do you know your holy days of obligation and when
these solemnities are not a holy day?" Concerning holy days of
obligation in the United States, if the feast falls on a Saturday
or a Monday, then it is not an obligation to go to Mass on that
day unless it's Christmas Day or the Feast of the Immaculate
Conception; those are the two exceptions. So, if All Saints' Day
or the Assumption of Mary falls on a Saturday or a Monday, then
while these are still solemnities, there is no obligation to attend
the Mass on those days. To further complicate things, we have
Ascension Thursday, which is a holy day of obligation. However,
in many parts of the United States and throughout the Catholic

world, the Ascension Thursday obligation has been transferred to Sunday. So, the seventh Sunday of Easter in many areas is called Ascension Day. Now, in certain parts of the United States, especially in the Northeast, the Feast of the Ascension still falls on a Thursday, and it's a holy day of obligation. Corpus Christi is another one where it's celebrated in Rome, for example, on Thursday as a holy day of obligation, but in the United States it's been transferred to a Sunday. It can complicate things a little, but holy days of obligation are normally announced in parishes the week before, so that people have plenty of time to prepare. To summarize: if a holy day of obligation falls on either a Saturday or a Monday, the obligation is not there to attend except for Christmas Day and the Feast of the Immaculate Conception. If Ascension Thursday has been moved in your area to Sunday, then you obviously do not have to attend on Thursday.

Fr. Trigilio: We also need to address that the priest mentioned in the question told people that it's not a sin to miss the Mass. That is wrong. That is not Church teaching. That is not Church discipline.

Fr. Brighenti: However, this priest is leading the parish into confusion, and because they might believe that what he's saying is true, their culpability could be reduced.

Fr. Trigilio: Indeed, the people themselves are not going to be guilty if they don't know any better. The priest, however, is going to have on his conscience the fact that he gave people misin-formation. It's like that old axiom attributed to St. Augustine which says, "When in Rome, do as the Romans do." If you're in a location where your Ascension Thursday has been transferred to a Sunday, then you don't have to attend Mass that day. North of the Mason-Dixon line, we still honor the Ascension on Thursday. Here at EWTN, people tune in and they'll say, "What happened with those poor Franciscans? What are they doing down there? They're not celebrating the Ascension." Well, that's because Ascension Day has been moved to Sunday in their region, but we're airing in Philadelphia where the Ascension is still celebrated on Thursday. You go by where you're located. But if you know that it's a holy day of obligation, and it's not a Saturday or a Monday, then you've got to go unless you're prevented by inclement weather or a serious illness.

Fr. Brighenti: Granted, this change regarding Ascension Thursday was for pastoral reasons, because Saturday and Monday were too close to the Sunday obligation, and it was considered a burden attending Mass two days in a row. However, this has led to some confusion. When in doubt, ask your pastor. There's also a liturgical calendar that you can get which will tell you which holy days are of obligation.

Fr. Trigilio: Most parishes give out calendars near the end of the year for the following year, and the holy days of obligation are marked on there for your area.

11. New Age

I got involved in New Age and the occult without knowledge that it was wrong. It started with consulting a psychic through a mutual friend. I thought the psychic was someone chosen by God, because she told me things about myself that no one else knew. I am not actively having problems with demons. I tried to get help from priests, but they are clueless and have honestly told me that they do not understand how to help me. What is the Catholic Church doing about educating priests and the faithful on how to recognize and combat New Age and the occult? I've met many other Catholics who are having problems with evil spirits and who think their experiences are from God.

Fr. Brighenti: First, we can confidently say that these psychics and their abilities are not from God.

Fr. Trigilio: The thing you have to be wary of, even though you were not aware of the implications, are that psychics are either phony charlatans out to take your money, or worse, they're in league with the devil. If they're giving you accurate details, hidden or secret information that only some supernatural force would know, then this isn't from God. God doesn't like to pull fast ones on you or throw a secret at you to make you feel bad about yourself. But the devil, who knows many things, including our deepest, darkest secrets, will use that information to his advantage. Some of these psychics, though, are rather skilled at pretending to be authentic. They have ways of picking up on details so they seem to know things about you that they really don't. But regarding the ones that would appear to be legitimate, anything that's considered confidential is within the purview of your privacy, and God respects that. That's why when you go to Confession, you go privately to the priest. What you tell the priest is kept confidential. We're not allowed to tell anyone. Not even the pope can get us to spill the beans, so to speak. So, why would God allow some other human being access to this information? When you're dealing with the occult and the psychics, remember you're getting close to the devil. When you dial Hell, the devil will pick up the phone, so be careful.

Fr. Brighenti: In other words, you're playing with fire. People think the Ouija board and tarot cards are just fun and games, but they can be a lot more than just that. They also go against the Commandment, "You shall have no other gods before me" (Exodus 20:3). We should stay away from things like psychics, tarot cards, Ouija boards, and so on. New Age incorporates a lot of these, and New Age itself is actually an old heresy that goes all the way back to the time of the Early Church. It just bears a new name today with fancy stones and crystals, packaged with sham spirituality. The Vatican even came out and said that Reiki, a New Age practice of "energy healing," should be avoided; we should instead spend our time growing closer to God through reading the lives of the saints, reading the Scriptures, Eucharistic Adoration, devotion and attending Holy Hours, and getting involved in the parish in works of charity. These are the things that are important. New Age is really a waste of time, but it could also lead into something more demonic.

Fr. Trigilio: That's what's scary. The least you could lose is some money and your self-pride. The worst you could lose is your immortal soul. There's a reason why they call it the "occult." It is hidden and secret; it's not in the open. Remember, Jesus is the Light of the World. He said you don't light a candle and put it under a bushel. The devil, on the other hand, is the prince of darkness. He hides in the shadows. He doesn't want to be recognized. It's obvious why he's not going to first appear as something that's actually satanic, because people may recognize it and stay away. But when they look at the fortune tellers and their tarot cards, they seem harmless. That's the devil's work, appearing as an angel of light to deceive you, as his true form would scare you away. If you see a horned beast with goat legs and bad breath, you're going to run. But if he appears as some little old gypsy lady peering into a crystal ball, you'll figure it's just a gag and give her five bucks. Be careful. She's either going to rob you, or you're going to be lured into the occult. It's not that people are not sophisticated enough to know the difference, but I think people have a neo-Gnostic tendency. Gnostics were ancient heretics who said salvation was secret. That's why their name comes from the Greek word *gnosis*, meaning "knowledge," but in this context it is specifically that of a "secret," religious variety. It revolves around this idea that you're going to find something that nobody else knows. The Christian religion, however, is out in the open, in plain sight for everyone to see. Jesus told us to go to the four corners of the earth and preach to all the nations. The candle is placed on the lampstand. It's public, whereas the occult is secret with its disguised covens and undercover devil worshippers. It's all hidden under the dark cloak of night, because that's how evil flourishes, in the shadows; whereas, the good is always out in the open. Stay away from the occult like the plague.

Fr. Brighenti: The priest mentioned in the question may not know the severity of all these issues that you're in and can't give a full judgment. He probably doesn't have all the pieces, although it was explained very well in the question.

Fr. Trigilio: If you just said, "Father, I delved into New Age for a while," most priests would likely say, "Okay, well, don't do it again." But if you said you're looking into it more and more, that's where a priest needs to really get involved and warn you of the dangers of the occult.

12. Gluttony

Is gluttony a mortal sin? I am obese and use food to numb my feelings and emotions, just as a drug addict uses drugs or an alcoholic uses alcohol. When I overeat, I do so with full knowledge and consent.

Fr. Brighenti: Before we even get into the idea of sin, we need to know that numbing ourselves with food, drugs, alcohol, or medication is never a good method. When you rely on these things, you're simply avoiding the problem or the issues that you have. Psychologically, I would say you need to address the issues. Why are you numbing yourself with the food? Why are you doing this? Because you're suppressing something that you really need to deal with. I would also say you should be bringing this into your prayer life. Remember, we pray as a body and soul together. We're a composite. This is something that is touching you in a very strong way, because you mentioned that you are obese. Therefore, you need to bring this into prayer, and if you don't have a prayer life, then you need to start developing one now. Simply start by spending time before Jesus in the Blessed Sacrament, and take the daily Scripture reading with you. We mentioned before that you can get that from *The Word Among Us*, the *Magnificat*, or on the Laudate app if you have a smartphone. You can then reflect on those daily readings through meditation, and then allow for some quiet time after that called contemplation. We call this process *Lectio Divina*. Praying the Rosary is very important as well, and so is making Confession part of your regular spiritual life, along with performing a daily examination of conscience. These are all things that will help you grow spiritually. Now, tackling the question head-on, it asked about sin. Gluttony is considered one of the Seven Deadly Sins, but do you know it is serious and do you freely do it anyway? That is between you and God, and the Sacrament of Confession and the examination of conscience will help you. Sometimes, psychological illnesses will reduce your freedom. I can't tell you if that's the case here. That's something only you would have the answer to.

Fr. Trigilio: That could be the case if she has an eating disorder.

Fr. Brighenti: An eating disorder would be one, but it doesn't take away the obligation to rid yourself of gluttony. For example, in the case of an alcoholic who is overindulging in alcohol, his free will can be reduced in the matter, but that does not take away the obligation to rid himself of the alcohol in his life. He still has that obligation to do so. These are some areas I would encourage you to research and begin to amend in your life.

Fr. Trigilio: Some of these afflictions may be treatable by going to a physician, or you may need some medication. The spiritual component will help you and doesn't have to compete with medical assistance; they can work in tandem. In one of our parishes, we have something called the TOPS program, or Take Off Pounds Sensibly. They try to incorporate a little spirituality into their weight loss goals. It's almost like an AA program for losing weight. In AA, they refer to this higher power, and they incorporate a spiritual dimension with the physical or physiological one as they try to help a person improve their health.

Fr. Brighenti: May I also suggest the twelve-step program, because those steps will work for alcohol, drug abuse, sex abuse, and so on. There are many versions of the twelve-step program, but one of them spiritualizes the steps through Scripture readings. There's a twelve-step program for Overeaters Anonymous as well.

Fr. Trigilio: Remember, as St. Thomas Aquinas tells us, anything that's an addiction will reduce your culpability, but it does not eliminate or dissolve the sin.[17] There's also some moral

---

[17] *Summa Theologica*, II, q. 76, arts. 1-4.

responsibility. It may move it from being a mortal sin to a venial sin, but you still need to work on it, because you want all imperfections removed from your life.

13. Chastity

What is the difference between being a single person who stays chaste and a person whose vocation is a call to chastity?

Fr. Brighenti: This is a very good question about chastity, because everyone is called to chastity. Single people are called to chastity. Married couples are called to chastity. They should not be thinking about adulterous relations outside of their marriage vows; they should be focused on their spouse. That means their thoughts and actions should be holy and pure. Finally, religious and priests are also called to chastity. They're living a celibate life and therefore need to be chaste in thought, word, and action as well. Word, too, is important, because sometimes our jokes can be on the unchaste side. Chastity is a virtue that everyone is called to live by, according to their state and their vocation in life. We need to remember that the gift of the physical act of sexuality is given by God in the Sacrament of Marriage to be shared between one man and one woman as husband and wife. In Pope St. Paul VI's encyclical *Humanae Vitae*, he reminds us that the two purposes of marriage are to bring forth life and to build up the covenant between the husband and the wife. Even though a couple may be older and beyond their childbearing years, the fact that they are not opposed to pregnancy and are not putting any device or taking any medication that would otherwise prevent pregnancy, they are still honoring the procreative side of human sexuality. Anything beyond that, however, is morally wrong. What would that be? Masturbation, same-sex acts, sex outside of marriage, or adultery; as well as pornography, the latter because it tantalizes our minds to commit sin outside of the marriage bond or out of our chaste or celibate vows. The question asks the difference between a single person and a religious, and that's where celibacy comes in. Of course, Fr. Trigilio and I made a promise of celibacy to our bishop as priests. Like the religious, be they Franciscans, Dominicans, or Carmelites, we have taken a vow of chastity and are therefore living in celibacy. Chastity is a virtue to help us live in whatever state we're called to. There's a great book we were given in seminary called *The Courage to Be Chaste* by Fr. Benedict Groeschel, where he speaks about chastity in the different states: the single person, the married couple, the people that are in vows, and the Holy Orders.

Fr. Trigilio: When someone speaks of chastity, people often think of the vow of celibacy that a monk or a nun takes, where they will not marry and will abstain from all sexual relations for the rest of their lives. But chastity is a much broader idea. It's purity even within marriage, because a husband or a wife can sometimes treat their spouse as a sexual object, which is what happens when artificial contraception is used. When you separate the unitive and the procreative, you're separating love from life. What occurs is this sinful tendency to treat the other more as an object, as opposed to living a holy life together in a covenant, where the couple is open to whatever God has in store for them. Whereas when you start focusing on "me," "my desires," and "my fantasies," you begin missing the point of marriage. I tell couples on the day they're getting married that when they say "I do," that's sort of the last time you can use the first-person pronoun, because from now on it's not about "me" and "mine." It's now "our" life and "our" marriage; it's about "us" and what "we're" going to do. Chastity in marriage is as much a reality as it is for priestly celibates in the Church or for the consecrated religious. Some people snicker at the concept of chastity, because they tend to think of the infamous chastity belt, where the medieval knights who went off to the crusades were rumored to have put these cumbersome devices on their wives or daughters to protect them from any amorous affectations while the knights were away, although modern historians have discredited this myth as being dubious. In reality, chastity is a wonderful, wholesome virtue that everyone's asked to embrace, whether married or not. Human sexuality is a gift from God. We're not animals who have relations merely out of instinct because they're in heat. As human beings, we choose. We have free will to act morally and use human sexuality in accordance with God's law.

Fr. Brighenti: Chastity is the virtue that helps us fight against the vice of lust, which is one of the Seven Deadly Sins, and it is very much alive in our present society: in our movies, our media, our language, and our jokes. We treat people as objects when we're not living a chaste life. If a husband and wife are practicing artificial contraception, it's a sin because they're treating the other as an object. Remember, human sexuality involves our intellect. It is a conversation, so to speak, at the deepest level. If we're putting a barrier in that conversation, as opposed to practicing Natural Family Planning, then we're holding some part of ourselves back and not giving fully in that conversation.

Fr. Trigilio: Unfortunately, we live in a culture where we're becoming increasingly tolerant of impurity. I hate to say it, but it's coming more and more from among young women. Impure things you would have heard back in the old days from a couple of guys at the bar, or sailors, or soldiers on leave, you hear today from young women.

Fr. Brighenti: It's coming from our Hollywood movies and shows. It's the whole idea that a chaste and virtuous person is something to look down upon in our modern society. Chastity is actually freedom, as the bonds of lust and impurity weigh us down and take us away from who we are as humans. We're not animals. We have an intellect and a will, and we're rational beings. The things that we see in the media and in Hollywood are really reducing us to banality.

14. Struggling with Same-Sex Attraction

I desperately need spiritual help, as I am in the middle of a great fight, and I feel unable to resist the enemy's advance. My problem is that I think I am gay, but I don't know what to do about it.

Fr. Trigilio: That's an honest appraisal of your situation, and we certainly want you to know that we're keeping you in our prayers. Whether or not you have the homosexual orientation is not the point at hand. If you have a heterosexual or a homosexual orientation, all sexual activity is restricted to the sanctity of marriage, which is between one man and one woman, and for a Catholic it must be under the blessings of Holy Mother Church.

It is not precise or accurate to say some *is* gay or lesbian. You and I identify ourselves as human *persons*. A human person has a sexual orientation or inclination. But it is in our free will and in our intellect that we are made in the image and likeness of God. We are children of God. People need to identify and take ownership of their personhood. Sexual orientation is only one aspect of our lives. My brother had Muscular Dystrophy. He had a physical disability, but I would never identify him solely as a disabled person. No, he was a human person. A human being. So, we should not look at people only through the one lens of their sexual attraction.

Each and every one of us is called to live according to the Ten Commandments. Whether you're gay or straight or someone who's got a homosexual orientation or a heterosexual one, we're all asked to live in chastity. The Ten Commandments apply to all human persons. For instance, priests, as male celibates, make the promise to live in celibacy so that we don't take a wife for ourselves, but we're also asked to live a chaste life. Similarly, a husband has to remain faithful to his wife, and the wife to her husband. They're not to be unfaithful or fool around on their spouse. Too often, people make it sound as if your sexual orientation gives you *carte blanche* to have sex with anyone as often as you want. That's wrong. The same Ten Commandments apply to everyone.

Fr. Brighenti: Priests, religious, singles, and married couples are all called to exercise the virtue of chastity within their own specific calling in life. There's a wonderful book called *The Courage to Be Chaste* by Fr. Benedict Groeschel that came out in the 1980s, where he addresses each one of these individual states in life. It's a very simple book to read and it is very down-to-earth, as all of Fr. Groeschel's writings are. The other thing I would recommend is to look up this great Catholic organization called Courage International, as opposed to one that's not been sanctioned, such as Dignity, which does not promote a chaste lifestyle. Courage International has several chapters, and this group will encourage you to live a chaste lifestyle and to interiorize your spiritual life, because that's where you're going to fortify yourself. Fr. Arrupe, a former leader of the Jesuits, used to say that the more you fall in love with Jesus, it changes everything, and the more you fall out of love with Jesus, it changes everything. Start your prayer life. Start your interior life. Start praying and allowing for contemplation, for the Lord to speak to you. Practice *Lectio Divina*, the praying of Scriptures and meditating on them in order to grow in your interior life, because that will be your fortification. That will be your citadel wall that will help you in your fight against temptation. Follow this up with a good support group like Courage International and then *The Courage to Be Chaste* by Fr. Benedict Groeschel. These are all good steps. If you're having difficulty finding either of these, you can contact your local pastor or your diocese, and they may be able help. There are plenty of solid, Catholic support groups out there, and there are many Catholics who are living a good and happy and healthy life of chastity. You will persevere.

Fr. Trigilio: And don't think that you're alone in this struggle, because regardless of someone's orientation, we're all struggling with chastity. I remember Fr. Sullivan telling us in the seminary that we're always going to be tempted in the flesh until we're six feet under. Whether you're an old man, middle-aged, or a teenager, you will always struggle with the temptations of the flesh, and the only thing that's going to be of any help to you is God's grace. That means the sacraments, going to Confession regularly, doing mortification, and making retreats for your spiritual life are your best tools in this fight. We all struggle in different ways and with different temptations, so remember that you're never in this on your own. However, the world wants you to give in to whatever weaknesses you have, but you must resist. Consider an alcoholic, who struggles every day to stay sober; some days are going to be better than others, but he must struggle every single day for sobriety. It will get easier.

Fr. Brighenti: Now sometimes with homosexuality, there's pornography involved. If that's the case in regard to this question, then that's certainly not going to help your chastity. I would suggest a couple of tools. Put your smart devices in lockdown mode, so that you can only go through one website. There's an app called My Mobile Watchdog that filters out all these impure websites, so if you attempt to go to a bad site, the app will bark to warn you that you shouldn't go there. There's another program called Covenant Eyes for your computer, and while it doesn't stop you from accessing bad websites, it keeps a report and alerts whoever you designate as your mentor in this matter, whether it's your spiritual director or your father or mother.

Fr. Trigilio: Pornography is so pervasive for so many people, regardless of their orientation. There are places trying to perform reparative therapy, and I've seen some success in getting people who think they're homosexual to become heterosexual, because they can obviously then be able to get married and have a family. I don't know if it's necessarily successful in all cases, but it's worth looking into, because the jury is still out on what exactly causes this to happen. Is it genetic? Is it cultural? Is it the environment? Psychological? I tend to think that it's a little bit of everything. But again, regardless of where you're coming from, we're all under the same Commandments, and we're all under the same purview of following God's will.

Fr. Brighenti: It normally takes about ninety days to detox yourself from a pornographic addiction, because it's so highly addictive that you've been trained to turn to it automatically, like a self-reward system. That's why putting these limits on your devices and computer and actively trying to overcome pornography will help you in your chastity and ultimately help you resist falling into the act of homosexuality.

Fr. Trigilio: We had Matt Fradd give a talk to our Confraternity of Catholic Clergy this past summer. His advice was pivotal on this issue, so if you're ever able to listen to any of his talks, I would highly recommend it, and I recommend to our brother priests to invite him to come to your parish or diocese to talk, because this is a big issue in our world today.

15. Giving to the Church

How do I know how much to give to the Church? Is it how much I feel is affordable, or a flat ten percent of my income? From the Gospels, it seems Jesus was more interested in the state of one's heart and not the amount of money a person donated. However, the Church needs funds to grow and survive. How do we reconcile this? Secondly, my mother passed away suddenly without receiving the last rites. Will this affect the salvation of her soul?

Fr. Brighenti: First off, we send you our condolences. This is a very interesting question, as Our Lord gave a subtle teaching on giving when He praised the widow (in Mark 12:41-44) who gave away the only two copper coins to her name, which percentage-wise was far greater than the large amounts given by the wealthy people. Those two coins were from this woman's want and not from her surplus. This is where the heart comes in, because she gave with confidence, and she gave with trust, and she gave knowing that the Lord cannot be outdone in His generosity and that she will be blessed for trusting in Him. She did not look back and regret that she had given too much or maybe consider to skip giving next week because she didn't think she'd have enough to make ends meet. When we give, we must always remember never to look back. We give out of generosity, and we also know that the Lord will bless us in our generosity. The ten percent of your total income is a good benchmark, and some people will give five percent of that to their parish and another five percent to various charities that are important to them. That's what we call tithing, and we don't only tithe with our money or material possessions, but we also tithe with our time and our talents, and this whole package is called stewardship. The Diocese of Wichita in Kansas is a shining example of tithing, as practically every parishioner is doing so; and because they tithe ten percent of their income, they can send their children to Catholic school for free. Not only Catholic grammar school, but also Catholic high school, and this is a wonderful testimony of where people are giving to the Church, and God is blessing them in their generosity. Their schools are also experiencing several vocations because of the Catholic education system and the good sisters that teach there. They have over fifty-eight vocations for a diocese that has just over one hundred thousand Catholics, which I think is marvelous. When I went there for the installation of the new bishop, I saw this tithing in action and the stewardship of the people who were truly on fire in their faith. Don't be stingy with the Lord, because the Lord will be generous to you.

Fr. Trigilio: When you look at Scripture, particularly the miracles of Our Lord, He was not stingy when He turned the water into wine. He took enormous jars filled to the brim with water and turned them into the best wine. Likewise, with the loaves and the fish; there was so much left over that it could fill twelve baskets. God's not stingy, but sadly people tend to be, and we want to know, particularly as pastors, that we can count on enough funds to keep the parish running, as the electric and gas companies don't care if you're a church or not. You need to pay your utilities, you need to pay insurance, and the rates are always going up. I know some Protestant pastors have the benefit of people coming in and relaying how much they can pledge for the year. This way, the pastors know they have a viable budget to work with, whereas we don't have that as priests. We make an educated guess and assume it will be like the previous year or maybe better or possibly worse. We never know, and there are people who can't always give ten percent of their income, but they can at least give ten percent of their time or talent, and ten percent is not some magic number; what matters is that you put charity first. Make it a priority to say to your family, "How much can we afford to give?" as opposed to "What's left over?" The spare-change mentality is not going to work too well, and it's not like you're leaving a tip at the restaurant. Your parish and your diocese depend on you, and if you don't support them, that's why some churches end up closing. In regard to the last part of the question about his mother not receiving the last rites, all that matters is if she was in the state of grace, and if so, then there's nothing to worry about. I would, however, suggest that you get Masses offered for her soul, and that you pray for her soul from this moment on. The last rites are preferred to ensure that people receive the Anointing of the Sick, the Viaticum, and the apostolic blessing. But sometimes it just isn't possible, because of the circumstances regarding the death.

Fr. Brighenti: Now, just because she didn't receive the last rites, she might have been anointed several times, as her son sounds like a very responsible and devout Catholic. So, I'm sure that part of it was his respect for his mom under the Fourth Commandment to honor your father and mother, and I'd bet he made sure that during the course of her illness, the priest came and heard her confession and anointed her. If she had already received the Anointing of the Sick and Confession and was in the state of grace, then there's nothing to worry about.

Fr. Trigilio: One must be in the state of grace (that is, free of mortal sin) when he or she dies to enter Heaven. Getting the last rites, being anointed, going to Confession, getting Viaticum and the apostolic blessing are an excellent way to prepare for death, especially if imminent. If, through no fault of their own, a dying person is unable to get the last rites, they just need to make a good act of contrition.

Fr. Brighenti: We trust in God's mercy. Sometimes when we anoint people in the nursing home on a Monday, they can take a turn for the worse by Friday and die without receiving the Anointing of the Sick. But they had at least received it during the course of their illness, when they were also preparing and receiv- ing the Viaticum and the apostolic blessing. But again, whether that happened or not, or whether your mother received the last rites or not, you should still have Masses said for the repose of her soul, and that's a time-honored custom to pray for the dead. So, please have a Mass said for your mother on her anniversary, or sometimes on her birthday, as these are wonderful times to have Masses said for the faithful departed.

16. The Seven Virtues

Recently my brother asked me, "What are the seven virtues?" I guess the topic came up in a conversation in his office at Christmastime. I am thinking about the classic virtues of purity, honesty, chastity, prudence, and forbearance, but I can't seem to remember exactly what the seven classic virtues are. Can you list them for me?

Fr. Brighenti: So, it appears the question is mixing a few lists of virtues. I think the best way to clarify this is to take them apart and list them separately. The first virtues we could talk about are the theological virtues, which are faith, hope, and love (which is also called charity). Often when we're starting the Rosary, we pray the first three Hail Marys for an increase in faith, hope, and charity. The next set of virtues we could talk about are the four cardinal virtues: prudence, justice, temperance, and fortitude (or courage). Another way of looking at it would be to compare the seven deadly sins with their corresponding virtues, which are a medicine to help break those vices.

The seven virtues and the seven deadly sins they counter are listed as follows:

> Humility conquers pride, the king of all vices.
> Generosity conquers greed.
> Patience conquers wrath.
> Kindness conquers envy.
> Chastity conquers lust.
> Abstinence conquers gluttony.
> Diligence conquers sloth.

Fr. Trigilio: Depending on how you look at it, you can either combine the four cardinal virtues with the three theological virtues to get seven virtues total, or you could take the seven virtues that correspond to the seven deadly vices. Either way, there's nothing written in stone, and there are only seven virtues, and just like there are different gifts and fruits of the Holy Spirit, there are different virtues depending on what you're looking at. But these are the ones commonly mentioned by the Doctors of the Church.

Fr. Brighenti: Bad habits or vices are learned and can be broken by good habits or virtues, which can also be learned.

Fr. Trigilio: It's important to point out that even as decadent as the Romans had become at the decline of their empire, in their prime the Greeks and Romans and pagans in general, through the light of natural law alone, realized that human beings have the potential and capacity to live a virtuous life. The need to practice the virtues is within the realm of everybody's purview. It is in the theological virtues, the life of holiness, where you need to cooperate through God's grace. On a very natural level, anyone and everyone can and ought to be at least virtuous, and they can then advance from there, because grace builds upon nature from virtue into holiness.

17. Bad Words and Unwanted Thoughts

When unwholesome words or thoughts creep into your mind, how do you dismiss them, and should you feel guilty after you've done so?

Fr. Trigilio: I would never feel guilty about dismissing unwholesome thoughts. That's what we're supposed to do. When the thoughts are involuntary, that is, we did not intentionally conjure them, that in and of itself is a consequence of Original Sin. We do not have complete control over our passions all the time. When we deliberately elicit immoral thoughts or images, then we are culpable.

It may be difficult to dismiss these thoughts, and particularly so if you're struggling with impure thoughts of a sexual nature or thoughts of anger and revenge. Lust and wrath are both very powerful emotions within us, and trying to get rid of them can be more difficult than most would imagine. One remedy I suggest to people as I hear their confessions or give spiritual direction is that when you feel some of these thoughts coming on and you're struggling to repel them, rather than getting yourself frustrated, try to conjure up in your mind an innocent and humorous event, thought, or recollection of one of your favorite movies, like when something funny happened to Jonathan Winters in *It's a Mad, Mad, Mad, Mad World*.[18] You laugh a little bit to yourself, and you're dissipating all this pent-up energy. It's then more difficult to jump from that little state of innocent humor back to thinking of the impure or angry thought. This method isn't always going to work, but I find that it sometimes works better than praying harder. And it's not that God doesn't hear our prayers; it's that, as human beings, we are wired with a complex psychology.

Fr. Brighenti: The question also mentioned bad words, and I'll give a technique, too, especially if the use of these words involves taking Our Lord's name in vain. After you say the Act of Contrition at night and call to mind that you slipped up, recite the Divine Praises. A bad habit takes time to accrue, and likewise, changing the bad habit over to a good habit will also take time to accrue. By saying the Divine Praises, which praise the Lord's name, we call to mind that this is how we should be using His name, and slowly but surely this reminder will help you overcome that temptation to take the Lord's name in vain in times of anger and despair.

Fr. Trigilio: I have also heard people recommend, particularly when they're getting angry, to replace bad words (that is, swearing) or using Our Lord's name in vain (which is blasphemy) with innocent, harmless words, which maybe only you would understand when you're upset. People may give you a strange look, but this method could be of great benefit to you. I remember many times hearing one of my relatives yell "Sugar!" whenever

---

[18] Directed by Stanley Kramer (United Artists, 1963).

something bad would happen. Try finding a substitute word or even a different language to use so that you avoid using profanity, and absolutely stay away from uttering blasphemy. In regard to impure thoughts, think of something else, not always necessarily something funny, but something benign.

Fr. Brighenti: You know, the nuns taught us that, in times of trouble or accident, we should call upon Our Lord and invoke the names of saints in a reverent manner. So often, they would say, "Jesus, Mary, and Joseph, come and save souls. Pray for us." By doing this, you're retraining your brain, which takes about ninety days to do, by turning it from the bad reward to a good reward. There are some great techniques available to you. Keep at it, and you will persevere. Praying the Litany of the Holy Name of Jesus on a regular basis is another help.

18. Celebrating Halloween

Does the Church have an official position on celebrating Halloween? I've heard conflicting opinions from different people, all of whom are good Catholics. I used to love Halloween when I was a kid, but now that I have kids of my own, I'd prefer to go to an All Saints' Day party rather than a Halloween party.

Fr. Trigilio: As Fr. Brighenti and I can attest to, when we were growing up, Halloween for us was just a fun time. Nobody took it too seriously. There was not the mayhem we see today with mischief at night and people vandalizing private property. We didn't have the occult side of it. People didn't dress up as demons and ghouls, but rather, like Bela Lugosi's Dracula, Boris Karloff's Frankenstein, and Casper the Friendly Ghost. It was innocent fun, and no one took it seriously. But today, because there has been occultic dimensions added to it and adults are now getting involved, it's no longer seen as just a day for children to have fun. The costumes are gory and realistic; they're not just frightening; they're plain sickening. I would have plenty of hesitation as a parent today. However, if you become too strict and prohibit Halloween completely and isolate your kid, he or she may try to sneak out and discover what Halloween is all about. I would definitely emphasize to your children that the origin of Halloween is All Hallows' Eve, the day before what we as Christians call All Saints' Day. Encourage your kids in your local Catholic school or your CCD (Confraternity of Christian Doctrine) or religious education program to dress up so that they can celebrate the lives of the saints. If they want to go trick-or-treating, that's fine, but make sure the costumes aren't ghoulish or satanic. I would be concerned they could be sucked into the occult aspect of the holiday. What's more bothersome is that there are more adults who celebrate Halloween than Christmas or Easter.

Fr. Brighenti: They also say that Halloween is the second-most-decorated holiday in the United States after Christmas. Now, All Hallows' Eve is where we get the name Halloween, and it comes from Middle-English terminology. However, being a secular society, we've really lost the connection between All Hallows' Eve with All Saints' Day. When I was pastor, we instituted saintly costumes and had a procession of the saints on All Hallows' Eve. We said the Litany of Saints, and the children would come dressed as saints and give a little background on the saint they represented and the meaning of the symbols they bore. It was a great learning experience for them. After that, we had trunk-or-treat, where the Catholic school's PTA would provide treats from their cars in the church parking lot. It was all very well-managed. The principal, Sr. Gloria, would then have saints-and-angels games in the gymnasium. We were highlighting what the feast is supposed to be about: All Saints' Day. Like you said, however, if they want to have other costumes when they go trick-or-treating in their neighborhoods at night, then they should dress up in fun, innocent costumes such as a robot, Charlie Brown, Superman, or Batman, and so on.

Fr. Trigilio: It's important that we remind our young people that Christmas and Easter are the two primary Christian feast days, but we should also put emphasis on All Saints' Day and other feast days in order to reclaim their religious origins in modern holidays. We should be careful not to blow things out of proportion though, as that's going to frighten our kids or make them wonder what's so dangerous about Halloween, for example. On another note, October 31 is also Reformation Day. It was ironic that we had some Protestants in the neighborhood come over and wish us a "Happy Reformation Day." It was actually a very sad day when they left the True Church. We should pray for Christian unity, but without diluting our doctrines or denying our disciplines. Back to the original question, by all means, as a good parent, you want to teach your children the Faith and how to live a Christian moral life. Emphasize the All Saints aspect and denounce the occult, diabolical, secular dimension.

19. Euthanizing Animals

Is it a sin to put down a family dog that has behavioral problems, without first exhausting all other options of finding a new home for the dog?

Fr. Brighenti: Unfortunately, we don't know the severity of the behavioral problems, so it will be difficult to answer this question directly. Was the dog attacking people or maiming children? Aggressive animals that can harm humans cannot go for therapy like human beings do. If it will attack and harm, if not even kill, then yes, that dog needs to be removed from society, because it is dangerous and could kill somebody or maim them for life. If the behavioral problems do not involve aggression but are more of a nuisance, such as the dog doing its business inside or chewing furniture apart or barking uncontrollably and disturbing the neighbors, then these things can be fixed with proper training. If you took on the responsibility of owning a dog, then you really need to have a little patience and train your furry friend or take it to dog school. Some pet stores even have centers where you can attend classes and learn how to train your dog.

Fr. Trigilio: Animal life is unlike human life, which is sacrosanct and can never morally and directly be taken away from an innocent human being. We don't euthanize people, but we do euthanize animals when they're suffering and there's no hope of them recovering, or if their treatment is too costly, but not just for mere inconvenience, as that would be a matter of injustice to the animal. The animal deserves better than that; however, we must be careful not to elevate animals higher than humans or even at the same level as humans. Animals can make fine companions, and you can certainly come to appreciate them in your life, but you cannot regard them as human beings, because they do not have immortal souls made in the image and likeness of God. You have to consider these things when contemplating the best course of action for a dog that's biting people: whether you should try to change its behavior or put the dog to sleep. However, this is where the Humane Society comes into play; if you can't handle your pet, they can try to find it a new owner who can.

Fr. Brighenti: Normally, a dog that has a severe behavioral problem has already been adopted, and you should already be aware of the responsibility you are undertaking. When you get a small puppy, either from the Humane Society or the pet store or from a friend, you are now responsible for training that dog. It will learn those behaviors, the good ones and the bad ones. You have the opportunity to encourage the good behaviors while suppressing the bad.

Fr. Trigilio: When I got my pet cat, I was asked for references. Yet people can have children without references and abortions so easily, but with pets we're suddenly so protective. It's like saying, "Save the whales, but forget the unborn child!" We must keep things in their proper perspective. Animals deserve our consideration, but never on the same level as humans. Human beings can participate in redemptive suffering by uniting their personal cross with Christ and His Cross. Animals cannot share in redemptive suffering, so placing them out of their misery is not just pity but compassion and kindness. When my cat got feline leukemia and had to have a leg removed, he was fine for a while, but then the cancer returned and caused great pain and misery. I had the vet put him down as it was not fair to him to suffer. You and I can offer up our sufferings, but animals cannot, as they do not have a rational intellect and free will. On the other hand, pet owners can use medicinal means (if they can afford it) to heal or cure their animals, as long as they do not neglect their primary responsibility to their own health and that of their family.

20. Giving Money to the Needy

Is it considered giving alms to help someone financially who is only in need because they are not a good steward of their own money, or is it only enabling them?

Fr. Trigilio: It would depend on the circumstances. If this person was a compulsive shopper, a gambler, an alcoholic, or a drug addict, then giving them money directly would enable them. If they're simply not prudent with their money, it would again depend on the circumstances. If they need money to pay the electric bill or for prescriptions, you could give them money knowing that they're probably not going to pay you back, but you could also argue that they should have been more prudent and saved money for these expenses. But to give them money so they can buy the latest toy at the store or order something frivolous online is absurd, and that's where you say no. Almsgiving is giving to someone who's in genuine need.

Fr. Brighenti: When I was pastor, we established the St. Vincent de Paul Society in our parish, and it's a wonderful organization that gives out money and essential things to people who are truly in need. But first, they go to peoples' homes and investigate. Are they blowing away all their money on cigarettes? Sometimes we discovered that was the reason why their phone bill was unpaid and why their rent was late. The Society wants to make sure that these people are not wasting their money on these unnecessary things. They then try to help the people financially and find them a job if they don't have one, or a second job if they already do. They try to do a service to these people by helping them get back on their feet, and their investigation of the homes is an excellent approach to this. It is prudent always to understand why someone is in need of financial support before giving them what they ask for. Priests and parishes should never, or rarely, give cash. It is better to pay an electric or utility bill directly, as sometimes people spend the cash on foolish or frivolous things and not on their legitimate debts and expenses. Prudence first, always.

21. Perfect Contrition

How do we know if our confessions of mortal sins are in the form of perfect contrition and not just out of fear of punishment? I know what the fear of punishment feels like, but I don't always feel the "love of God," although I do wish I did. I've heard that faith is not necessarily about feelings but an exercise of will. In this case, is confessing done so out of love for God, or am I missing the point? Is it even possible for someone who lived a sinful life to make a perfect contrition?

Fr. Brighenti: First of all, when you go to the Sacrament of Confession, the minimum that is required is an imperfect contrition; but as you become more consciously aware of sin throughout your life, the more you grow in love with the Lord. When you give up even your habitual sins or the fond memories of such, you climb the ladder in your spiritual life, and that imperfect contrition will become perfect.

Fr. Trigilio: What would be the motivation for an imperfect contrition?

Fr. Brighenti: The motivation, as the Act of Contrition says, is the fear of the pains of Hell.

Fr. Trigilio: It's not necessarily a selfish motive, the fear of punishment. When we were kids, we basically did whatever our parents told us, because if we didn't then we got punished. The perfect motive, however, is not your fear of punishment; it is your love of God. It becomes not so much that you're afraid of Hell, but that you're afraid of offending Our Beloved Lord and Savior.

Fr. Brighenti: Also, if you can't receive the Sacrament of Confession because you're on a sinking ship or a crashing plane and there is no priest available, you need to then make an act of perfect contrition where you're sorry for your sins because they hurt and offended God, and not only because you're afraid of going to Hell.

Fr. Trigilio: I will say I certainly wouldn't want to rest my eternal salvation on hoping that I got that act of perfect contrition, and that's why we encourage people to go regularly, faithfully, and consistently to Confession, at a minimum of every three months, though optimally every month, if you can make it. The Church says that at the minimum, we should go to Confession at least once a year. But Confession shouldn't be viewed as an obligation; it's an opportunity to purify our souls and obtain the grace to better avoid sin from that moment on. Would you opt to shower or brush your teeth only once a year? I didn't think so. How much more attention, then, should we give to our immortal souls?

Fr. Brighenti: The more you practice a daily examination of conscience and pray the Act of Contrition, the more conscious you become of your sins. You can also grow in your spiritual life, either through Eucharistic Adoration or praying the Scriptures with a practice called *Lectio Divina*, where you meditate on the text, have a quiet moment of contemplation, and let the Lord speak to you. The more you grow in the love of the Lord, the more He will reveal these imperfections in your life, and the more you'll want to change and rid these evil things from your life, because God is coming in and filling up those spaces that are left void. Increasing in your spiritual life should be your top priority, and you'll want to go to Confession more frequently, not only to be forgiven of your sins, but also to receive the grace to help you avoid sin in the future.

22. Respect for Life

A friend of mine is seriously considering coming back to the Church after a long absence of several years, but she has reservations about certain issues of doctrine, particularly regarding abortion. I am afraid to really reach out to her due to past experiences with losses of patience and charity. Is she allowed to receive Communion? If not, how do I go about telling her?

Fr. Brighenti: First off, if your friend has been away from the Church for a while, then she's going to need to go to the Sacrament of Confession before she can receive Communion, and she may want to update her faith a little as well. Unfortunately, a lot of people think that when they receive Confirmation, they're done with learning the Faith, but this simply isn't true. We should be learning our Faith every day of our lives, as you will always find something new. That said, I would encourage your friend to go to a parish Bible study or make an appointment to talk with her parish priest. She should have these conversations so she can make a good sacramental confession before receiving Communion, and this might help her catch up on some of the doctrines that she might be confused about. Another thing I would tell your friend is that we don't have the choice as Catholics to pick and choose what we want to believe and not believe. Our Faith is given and revealed to us through Sacred Tradition or Sacred Scripture, and we have to believe it and accept it. We may experience difficulty in understanding, but this should lead us to prayer and research, not the denial or rejection of certain doctrines. Also, perhaps your friend may have had an abortion, and maybe she's going through a difficult time and is struggling to reconcile this in her life, or maybe she doesn't want to deal with it. If that's the case, then she should look into a program in the Church called Project Rachel, which helps women who have had abortions to reconcile themselves, and it's a wonderful counseling tool. It would be vital to read the consistent teachings of the Church in this area as well. Pope St. Paul VI addressed abortion in his encyclical *Humanae Vitae*, and he said that if we don't respect life from its beginning, and if we practice artificial contraception, there would be ramifications in the years to come. Two of these ramifications he mentioned were abortion and euthanasia. Unfortunately, these things have become legal in many places worldwide, just as he predicted back in 1968.

Fr. Trigilio: Also, if you feel a little nervous about preaching to your friend, find out if there's a mission being preached in your local area. When Fr. Wade from Fathers of Mercy came to preach a mission at my parish, we sent word to all the surrounding parishes. Many people brought friends with them who knew their theology, but their morality or practice of the Faith was a little fuzzy. They didn't accuse their friends of needing some maintenance on their faith, but it was just an invitation to listen to a priest and maybe go to dinner afterward. Father would preach and give them the pure teachings of the Catholic Church and tell them what is right and what is wrong. Father said that there were a lot of good confessions following the mission, as people were having the light shone on areas where they needed to amend their lives. Some realized they had to make a choice between remaining Catholic or abandoning the Church altogether. Many souls are saved at these missions. Inviting somebody to a mission or a retreat may be a gentle way of letting them find out their faith needs to be spruced up a bit.

Fr. Brighenti: I remember, when Father was coming to your parish to do the mission, you told people in your parish to invite someone who hasn't been to church for a while. You had asked them to participate in this mission. I also remember Pope Francis recently talking about "throwaway culture."[19] Part of this culture is abortion. Even our present teaching addresses this crucial issue. Also, remember that abortion mills don't like to show women sonograms, because that allows them to see the live baby within them. If this friend is suffering from a past abortion, it may be hard for her to reconcile.

Fr. Trigilio: Definitely keep her in prayer.

23. Scandal

I was told that if you create a scandal, all the good things you have done in your lifetime up to the point of that scandal are wiped away. Is this true? Where would I find this in the Catechism?

Fr. Brighenti: In the *Catechism*, scandals can be discussed in the section dealing with the Sacrament of Confession. We give scandal by our examples, but if we're striving to live good and virtuous lives, then hopefully we're not giving scandal. However, as we see in the newspapers and hear about on television, there is plenty of scandal in our world. A person who commits scandal is guilty of mortal sin, and the merits they may have accumulated prior to then are no longer applied to them. Once they go to Confession, however, the merits that they've lost can be restored. The scandal might still linger on though, so they may have to work out their penance for a time to overcome that scandal and

---

19 Carol Glatz, "Economy Lacking Ethics Leads to 'Throwaway' Culture, Pope Francis Tells Council for Inclusive Capitalism," *America*, April 7, 2020, https://www.americamagazine. org/politics-society/2019/11/11/economy-lacking-ethics-leads -throwaway-culture-pope-francis-tells.

to make a true repentance. I often think of that scene in Spain, where the penitents follow in the procession. This act is carried over from the Middle Ages, when people who had committed a public sin were given a specific type of penance. They would walk behind the saint and dress in certain clothes to diminish the pride within themselves and work out their penitential life in a public form since their scandal was public. Somehow, this has got to be done today in the lives of those who cause scandal.

Fr. Trigilio: One of the topics that this question touches upon is restitution, and how the divine mercy of God runs parallel with His divine justice. Even someone as holy as Mother Teresa of Calcutta could have wiped out all the good that they have done with one mortal sin at the end of their life. It takes only one act of mortal sin to destroy the life of grace, yet grace can be restored by going to Confession and being truly repentant, receiving the absolution of Christ through the Sacrament. All that good they have done would then come back to them, meaning that it's not lost forever, but it does have the potential to be. This is why you can't bank on what you've done in the past and figure you've stored up credit or brownie points on your account. This was the sin of Pelagius, who thought he could earn his way into Heaven. As Catholics, we don't believe in salvation through works but through faith and works, where any good that you do is because of God's grace animating and empowering you. It's the grace of the Sacrament of Confession that not only absolves your sin but restores the value of the good works that you've done. Some people do things but don't have the right motivation; they do things for show, so other people will think well of them. Instead, we should be doing good because we've been motivated by love of God and neighbor, otherwise our good is meaningless.

Fr. Brighenti: When we were doing our *Web of Faith* show live in a parish, there was a question about plenary indulgences, and I remember you said that if you had even an attachment to a fond memory of sin, you would not be able to receive plenary indulgences. You must detest even the memories of your sin so that you'd be fully receptive to that plenary indulgence.

Fr. Trigilio: If that is the case, which unfortunately most of us find ourselves experiencing from time to time, the indulgence would then naturally default from plenary to partial. You still receive some benefit for your efforts, but you don't receive the fullness of it because you still possess some fondness or attachment to sin.

24. When Can't You Receive Communion?

When am I not allowed to receive Communion? For being disrespectful to my mother? For slapping my little sister?

Fr. Brighenti: We should make a firm distinction between objective matter and the subjective culpability of the sinner. If the act is a grave matter, then it's always objectively wrong. The Ten Commandments help us define this area. Dishonoring your father or mother can objectively be a grave matter, but subjectively, do you know it's wrong? Do you do this wrong willingly? Is the gravity of this disrespect a trivial matter or a serious one? If you were being psychologically or even physically abusive to your mother, then this would certainly be a grave matter. Concerning the act of slapping your little sister, is it done so out of a sibling rivalry, or is the matter more serious, such as involving revenge? We've seen how sibling rivalry can become dangerously revengeful as people grow older. This would be an objective matter and always a grave one at that point. However, you should always strive to avoid doing these things, even if the sin is venial. You should always strive to respect your mother and always strive to get along with your siblings, even though it might be difficult at times. I know that as a little brother, I was in my older sister's way a lot of times when she was a teenager and I was just a kid. Thank God she never held any grudges toward me, as today we're very close. If you're asking this question, then you seem to know already that being disrespectful to your parents and slapping your little sister are not right, and therefore you want to have your soul in the most perfect condition you can for receiving Communion.

Fr. Trigilio: If the sin is a venial one, you can use sacramentals, such as holy water, which would immediately remit the venial sin, and you can also confess those as well. I remember back when I was a child, as well as hearing confessions as an adult priest, that most young peoples' sins often consisted of disrespecting their parents, fighting with their siblings, telling a fib, or not saying their daily prayers. These things don't reach the level of a mortal sin at that age, but they are still a matter for the confessional. We need to also touch on the fact that adults can fall into these sins, because often times they get the idea that honoring parents is only a Commandment for children. But when your parents are elderly, it may be more difficult to be patient with them and to stay attentive to their needs. I've seen some very sad situations where people in the nursing homes or hospitals are never visited by their adult children. The elderly are totally neglected, and this is worse than a little boy or girl not respecting their parents. In this case, an adult (either through negligence or spite) is deliberately ignoring their parents. It's a different case for those who may be overwhelmed because they're the caregiver and may need some time off. But if you don't even try to visit or show any concern, that is selfish and a form of abuse.

Fr. Brighenti: You reap what you sow. If this is the example you're giving to your children, be prepared to suffer the same.

Fr. Trigilio: Matthew 7:12 says, "So whatever you wish that men would do to you, do so to them; for this is the law and the prophets."

25. Receiving God's Forgiveness for Our Sins

I have done so many terrible things in my life that I wonder if God will truly ever forgive me. I pray every morning and every night, but I just don't think that's enough. I love Jesus with all my heart and soul, but I don't think He's happy with me. How do I make things right in God's eyes?

Fr. Brighenti: You may have already, but I would definitely suggest that you go to the Sacrament of Confession. It is in this sacrament where we receive God's forgiveness through the words of the priest in what's called absolution, where Jesus absolves us of our sins. The priest acts in the Person of Christ since he is ordained to be an *alter Christus* (another Christ). The priest does not say "Jesus absolves you;" he says, "I absolve you." He can only say that because at that very moment Jesus is speaking to you through the priest. Jesus takes the Blood that He shed on the Cross and applies it through the Sacrament to our soul. If we confess our sins, and we're truly sorry for our sins, and we make amends to try at that moment not to do them again in the future, we then receive absolution. After performing our penance, the Sacrament of Confession is complete. If you're not already, then you should start going to Confession and making use of the grace available in this sacrament. Don't ever be afraid to go to Confession, as many people seem to be, because God rejoices over the return of a sinner through this sacrament. Please be encouraged to make use of Confession, in which a priest is the mediator, standing in between God and man. It's Jesus Who is using the priest, and it's Jesus Who is absolving, as the words of absolution are given in first person: "I absolve you from your sins." The Lord wants to forgive us and wants to help us. We call that grace, His very life within us. It's like a healing balm or a salve, and it strengthens us to avoid sin in the future.

Fr. Trigilio: People often feel embarrassed to confess their sins, but as the saying goes: "The only stupid question is the one you don't ask." The same applies to this sacrament; "The only bad confession is the one you don't make." The only unforgivable sin is the one that you don't confess. There is not a sin out there that you can't tell to a priest. Now, there may be instances where the priest will ask you to come back later for absolution, though this is in extremely rare cases. For example, if a priest violates the seal of Confession, if someone desecrates the Blessed Sacrament, or if someone tries to kill the Holy Father — these are such occasions that a priest must travel to Rome and secure the Holy Father's permission to lift the censure on that person. But even the sin of abortion, which is a terrible evil, can be forgiven by any priest. Pope St. John Paul the Great extended that ability during the turn of the millennium to every priest, while it used to be a reserved penalty. Even if you've had more than one abortion, you can go to any priest and confess those sins. There's no reason to ever feel embarrassed or be afraid of Confession. The devil is the only one who wants you to stay home. He's the only one who wants you to be quiet and not admit to what you've done. The priest is happy, not that you committed sin, but that you're repenting. As Scripture says, "Just so, I tell you, there will be more joy in heaven over one sinner who repents than over ninety-nine righteous persons who need no repentance" (Luke 15:7).

Fr. Brighenti: You must remember that Confession is the medicine that can cure your soul, and we priests have heard everything before, so you're never going to scandalize us. We're here to help you. That's part of the spiritual life. However, maybe your need isn't a sacramental one but a continuation in your conversion. Maybe this is something where you need to make an appointment with your parish priest in order to gain some knowledge in certain areas. I would also suggest you take a retreat. They have great laymen and laywomen retreats, often on weekends. They start on a Friday afternoon or evening and go on until Sunday. You can take extended retreats called "Ignatian retreats" that last for seven to nine days.

Fr. Trigilio: You could try an Opus Dei retreat or a Cursillo weekend. There are so many options available.

Fr. Brighenti: Right here in Birmingham at the Casa Maria, the sisters have retreats almost every weekend. These are things that could help you in this struggle that you have. I would definitely go to Confession, attend Mass, pray the Rosary, and read the Bible. Then consider seeking spiritual direction from a priest and perhaps even go on a spiritual retreat.

26. Praying in a State of Mortal Sin

When a person is in a state of mortal sin, is there any point to praying? Can God, the angels, or saints even hear his or her prayers? If so, do they do any good? I ask this because I am a twenty-two-year-old man, and I am struggling to be a good Catholic. I worry that I cannot make a true confession because I do not have a firm purpose of amendment.

Fr. Trigilio: This certainly is not an uncommon occurrence, as both Fr. Brighenti and I can attest to in hearing confessions and giving people spiritual direction. The two poles that people fall between are the lax conscience and the scrupulous one. The lax conscience doesn't see sin where there is sin, and the scrupulous finds it where it doesn't exist. We have to admit that when you're in the state of mortal sin, you're not going to benefit from any spiritual graces, because you're dead in the life of grace when there's mortal sin on your soul. However, you can still pray for the grace of repentance while in mortal sin, because without God's grace you can't so much as be sorry for your sins. You need to ask for the grace to feel remorse for your sins and seek Confession, where you will be absolved. But consider that the Lord is not going to ask you for a perfect life. He knows both you and I make mistakes. That's why there's no limit to how many times you can go to Confession. We don't punch a card, like at the grocery store, and realize one day we've maxed out on our absolutions. You do, however, want to do your best to avoid sin, especially when you're shaking off a bad habit, where it's going to take longer, whether the sin is swearing or an addiction to pornography. It may take you a while, but with a firm purpose of amendment you can continuously decrease that addiction and hopefully get to the point where you won't ever do it again; but you're not making an absolute moral certitude where you know for sure you never will. But as long as you're willing to move in that direction, I as a priest can give you absolution, even though you know you may fall again in the future. This is different from the people who say to themselves or to the priest that they don't want to stop sinning, like if they intend to continue an illicit affair that they're having.

Fr. Brighenti: We also have to remember the three requisites for a mortal sin: it must be a grave matter, you have to know it's a grave matter, and you have to do it freely. We touched upon the sin possibly being a bad habit that's been developed, and a habit will reduce our free will, but the perfect remedy to break a bad habit is by establishing a good one. The Sacrament of Confession is a good habit, because you're receiving grace from the Blood of Our Savior on the Cross in that sacrament to promote spiritual healing. When I was a pastor, I would always tell my grade-school students that when you're confessing a mortal sin, the Sacrament of Confession is like an antibiotic that is given to pneumonia victims. Confession also builds up the vitamins, so to speak, to resist even venial sins, or those that are not mortal. It's the sacrament that will combat sin and fortify your soul so you will be more resistant to sin in the future. You should constantly go to the Sacrament of Confession, because that will help you in your firm purpose of amendment. It may not be perfect at that moment, although you may want to stop sinning and are making the pledge to stop doing so at that time. But through repeated use of the Sacrament of Confession, your soul will be disposed to God, and you will begin to see, through the light of the sacrament, how this particular sin you struggle with darkens your soul.

Fr. Trigilio: That's so true. Another excellent analogy, which I found useful with the RCIA (Rite of Christian Initiation for Adults) process, was the difference between a malignant and a benign tumor. The malignant tumor can kill you, while the benign tumor, although it will not kill you, can be quite unsightly at times. No one's going to want to walk around with a big lump growing on the side of their face, so they're going to want to have it removed. That's the way we should be in regard to venial sin.

We don't want to ignore them simply because they're not killing our souls. Today, people are so casual about venial sin, and it does actually threaten their souls, because it can spill into mortal sin, and people can be so casual today about that, too.

Fr. Brighenti: Concerning the question at hand, I would have to say that God is definitely working in this person's life. As long as we open the door just a little, God can work miracles within us, as imperfect as we are. That one confession could be most powerful and changing, so don't shy away from the medicine that can restore your health.

27. Living a Christian Life While Struggling with Depression

How is depression the work of the devil? How can one continue to pray and read spiritual books amid extreme anxiety, lack of energy, not sleeping, and taking medicines religiously? What spiritual exercises and postures could one do in order to overcome depression, other than daily Mass, praying the Rosary, going to Adoration, going to Confession weekly, reading Scripture, and watching programs on EWTN?

Fr. Brighenti: First of all, depression is not the work of the devil; it is part of our human condition. After the Fall of Man, there was an imbalance in nature, and we've since become prone to illness, sickness, and depression, which would be a mental illness. Combating depression spiritually is certainly the best thing you can do, and it seems like you are already doing that, but don't feel bad about pursuing counseling, as there is nothing wrong with that. Find a good Catholic counselor that shares our values. You can probably locate one through Catholic Charities. Spiritual direction and counseling go hand in hand in these kinds of struggles. Counseling will help you with your mental issues, along with your prescribed medications. In getting to the root cause of your anxiety and why you're not sleeping, that's where a counselor or psychologist or a psychiatrist can assist you, but you'll want to find one that shares our values. That is very important.

Fr. Trigilio: In moral theology, we make a distinction between being depressed, which is a mental condition that can be treated, and despair, which is a spiritual condition that you want always to fight against. Sometimes, people who are depressed can fall into despair. They are doing their best to battle this particular situation. We personally know a number of people who have battled clinical depression. They each did the best that they could, and some of them were able to overcome their battles or at least keep it managed. Despair is something you want to avoid, and the only remedy for it is hope. You fight despair by clinging to and praying for hope. Mary is Our Lady of Hope, because she was able to fight off any type of temptation to give up, despite all the struggles and shortcomings she endured during her life and the life of Christ.

28. Can Homosexuals Be Saved?

I need help answering a question from my teenage daughters. I read in 1 Corinthians 6:9, "Do you not know that the unrighteous will not inherit the kingdom of God? Do not be deceived; neither the immoral, nor idolaters, nor adulterers, nor homosexuals, nor thieves, nor the greedy, nor drunkards, nor revilers, nor robbers will inherit the kingdom of God." We all know what it is to be saved: that a personal trust in the Lord Jesus Christ is the only way to Heaven. This verse says to me that those who engage in homosexual behavior are not saved. My daughters disagree; they both know a teenager who claims to be homosexual and saved. I told them this is not possible.

Fr. Brighenti: You're certainly on the right track, and I would have to say that this is a very complex question. First of all, it is objectively a very grave matter to have homosexual acts. This topic centers around the Sacrament of Marriage which is only between a husband and a wife, one man and one woman, and this gift of sexuality is not given to anyone else. More importantly, the idea that this homosexual feels that he's saved comes from a Protestant understanding that salvation is only an act of faith. In the Catholic perspective, we believe in both faith and good works. We're therefore judged on our expressions of our faith. There are sins of commission (doing things you shouldn't do), and there are sins of omission (not doing things you should do). The Church's official understanding of same-sex attraction is that it is a disorientation. A person who is homosexual and tries to live a chaste life, and might be doing so with the help of a good Catholic support group like Courage, is not going to be condemned, because they're not committing the act. It's the act of homosexuality itself that is a sin. The inclination is not a sin, as it's only a disorder.

Fr. Trigilio: You touched upon an important truth here that salvation isn't a one-time act where you accept Jesus. That's the beginning of your spiritual journey, but now you have to live the Faith, and this means you live a moral life and follow the moral law, particularly the Ten Commandments. A heterosexual is under the same moral law as a homosexual. The orientation or inclination of homosexuality, however, is disordered. The acting-out of any type of sexuality outside of marriage, outside the covenant between a husband and a wife, is considered sinful and immoral. Regarding the salvation of a homosexual, I believe it was either Fr. Groeschel or Fr. Rutler who described it on one of their programs where if somebody is drowning outside a boat and you throw them a life preserver, you're providing them the means to be rescued, but they're not actually saved until they get back onto the boat. Jesus is the only One who provides the lifebuoy, but we have to cooperate with it. We have to allow ourselves to be saved, and being saved means you're in Heaven. You're only saved after you've left this planet and are standing in the presence of God. It's a future event yet to happen.

Fr. Brighenti: I would suggest that the two daughters encourage their friend to seek out that wonderful Catholic organization called Courage.

Fr. Trigilio: Absolutely. Fr. Harvey, God rest his soul, was so tremendous in working with Courage, as opposed to other groups that do not espouse the teachings of the Magisterium.

29. Contraception and Natural Family Planning

Could you please talk about contraception in a Catholic marriage? I have four children and was told I could not receive Communion if contraception is being used.

Fr. Trigilio: This is not an uncommon question. I highly recommend that you read Pope St. Paul VI's encyclical, *Humanae Vitae*, wherein he describes the two purposes of conjugal love between husband and wife: love and life. Love is the unitive aspect which brings the couple together, and life is the openness to procreation. Those two have to be present whenever there's an act of conjugal love. When a separation occurs, it goes against God's will, and that's when it becomes sinful. This is why both artificial contraception and artificial conception are considered sinful in the eyes of the Church. For instance, these *in vitro* fertilizations that take place in the test tube and then later placed inside the womb are as wrong as artificially taking hormones or using devices that would prevent conception from taking place. Now, you can use Natural Family Planning, which has been shown to be just as effective as anything else if you do it properly. There's even a newer aspect of that now called NaPro Technology, and it's for couples who want to conceive but also want to space out their births. This is done by using the natural processes that are involved within the woman and the man's physiology and taking advantage of the infertile periods. This is considered a natural means. But when you're using medications or devices, this is not natural. Again, this applies to both having children and avoiding children. You want to be open to both love and life.

Fr. Brighenti: In Pope St. Paul VI's encyclical *Humanae Vitae*, which is very concise and easy to read, he predicted that terrible things would take place if we violated the sanctity of life at its conception, and this was back in 1968. If something is rotten at its core, there are going to be ramifications in everything that derives from it. Artificial contraception is not only forging a lie between the husband and the wife in their communication and the intimate self in love, but it will later affect all other life-related issues. Pope St. Paul VI predicted that the divorce rate would drastically increase and that there would be less respect for life outside the womb. Not only do we see widespread abortion today, but we also see a push for euthanasia, the outright murder of our sick and elderly people and the withholding of basic medical treatment for them. Unfortunately, all of these predictions have come to pass, and this is because we're not respecting human life from its infancy. Pope St. John Paul II, on the twenty-fifth anniversary of the publication of *Humanae Vitae*, reminded us that these evils now occur, and their root can be traced all the way back to artificial contraception. These were groundbreaking predictions in Pope St. Paul VI's letter, and we can now see that there have been major impacts on modern society as it disregards the teachings of the Church. With divorce, we see the breakup of the family, and with the breakup of the family we see instability among the children. With instability among the children, we also see a decline in vocations, because vocations come out of good, strong families. We also know that people from divorced families generally do not succeed as well in obtaining further degrees as compared to those who come from stable families. This doesn't mean that vocations and higher education don't occur for people from divorced families, but these things are simply not as prevalent as they are with children who come from stable ones. These present crises can all be traced back to the articles of contraception.

Fr. Trigilio: I remember when Pope St. Paul VI first issued that letter. People called him a fearmonger. They accused him of taking things out of context, and they claimed that they wouldn't happen, that we wouldn't see a proliferation of pornography and abortion. There were even theologians who were opposing the document in an act of dissidence, yet everything the pope said came true, and it is truly an insightful document to read. Instead of contraception, you should try NaPro Technology or Natural Family Planning. This is a valid option in the Church, and the benefit of its practice is that it's a team effort. You work together. There's never the blame game, where the husband might accuse the wife of not taking her pill or failing to use an artificial contraception device. You're both in this together, because marriage is a team effort.

Fr. Brighenti: There are a couple of points I'd like to make in this regard. We had couples in my parish who were certified by the diocese to teach Natural Family Planning, and they readily put their names in the bulletin. So when I had couples that were getting married, I would send them to these instructors. The interesting thing about Natural Family Planning is that it follows through even when a woman is going through her changes in life. There are specific things required for either fertility or infertility to exist, and Natural Family Planning is about ninety-nine percent effective. It's very effective. Do not be afraid of using NFP for spacing out pregnancies, but don't abuse it to exclude children either. It's important for this to be taught by someone who is well-catechized in Church doctrine. It's interesting that doctors will readily prescribe Natural Family Planning for those couples who have a difficult time conceiving, but those same doctors won't promote NFP for spacing out children, and this is because the doctors wouldn't get any money from the drug companies. In addition to practicing NFP, consider finding a good Catholic doctor who can assist with this, and there are always some in every diocese.

Fr. Trigilio: Both the Couple to Couple League and the Catholic Medical Association are great vehicles that can help you with these things. It's startling when you see the staggeringly low birthrate in Europe, and especially in Italy, France, Spain, and Germany. The birthrate is about 1.1 children per couple, yet you need at least two or more per couple to keep the generation going. They project that in ten to twenty years, it's going to reach such a dangerously low level that you may witness entire cultures disappear. Meanwhile, the Muslim families are having six to eight children per couple. Just by mere mathematics, Christian

Europe is going to die out unless they realize what contraception is doing to their culture.

Fr. Brighenti: I just read recently that the United States has had a severe decline in the birthrate, and if it weren't for immigration, it would have been even lower.

Fr. Trigilio: The downside is that once immigrants become acclimated to our society, they then adopt this contraceptive mentality, and the birthrate then continues to plummet.

Fr. Brighenti: We are seeing the opposite of the population explosion which the "experts" claimed was going to happen in the 1960s. The population is actually in dangerous decline, and because of this there are not enough people in the workforce to support our life, our culture, and our society. We are witnessing a sharp decline in population, and in fact, Italy has a zero-percent birthrate. They're not reproducing at all.

Fr. Trigilio: The Italian government even offered the people money to have children, and even that didn't work.

Fr. Brighenti: The government also asked for people who had immigrated to Argentina or to Canada to come back to Italy to repopulate it. That's how bad and serious this is. You can clearly see all the evil effects that take place when the root itself is evil. It's going to manifest in countless ways and take its toll on every aspect of society.

Chapter 4

Prayer

1. Devotion to The Blessed Virgin Mary

My husband recently converted from Protestantism to Catholicism, but he doesn't understand the Catholic devotion to Mary, such as praying the Rosary. Can you help me explain our devotion to Mary?

Fr. Brighenti: This is a point in the Catholic tradition that many of our Protestant brothers and sisters stumble over. We have only one Mediator between God the Father and man, and that Mediator is Our Lord Jesus Christ, but we also have many intercessors. Protestants often pray for each other, as do Catholics, but we believe that the saints are alive in Heaven and continue to pray for us from there, and that's where we get our intercessory idea of Mary being the Queen of all saints. I think that fundamentally many of the Protestant churches recognize most of our doctrines regarding Mary, because the Marian dogmas are also there to safeguard the doctrines relating to Jesus Christ and His divinity or humanity in one hypostatic union; as the Mother of God, Mary gave Jesus His sacred humanity. Besides the powerful intercessory prayer of Mary, she's also our number-one example next to Christ, as Our Lord praises Mary for not just being His Mother but because she is His first and best disciple. We see this when Mary accepted God's will at the Annunciation, and her last words in the Gospel are, "Do whatever He tells you." That's the key to understanding Mary, and the Rosary itself is purely Christocentric; when you pray the Rosary, you are literally praying the Bible. Each mystery of the Rosary is based on the doctrines of Christ, and it has a very profound way of teaching people their Faith. Before print became widely available, Faith was taught through a plethora of ways: stained-glass windows, sculptures and carvings, sermons, and devotions like the Rosary. There was once a heresy that plagued southern France called "Albigensianism," and St. Dominic victoriously preached the doctrines of Christ to these dissenters through the Rosary. For the last four hundred years, every pope has written about the power of the Rosary as a spiritual tool for our prayer life. Pope St. Pius V asked all Christians to pray the Rosary before the brutal Battle of Lepanto, which is where Christian Europe was almost overtaken by the Ottoman Empire, as the Christian forces were greatly limited in comparison to the huge navy of the Ottomans. It was by the intercession of Our Lady and through the power of the Rosary that the victory was won by the Christians. Hence, we have the Feast of Our Lady of the Rosary, which was first called the Feast of Our Lady of Victory.

Fr. Trigilio: There is so much that you can read, and there are so many documentaries that have been made on the Rosary and the Blessed Mother. As you said, Mariology and Christology are intimately connected; they back each other up. I often remind people of Mary's special relationship to Jesus. Yes, He is her Lord and Savior, just as He is Our Lord and Savior, too, but His humanity came from Mary, His Mother. If we profess that Jesus is True God and True Man, you then have to look at His humanity, that He has this special relationship with this woman who is more than just some biological factory; she didn't simply produce a body for Him to use, like something you'd see on the Syfy channel. He has a literal sacred humanity which Mary gave to Him. It's more than just DNA, and it's more than just genetics; Jesus gets the whole makeup of human feelings and emotions, laughing and crying, from His Mother. As God, He knows all things in His divine comprehension, knowledge, and providence, but in His humanity, He grows up and experiences life. Mary gave birth to Jesus, she nursed Him, she cleaned Him, she hugged Him, she kissed Him, she loved Him. There was a tangible connection and an intense love between a mother and her son, which we see at the Wedding Feast of Cana and then ultimately at the foot of the Cross at Calvary. Mary's role is not incidental, and it's not by necessity; it's by God's divine will.

Fr. Brighenti: There's a beautiful painting in the Guggenheim Museum that shows the closeness of Mary and Our Blessed Savior, Her Son, Who was trained in carpentry by St. Joseph, His foster father. The painting features Jesus and Mary in the workshop; Mary is busy about in the chest drawers, looking for the gifts that the Magi had brought, and Our Lord is stretching out His arms, and the sun casts a shadow behind Him that looks like a cross. In this picture alone, you can see the connection of the sacred humanity, the closeness of Mary and Our Lord in those quiet years before the Gospel that we don't know very much about. Mary always knew the purpose of those three gifts from the Magi: for Jesus to become the High Priest, Prophet, and King.

Fr. Trigilio: You mentioned the quiet or hidden years. Jesus died at thirty-three years of age. Thirty of His thirty-three years were spent with Mary and Joseph. That's a significant amount of time. For us to casually discount Mary as only incidental would make no logical sense whatsoever. Mary counted enough to not only be there at His birth but through the very formative years of His earthly life.

Fr. Brighenti: Fr. Miller, the renowned Mariologist, would say that Mary's *fiat* was not only meant for the moment of the Annunciation. Her *fiat* was also at the foot of the Cross and with the Church while waiting for Pentecost. Her *fiat* is even now in Heaven, and it's an example for us all, who should be saying the same thing Mary said at the Annunciation: "Thy will be done."

2. Consecration to The Blessed Mother

How can Catholics consecrate themselves to the Blessed Virgin Mary, when God commands us to love Him with all our heart, soul, and mind?

Fr. Brighenti: In no way does our devotion to Mary take away from our worship of Our Lord and Savior Jesus Christ. We worship the Lord with all our heart, soul, and mind, and we also honor the saints because they're in Heaven experiencing the Beatific Vision. Mary deserves the most honor, due to the special way she was redeemed in the womb of St. Anne through the Immaculate Conception, as well as to the role she had in salvation history as the Mother of God. Christ is Our King, and His Mother Mary is Our Queen; there are a slew of references to the Queenship of Mary in the Old Testament as well as in the Book of Revelation, and there is no competition between Christ and Mary in any way. Can you go to Our Blessed Savior for help? Of course, as there's no greater Mediator, but He also gave us devotion to Mary and the saints so we can all be connected on earth and in Heaven. When we consecrate ourselves to Mary, we are really consecrating ourselves to Christ, because the closer we come to Mary, the closer we will be to her Son Jesus Christ. This is the whole message of *True Devotion to Mary*, by St. Louis de Montfort.

Fr. Trigilio: There is a lot of allegorical language that's often used, such as "Slaves of Mary," and I think that sometimes bothers people. Our elevation of Mary is not in any way meant to make her into a goddess or to give her worship or adoration, which are due to God alone. But we do give her the highest veneration, which we call *hyperdulia;* and the honor we give to the saints is *dulia;* to God alone do we give *latria,* which is worship. Here's an analogy: All the relatives that are on my mother's side of the family are part of my family because I'm related to my mother, and if Jesus is truly Our Brother, which we believe Him to be, then His Mother becomes part of our family, too. The closer we get to His Mother, the closer we'll get to Him. In the same way, when a kid makes a new friend, at some point he'll want to invite his friend over to his house and meet the family. As a priest, one of the greatest things you can have is when somebody says to you, "Father, can I meet your mother? I'd like to talk to her," and you feel wonderful as the son because they're honoring you through her. In the same way, the honor we give to Mary is because of her relationship to her Son.

Fr. Brighenti: When a priest is ordained, his hands are anointed with the oils and wrapped in a *maniturgium,* and there's a beautiful custom where he will save a piece of the material to be placed on his mother's hands in the casket when she dies, as a symbol that she gave a son to the priesthood.

Fr. Trigilio: There is indeed a beautiful, intimate connection between the mother of a priest and her son, and this emulates the relationship of Jesus and His Mother. In consecrating ourselves to Mary, we're not detracting from or even diminishing our love, allegiance, or devotion to Jesus, because this is His Mother. This isn't His neighbor or His in-law; this is *His* Mother. Even though Mary did not give birth to His divinity, she did give birth to His humanity. A Person was born on Christmas Day, and that's why we can say, contrary to the heresy of Nestorianism, that she isn't just the Mother of Christ; she's the Mother of God.

Fr. Brighenti: Some of the greatest saints from the Early Church as well as the Church Fathers have written many beautiful things on Mary, especially regarding the doctrine of Christ. In fact, the reason why we had the Council of Ephesus to define Mary as the Mother of God was to combat a heresy at the time called Arianism and later Nestorianism. The dogmas based on Mary are because of Christ, Our Lord and Savior. There are so many excellent writers who have explained the critical role of Mary in Christianity, such as St. Bernard of Clairvaux, St. Alphonsus Liguori in *The Glories of Mary*, St. Louis de Montfort in *True Devotion to Mary*, and more recently Scott Hahn in *Hail Holy Queen*, where he uses scriptural references of Mary as Our Queen. These all show that wherever devotion to Mary is, honor and worship of God is even stronger, because bringing us closer to her Son is her sole purpose.

Fr. Trigilio: A very clever cousin of mine fell in love with a woman with whom he worked, and when he met her mother, he brought a dozen roses and candy for the mother and would even call her sometimes more than he would call the daughter. The mother really came to appreciate him, and she's the one who told her daughter to go out with my cousin and marry him. His whole plan was to get the mother to like him, because he knew that through the mother, he would build a connection to the daughter. Likewise, we get closer to Jesus through His Mother, Mary. They're not in competition, and Mary doesn't want to replace Jesus. After all, she's the one who said, "Do whatever He tells you."

3. Saints in the Eucharistic Prayer

I noticed that during the Eucharistic Prayer, certain saints like St. Clement and St. Polycarp are invoked. Can you explain why these particular saints are named? Also, why are they mentioned during some liturgies but not at others?

Fr. Brighenti: In the Roman Canon, which is one of the oldest Eucharistic Prayers that a priest can choose to say at the Holy Sacrifice of the Mass, there are two sets of saints listed: one before the consecration and one after. The first group consists of the twelve apostles (Peter and Paul, Andrew, James, John, Thomas, James, Philip, Bartholomew, Matthew, Simon, and Jude) and twelve early martyrs: popes (Linus, Cletus, Clement, Sixtus, and Cornelius); a bishop (Cyprian); a deacon (Lawrence); and laymen (Chrysogonus, John and Paul, and Cosmas and Damian).

Following the Consecration, there is another group of saints in the Roman Canon, fifteen to be precise. Eight are men (John the Baptist, Stephen, Matthias, Barnabas, Ignatius, Alexander, Marcellinus, and Peter) and seven are women (Felicity, Perpetua, Agatha, Lucy, Agnes, Cecilia, and Anastasia).

These names harken back to ancient Rome, in the time of the early martyrs. Mass was often celebrated near the tombs of martyrs to give them honor and to highlight their example for the people. It is an old tradition to add saints to the Roman Canon, and there's a book called the *Roman Martyrology* by Caesar

Baronius which includes the whole list of saints, along with some relevant writings about them. This is another way of honoring those saints through extensive prayer and reading about their lives. Eucharistic Prayer II only mentions the saints in general, while Eucharistic Prayer III presents the opportunity to honor the saint of the day in your devotions, feast-day celebrations, or parish. In recent days, Pope St. John XXIII added St. Joseph to the Roman Canon, and under Pope Francis the name of Joseph has been amended to the other Eucharistic Prayers.

Fr. Trigilio: In the Latin Rite, we have four typical Eucharistic Prayers, starting with the Roman Canon, which was used exclusively in what is now called the Extraordinary Form of the Mass. A priest would mention the names in the Roman Canon, and those names only. Then when the liturgy was revised after the Second Vatican Council, they allowed for a few options. They added parentheses around the names of saints in the text of the Roman Missal that can either be omitted or included in the Mass. In some of the other Eucharistic Prayers, you can mention the saint of the day. It's up to the celebrant, the priest who's offering the Mass, which of those four prayers he will use. There's also the Eucharistic Prayers for Reconciliation, which can be used during Lent, for instance, and there was also a children's prayer that had to be used in specific situations. Now, in the Eastern Byzantine liturgies, they invoke more of the saints throughout the whole Divine Liturgy so that their names would be mentioned several more times, based on whose feast day the Mass was said on. In the Latin Rite, we would insert their names not so much in the Eucharistic Prayer but in the Opening Prayer over the Gifts, or in the Closing Prayer, if the Mass falls on the Feast of St. Dominic or St. Francis of Assisi for example. The beauty of having some of these names from the Roman Canon is the continuity with the ancient martyrs of Rome and our belief in the communion of saints who are now in Heaven, literally uniting themselves with the Holy Sacrifice of the Mass that we're offering down here on earth. It isn't just about remembering the past, but it's connecting the past to the present and the future. When you're invoking St. Linus, St. Cletus, St. Clement, and St. Sixtus, you're not just rattling off a list of old popes; you're directly asking their intercession. It's like when Jesus said that God is the God of the Living, not the god of the dead. He's the God of Abraham, the God of Isaac, and the God of Jacob, and all three of them are alive right now with their immortal souls. That's the beauty of these invocations. Now, you may attend a parish where the priest always uses the same Eucharistic Prayer and never invokes the saints. It's a matter of taste.

Fr. Brighenti: It's ultimately the choice of the celebrant. However, there's a common liturgical custom where we would use Eucharistic Prayer III or IV on Sundays, if not the Roman Canon (Prayer I). Eucharistic Prayer II, which is the shortest of them all, is not usually used on Sundays but rather on weekdays. There are also two Eucharistic Prayers for Reconciliation and four Eucharistic Prayers for use in Masses with various needs (the Church on the Path to Unity; God Guides His Church along the Way of Salvation; Jesus the Way to the Father; Jesus Who Went About Doing Good). Again, the liturgical preference is solely up to the celebrant.

Fr. Trigilio: There's nothing wrong with politely asking your priest after Mass if he could use some of the other available prayers. It's not confrontational, as sometimes we priests like to hear these requests, although you'll get more distance if you ask it in a friendly, nonthreatening manner. Some folks might attend one parish where they don't have the Sign of Peace, and then visit another where they always have it. If you just ask Father without jumping on him, he'll tell you that this is the option he chose, but he may be grateful that you brought it to his attention. Another question might be why the priest is celebrating Mass *ad orientem* while the priest down the street is doing it *versus populum*. If you want to learn why, just ask Father in a friendly way, and maybe even email him or jot him a little note, kindly asking if he could explain in the bulletin someday so that the parishioners are better educated, as opposed to bombarding him with, "Hey, how come they don't do this over at St. Adalbert's?"

4. The Hail Mary

Please shed some light on the source and inspiration behind the part of the Hail Mary prayer that says, "Holy Mary, Mother of God, pray for us sinners, now and at the hour of our death."

Fr. Trigilio: The first part of the Hail Mary comes from the salutations of the angel Gabriel and later St. Elizabeth, as recorded in the Gospel of Luke. In fact, those salutations were the Hail Mary prayer up until the time of St. Thomas Aquinas. This second part came later, developing like pious tradition.

Fr. Brighenti: It was provided by the Church to remind us that we are sinners and that we need not only pray for one another, but to ask the saints to pray for us, and Our Blessed Mother is the most powerful intercessor of them of all. We should ask her to pray for us to the Lord that we be encouraged in keeping our baptismal vows, staying in the state of grace, and remaining close to her Son, Jesus. It is a beautiful way of concluding that prayer. Most people, Catholic or non-Catholic, hear the words of this prayer, especially during the Christmas season, where the wonderful renditions of the Ave Maria are played either by César Franck or Bach. The Hail Mary is part of our tradition and our history, but the majority of it comes directly from the Bible.

Fr. Trigilio: Exactly, and what better time to invoke Our Lady's intercession than at the hour of our death, just as she was there at the moment of Christ's death at Calvary?

5. Essential Prayers

Since I usually only go to church on Sunday, I find that I am in spiritual need of something to help me get through the week. What are some tips for prayer?

Fr. Brighenti: This is an excellent question. Padre Pio wrote in a beautiful passage that he divided the spirituality of his week in two halves. The first half of his week was spent in thanksgiving for the Sunday Mass that he had celebrated, and the second half of the week was in preparation for the next Sunday Mass, even though he celebrated Mass every day, in which he also divided his day in thanksgiving for that morning Mass and then in preparation for the next Mass. In your case, the Holy Eucharist nourishes your private prayer and devotional life, and likewise your private prayer life will prepare you in such a way that you're going to be disposed to receive the graces from the sacraments on Sunday. In your private devotional life, you can pray the Rosary. It's a laudable prayer to say every day, and there are four different mysteries to be prayed on specific days of the week: the Joyful, the Sorrowful, the Luminous, and the Glorious Mysteries. There's also the practice of *Lectio Divina*, where you meditate upon Scripture, whether as an observer of the scene or reading a commentary, say a little prayer, and then allow for some quiet time to let the Lord speak to you. You could read the Scripture of the day, or you could read the Scripture for next Sunday, which would be a great way to prepare for Mass. You can also find some wonderful books on the saints, such as the *Lives of the Saints*, by Fr. Alban Butler; *Roman Martyrology*, by Caesar Baronius; or *Saints for Dummies*, which we wrote. These books will give such great insight and inspiration and can be found in the EWTN catalogue. You should also pick up a book or two on theology, such as *The Soul of the Apostolate* by Jean-Baptiste Chautard; *Introduction to the Devout Life* by St. Francis de Sales; and *The Imitation of Christ* by Thomas à Kempis. Another idea is to make a visit to your church during the week at lunchtime for prayer and to join a Bible study or prayer group that meets during the week.

Fr. Trigilio: In addition to these terrific ideas, stay tuned to EWTN, whether it's on the television, radio, or internet, because one of the principal reasons why this network exists is to help people in their daily spirituality, whether it's to get them through the week or broadcast Mass for those who can't attend on Sunday. You can make a spiritual Communion by listening or watching the Mass from home. You can also watch the other programs on EWTN, such as Fr. Dubay's series; Fr. Levis's *The Voyage of Faith*; and Fr. O'Connor's *Catholic Beginnings*. I also recommend reading *The Way* by Msgr. Escriva, founder of Opus Dei. In addition to praying the Rosary, there's also the Divine Mercy Chaplet with lots of pious devotions. There are plenty of spiritual exercises you can do to keep your soul in shape, just like physical exercises do for the body.

Fr. Brighenti: Also, the question didn't say that he's not able to attend the weekday Mass. So, if you can make it to Mass during the week, that'd be even better. Every parish is a little different, but you can find Mass times in the morning, afternoon, and evening. Going to Mass one to two times during the week can really be beneficial to your spiritual health.

Fr. Trigilio: When I was at the Cathedral of St. Patrick in Harrisburg as a hospital chaplain, I was amazed at how many people would take the first half of their lunch hour to go to the noontime Mass, Monday through Friday, as part of their daily need and devotion.

Fr. Brighenti: Another thought is to do a work of charity, maybe to join a fraternal organization like the Knights of Columbus, who generally gather twice a month during the week. You could find not only fraternity but spiritual direction from a priest who may come as a chaplain, and you can also perform works of charity. St. Francis de Sales once said that part of our devotions is good works.

6. Explaining the Rosary

Who invented the Rosary, and how do I explain it to my Protestant co-workers? They say it's just a useless, repetitive prayer, but I have been taught that meditating on the mysteries makes a difference in our spiritual lives.

Fr. Brighenti: The concept of using beads to calculate your prayers has been a part of our tradition for many, many centuries. Even the Eastern Catholics have what they call "Jesus prayer beads." The Rosary we know today became popularized under the influence of St. Dominic, who used this spiritual tool as a teaching device to instruct people in the Catholic Faith. At that time, there were only three mysteries: the Joyful Mysteries, which centered around the birth of Christ; the Sorrowful Mysteries, which centered around His Passion; and the Glorious Mysteries, which centered around His Resurrection and Mary's Assumption into Heaven, which prefigure our own resurrection. Pope St. John Paul the Great added the Luminous Mysteries, which center around the public ministry of Christ. As you can see, the mysteries themselves are quite Christocentric. The prayers themselves are also Christocentric and can be found directly in the Bible. The Hail Mary prayer is taken from the Gospel of Luke's salutation given by the angel Gabriel at the Annunciation, and then from St. Elizabeth's greeting, and thus the prayer centers around Jesus. For the last four hundred years, every pope has written on the power of the Rosary. It is one of the strongest spiritual tools in every Catholic's arsenal. It's also used in meditation, in which the Hail Marys become a backdrop as we turn to contemplation. Many saints have written on the efficacy of the Rosary, so there's plenty of history and tradition that backs up the use of this prayer.

Fr. Trigilio: I think it's so crucial to remind people that the Rosary didn't just fall out of the sky one day. A lot of thought was put into this devotion, and the original Rosary of St. Dominic actually consisted of one hundred and fifty beads. We're using an abbreviated version today, only about a third as many beads, because the original was considered too much for the average person. The one hundred and fifty beads go back to Jewish times when people would recite the one hundred and fifty psalms from memory, and they needed to know where they left off. They did this by tying these little knots into a rope, and this practice was the precursor to the one hundred and fifty beads that St. Dominic then transformed into the Rosary, under the guidance of the Virgin Mary. As stated, it's a deeply

Christocentric prayer, and just like the Our Father, the Hail Mary comes straight out of the Bible. These prayers are not artificial inventions of man but were taken from the Word of God and applied in a particular way, enabling people to connect themselves to the life of Christ. Sometimes, people will look only at the fact that people recite the Rosary by saying several Hail Marys and Our Fathers, and they'll argue using Matthew 6:7 to "not heap up empty phrases as the Gentiles do." Yet immediately after that verse, Jesus then gives us the Our Father. The pagans say words for the sake of saying them; Christians pray, and it's not considered repetitive to use the prayers that God Himself prescribed in Sacred Scripture.

7. The Purpose of Litanies

What is the purpose of the repetitive recitation of litanies? Do they compare in grace to saying novenas? At night, I read and pray short powerful prayers to give me peace in order to sleep. Any suggestions?

Fr. Trigilio: Litanies were first started in a communal fashion where there is a leader, like when you attend the Easter Vigil at your parish where we typically have the Litany of Saints, an ordination of a deacon or a priest, or a consecration of a bishop. During the litany, the leader lists the names of the saints, like St. John the Baptist, and the people respond, "Pray for us." Litanies can also be done privately at home, or you can do them by yourself in church, but the antiphonal of going back and forth between the people and the leader was originally designed in that communal, rhythmic fashion, and it's meant to orient the whole congregation on these particular themes. Some litanies, such as the Litany of Loreto or the Litany of the Virgin Mary, are primarily designed for when you're praying the Rosary with a group. I do know some people who pray these privately as well, but they're really not composed for one person, though they can still be used. They're meant to build an interior rhythm, just like reciting the Hail Mary a number of times in the Rosary, and this helps you get into meditation where you can transcend the words and dig into the concepts as you're saying, "Pray for us. Pray for us." There are so many litanies you can pray and lovely titles for the Virgin Mary and all the different saints.

Fr. Brighenti: That's right. In the Divine Office, also known as the Liturgy of the Hours or the Breviary, some of the psalms are written in a litany format. The Prayers of the Faithful either in the Divine Office or during the Mass are also considered a minor litany. The *Kyrie* at the beginning of Mass is a penitential litany, and in the Byzantine Church there are countless others. Litanies have been part of the Jewish custom and our Catholic liturgy, as well as the tradition of our Byzantine brothers and sisters. There are specific Latin Rite litanies that can be prayed in church, such as the Litany of Our Lady of Loreto, the Sacred Heart, the Holy Name of Jesus, and the Litany of Saints, and then there are some for private devotion. There are also litanies for specific saints, such as the Litany of St. Lucy and the Litany of St. Anthony of Padua, and there are litanies for specific needs as well. There's a beautiful litany written by Cardinal Merry del Val called the Litany of Humility, which is very poignant. Litanies are just a type of prayer to help us grow, along with the other sacramental tools in our spiritual lives. There's also *A Prayerbook of Favorite Litanies* by Fr. Albert Hebert, SM, available in the EWTN catalogue. I keep a copy in the chapel at the seminary, and I use it sometimes for inspiration during my Holy Hour.

8. Prayer for Struggling with Depression

What do you find to be the best spiritual remedy for healing from anxiety and depression? Please pray that I have hope and trust in Jesus and know His presence, so I won't feel lonely.

Fr. Brighenti: Unfortunately, because our society has become increasingly more dependent on technology, less personal, and more individualistic, we see widespread anxiety and depression in the world today. Before this time, when the family was intact and folks were gathering in their neighborhoods and involved in their local parishes, people knew each other and built authentic friendships. Today, there's an apparent distrust among people, and I think a lot of this stems from social media. Instead of talking to their neighbors, people today rely on texting, emails, Skype, Twitter, or Facebook to build connections. This tendency is adding to the problem of isolation in our society. A great devotion to address depression would be the Divine Mercy, received through an apparition of Our Lord by St. Faustina, a Polish nun who was canonized by Pope St. John Paul the Great. The whole message in this devotion is that this is the time of mercy, right now in our lives today. Hope doesn't exist after life, because it's too late then, and we'll hopefully be standing in the presence of the Lord. But for the moment down here, we are hope-filled Catholics. No matter what we experience, be it our own illnesses and disappointments or national and global tragedies such as war, we can still say we are hope-filled Catholics. These depressing things don't destroy us, but we can bring them to prayer and move on with hope in Christ. Another great avenue for fighting depression would be the saints, as they're in the pipeline, so to speak. Some of the saints lived very heroic lives under the worst conditions imaginable. Consider St. Margaret of Scotland, who had a total ogre for a husband. It was through her gentility and her firm Catholic faith that he converted. St. Rita of Cascia was another one who had a husband who only converted due to his wife's faith. There are then those who had personal disfigurements, like St. Margaret of Cortona, and had to struggle with all these handicaps in life. Finally, there are those in the pipeline, like the Venerable Matt Talbot, who was a terrible alcoholic and came to his lowest level before having a conversion. It was through the Bible and the saints and his faith in the Catholic Church that he recovered. Hopefully, one day he will be a saint and a great inspiration for those who suffer chemical addictions, be it alcohol or drug abuse. These are all areas where we see hope in Christ and hope for the future.

Fr. Trigilio: That's the key. Hope is the best spiritual response to depression. Anxiety is basically worry, and worry is just the act of fretting over something that maybe you have no control over. There are the things that you and I can and must do, and those are things that we need to pay attention to, but the things we have no control over we need to let go of. If you're getting all discombobulated because there are things going on in your life that are beyond your control, such as family members who are sick or are dying, you need to understand that there's often nothing you can do to change those unfortunate circumstances. What you can do, however, is unite your suffering with theirs at the foot of the Cross. I have found that plenty of people in the hospital pray the Divine Mercy Chaplet along with the Rosary, and it helps them focus on greater things other than their aches and pains.

Fr. Brighenti: When we visit shut-ins or go into the convalescent homes, a lot of the people we meet are depressed because they can't do what they used to be able to. One of the things I tell the shut-ins is that they are now a powerhouse of prayer. You can offer up your prayer, your Rosaries, and your sufferings for those who are out in the world, for those who are going through a marital crisis. I always give shut-ins both people and intentions to pray for. This also helps make them feel that they are still part of the Mystical Body of Christ, because they can be useful in offering their suffering in prayer for someone who needs it.

Fr. Trigilio: An excellent point. I remember when I was in another parish during the Iraq War, and we had a lot of military people who were stationed overseas. Families were worried about their sons and daughters and husbands and wives. We turned to the people in the nursing homes and gave them each a name of a serviceman to pray for and told them to say a Hail Mary or an Our Father whenever they could for the serviceman. It put the people in nursing homes to work spiritually and got their minds off of their sufferings. They were praying for someone to come home safely, and this communion helped alleviate a lot of the anxiety the families were feeling. Unfortunately, we now live in a time where everyone with anxiety is put on medication, and I know there are some mental ailments that deserve pharmaceutical treatment, but sometimes your struggles can be alleviated through prayer.

Fr. Brighenti: Pour your heart out to Our Lord in the Blessed Sacrament, not just in formal prayer but in a real conversation. Then be quiet and allow the Lord to speak to you in return. That's going to be a great source of relief, along with *Lectio Divina*, by reading and meditating on a passage of Scripture, followed by silence and contemplation, ideally before the Blessed Sacrament. The Lord can speak to you and encourage and enliven you.

Fr. Trigilio: One person I would also invoke as a possible patron saint for people who are anxious is St. Martha, the sister of St. Mary. Remember, Jesus said, "Martha, Martha, you are anxious and troubled about many things" (Luke 10:41). She was fretting because she was trying to cook dinner for Jesus while her sister wasn't helping but was instead talking to Him. Martha was stressed out in the kitchen, banging those pots and pans around. She is someone I would invoke if you feel the tension and the stress levels rising.

Fr. Brighenti: Another one is St. Dymphna of Ireland. She didn't suffer depression or mental illness herself, but her father did, and he was actively trying to attack her. She had to run away. She's sort of the patron saint for those who suffer mental illness, including depression, by the fact she suffered due to her father's condition.

Fr. Trigilio: It's not to say that anxiety isn't serious, because I've seen it in both family members and parishioners. It can be very debilitating. People get panic attacks; they get anxiety attacks. These are problems you need to discuss with your doctor, but you must also incorporate your struggles into your spiritual life.

Fr. Brighenti: You need a holistic approach, including the spiritual, the physical, and the mental.

9. The Presence of God

I have been a Christian for over fifty years, and a few years ago I began asking the Lord to let me feel His presence in my life, yet I never have. Other believers seem to recognize God's presence in their lives, whether by praying in church, in personal prayer times, or in singing, yet nothing works for me. Why?

Fr. Brighenti: First of all, don't worry. Prayer is more than a feeling. Our rector here at the seminary, Msgr. Rohlfs, mentioned once that the last time he had a spiritual movement at Holy Hour was over twenty-five years ago, and yet he perseveres. It means more to God that we continue to pray and keep up with our spiritual duties and works of charity, even if we are not receiving any recompense here on earth. We do it purely out of love of and devotion to God. The fact that we're even doing these things is because we know there's a higher gift in Heaven which we're aiming for. I also have to say that you're in good company with many of the saints. St. Thérèse of Lisieux was spiritually dry in her prayer life for almost her entire time in Carmel, which lasted for at least seven years. Mother Teresa mentioned that she was spiritually dry after she had established the Missionaries of Charity in 1950; yet she pressed on all the way until she died in 1997. Again, prayer is more than just a feeling. The Carmelite saints have a great tradition in this department, and they'll tell you that prayer doesn't only happen in the brain; it happens deeper inside. We might be distracted mentally, we might feel dry spiritually, and we might feel that we're not getting anything out of prayer, but in reality we are. Prayer is God's work, and we need to show up and allow for that time, whether we feel it or not. Now, if you do experience a movement or a tremor or a hint of inspiration, that's just a little gift to keep you going. It's helpful, but it's not necessary for your prayer life.

Fr. Trigilio: Something Mother Angelica had mentioned numerous times on her show is that God gives us consolations only when we need them, and we don't get them all the time. They're sent sporadically and sparingly on purpose, because the motivation is not that we're doing our prayers for the consolation. It's not about what we get out of it, but that we owe this time to God. My prayer of adoration is a matter of justice, and I need to do it; but my reciprocation may not be a warm and fuzzy feeling, or that little tingling you get when you're out on your first date. I can remember the many times my mother would sit in the hospital room with my father for hours on end as he was getting a blood transfusion. They said nothing and were probably bored out of their minds, but that was married love which persevered because of their commitment. When we're praying, sometimes we feel like Mother Teresa, who said she felt at times God wasn't listening to her prayers or wasn't with her anymore. Yet she knew He was listening, and she knew He was there.

Fr. Brighenti: It was the same with St. Thérèse and all the other saints. They all experienced a dryness.

Fr. Trigilio: If you go back to C. S. Lewis, the reason why you endure dry spells is so you'll long for that moment in Heaven where there is no more dryness, where you have complete fulfillment. To give an analogy, and not to drift too far from the question at hand, Heaven is the full banquet. Earth is just the appetizer. Unfortunately, people are loading up on the appetizers instead of the main course, due to the cost of receiving it. The purpose of the appetizer is to whet your appetite, to give you a taste of what's to come. That's earth. The real meat is going to be in Heaven.

Fr. Brighenti: Another consideration is your personality. There are certain personalities that are not ever going to be movers or shakers in the prayer life, because that's how God made them. How are your relationships with other people? How we pray usually reflects how we deal with one another. So, if that's how you are in regular life, then there's not much to worry about.

Fr. Trigilio: It would be as if I went to a charismatic prayer meeting. Although it's not my cup of tea, I bless everybody who has the charismatic spirituality, because that's what they've been designed for, and it gives them fulfillment and satisfaction in their spiritual lives. Someone else may get it from Opus Dei, another from the Traditional Latin Mass, and someone else from more meditative or contemplative prayer. There are different spiritualties, and there are different modes of valid prayer in the Church that are designed for your particular situation.

Fr. Brighenti: Some people may not realize that there are four kinds of prayer, and we sometimes forget the two which give worship and thanks to God. We tend to pray the ones of contrition and petition, saying we're sorry and then asking for something. We need to spend time in Holy Hour and in our prayer life to give worship and thanks to God. Whether we feel warm and fuzzy on the inside is beside the point. It's our duty and obligation to give God praise, and we'll be rewarded more in Heaven if we're not receiving recompense here on earth.

Fr. Trigilio: When you dig into prayer, it's basically you and I communicating with God. You have to realize in our human experience that there are times when maybe you didn't want to call your parents or your grandparents, but you did it anyway because it was the right thing to do. It may not always be a pleasant experience, but it's right, and there's satisfaction in knowing that you're doing it.

Fr. Brighenti: And this doesn't apply to just one moment in your prayer life, but rather your whole prayer life. I would also suggest to allow time for silence, where you are not doing anything active. Don't worry if you get disturbed or distracted, but simply allow for that time to let the Lord speak to you deeper inside. You'll see that your overall experience in your prayer is going to change you, not just that one moment, but throughout the rest of your life.

Fr. Trigilio: More and more laypeople are finding value in the Liturgy of the Hours, praying the ancient prayer of the Church that every priest and religious are obligated to pray. These are the psalms with some other prayers attached to them, and these are prayed around the world every hour of the day. You can download an app for this prayer to your smart device.

Fr. Brighenti: If you're feeling spiritually dry, I would also suggest you go see your priest every once in a while. Maybe he isn't available for regular spiritual direction, but your priest is there for you. Make an appointment and talk about these things with him. He might have some great suggestions or spiritual saints to read up on. He is the spiritual wealth in your parish.

Fr. Trigilio: Make an appointment, or just ask him for five minutes after Mass sometime. Priests have a packed schedule, but they might be able to make room for you between Masses. Do that every couple of weeks or once a month, and you'll find it greatly beneficial.

10. The Merits of Eucharistic Adoration

I was recently engaged in apologetics with some friends. When I started to discuss how Eucharistic Adoration was very important to me, they asked me why I can't just pray in my room. To be honest, I felt hardpressed to answer them. How would one explain Eucharistic Adoration in a meaningful way?

Fr. Brighenti: You can certainly pray in your room. There's nothing wrong with that. In fact, Our Lord says to go to our room to pray, but He's also speaking of our interior room, and that's where our intimacy with the Lord in our interior life comes into play. Out of necessity, there are times where you do have to pray in your room, such as when the churches are not open when we would like them to be or we're traveling and we want to pray the Rosary or do our *Lectio Divina* and Scripture meditations. But when we're at church, where we have the Real Presence of Our Lord, and especially so at Mass or if the Real Presence is exposed on the altar during Adoration, that is the highest form of worship that we can attain. Why would we want to settle for prayer in our room when we can have it at a time when our Lord Himself is on the altar or during the Consecration of His Body and Blood?

Fr. Trigilio: Also, this isn't a question of either/or in the sense that you have to choose between praying in your room or at church. You can and should do both. Obviously, the time you spend before the Blessed Sacrament is going to be more precious, because you have that direct contact with Jesus in His Real Presence. You and I should want to show our love of Jesus by being with Him and spending time in His presence like St. Mary, the sister of Martha, who sat there listening to Jesus. Also consider that on the road to Emmaus, Jesus was made known to the disciples at the breaking of the bread. This is the earliest way the Church gave a name for what we now call the Mass or the Eucharistic liturgy. It is implicit in the Sacred Scripture that this is the pinnacle of the Christian Faith. That's why the early Christians got together at least once a week for the Eucharist, and this did not deny or discourage them from daily prayer outside of Mass.

Fr. Brighenti: Prayer is especially appropriate during Eucharistic Adoration, when Our Lord is exposed in the Blessed Sacrament in what we call a monstrance, this beautiful vessel with rays like a sunburst. Not only are we gazing upon the Lord, but the Lord is gazing back at us in the intimacy of that Holy Hour we spend before the Blessed Sacrament. Consider how when you're away from a friend for a long period of time, you start to grow apart. But when you make the commitment to go visit and spend time with your friend, to be physically in his presence and get all the subtleties of that conversation, you begin to solidify that bond. It's the same thing with visiting Our Lord in the Blessed Sacrament. He is asking us to be friends with Him, and we do this through prayer; and the most beautiful way is to sit in Adoration and soak up the rays of Our Lord in the monstrance.

11. Intercession of the Saints

Although I have been away from the Church for several years, through Pope Francis I am now considering coming back. However, one of the greatest setbacks for me is the intercession of the saints. The Bible in 1 Timothy 2:5 is very clear that there is only one intercessor: "For there is one God, and there is one mediator between God and men, the man Christ Jesus." Hebrews 12:24 likewise says, "and to Jesus, the mediator of a new covenant, and to the sprinkled blood that speaks more graciously than the blood of Abel." How can I ask a saint for intercession if Christ alone died for me?

Fr. Brighenti: I think there is some confusion here between the terms "mediator" and "intercessor." As the question pointed out, there is only one Mediator, and that Mediator is Our Blessed Savior Jesus Christ. He has redeemed us by His life, Passion, death, and Resurrection, and we celebrate this in the Holy Eucharist, the Sacrifice and Resurrection of Our Lord in the Mass. Being the Mediator, He brings our prayers to His Heavenly Father and then the graces and blessings from His Heavenly Father to us. The priest at the Mass is in the person of Christ (*in persona Christi*), but it's Christ Who is the Priest and Victim at every Mass. Now, let's talk about intercessors. An intercessor would be any of the saints, and they are not mediators, as Christ is the only Mediator between us and God the Father. Consider the prayer services held by Protestant churches where they pray for one another and their needs. The only difference between Protestants and Catholics in this regard is that we believe prayer continues beyond the grave, and this is because the saints are alive in Heaven. They can continue that prayer chain in Heaven just like we can on earth, and how much more so, considering these saints are already in the Beatific Vision and so much closer to the Lord. Revelation 5:8 paints a telling scene in Heaven where the saints intercede before the throne of God with bowls full of incense, which are the prayers of the saints. Their prayers are so very beneficial to us, just as our prayers are for one another.

Fr. Trigilio: It's so important for people to know the difference between "mediator" and "intercessor." An intercessor (*enteuxis* in Greek) is basically someone who asks a favor for someone else, whereas a mediator (*mesites* in Greek) is someone who bridges the gap between people. Jesus, Who is both God and Man, is the only Mediator that can bridge that gap between humanity and divinity, while even in the Bible, we see St. Paul refer to himself as an intercessor, asking for prayers from the Corinthians, Galatians, and Ephesians and praying for them. Jairus intercedes in the Gospel for his sick daughter (Luke 8:40-56), and a Roman centurion intercedes on behalf of his servant (Matthew 8:5-10). In each case, a human intercessor is making a request to Christ the Mediator for Him to help another person. This is intercession. The One Mediator is the same, Jesus Christ.

Our prayers to the saints in Heaven are nothing more than intercession. It's not mediation, but the saints instead are going to, interceding to, the One Mediator. Some people will wonder why we don't go directly to Jesus, and you can, but consider when someone comes to Fr. Brighenti and says, for example, that they're having surgery next week, and they want him to pray for them. Should he refuse to pray for them and instead tell them to go directly to Jesus? Theologically, he'd be correct, but he might get a fat lip if he treated a parishioner like that. People like to know that other people are praying for them and with them. It's not that we're praying to the saints as objects of adoration, which would be idolatry, but we're instead asking for their intercession, exactly like people would do in a prayer chain.

Fr. Brighenti: It's literally nothing more than that, so I don't know where the confusion comes from in regard to this topic. Again, our Protestant brethren are very used to asking for intercession from fellow believers in their own worship services. They're famous for their prayer chains.

Fr. Trigilio: Many times, they do better at that than we do as Catholics.

Fr. Brighenti: Exactly. So, asking intercession from the saints is the same concept as what we do here on earth among believers, but again, the saints are already in the Beatific Vision. They're closer to God than anyone down here, so how much more would we like to have these ambassadors bring our petitions before the Heavenly throne?

Fr. Trigilio: Let's go to the scene from the Gospel where the Roman centurion sends a messenger to Jesus to tell him that his servant boy is ill. The centurion is asking for favors for his servant boy, and he sends a messenger to ask for him. There are two intercessors going to the One Mediator.

12. "World without End"

In the Glory Be prayer, what do we mean by "world without end"?

Fr. Brighenti: The phrase "world without end" refers to the fact that God is not in or even limited by time, because He created it. He is always a present "Now." When we say, "Glory Be to the Father, and to the Son, and to the Holy Spirit. As it was in the beginning, is now, and ever shall be, world without end," we're saying "infinity" or "forever and ever," which we sometimes use in our prayer, especially at the conclusion of the Collect at Mass or at the doxology.

Fr. Trigilio: The phrase "world without end," or "*in saecula saeculorum*" in the Latin, is a manner of speech. Some people get so hung up on this phrase, but it's just a way of speaking that describes something that's challenging to describe. You're talking about things that go beyond our experience, which is spatial and temporal. We're trying to describe things that are timeless, and our language is not adequate to do so.

Fr. Brighenti: Yes, and consider in the Scriptures where it says that there will be a new Heaven and a new earth. It's referring to eternity, and that's without end. That attribute, of course, is God, because God always was, always is, and always will be.

13. Going to Adoration

What are we supposed to do during Adoration? Can we say the Rosary or the Stations of the Cross?

Fr. Trigilio: When you are at Adoration of the Blessed Sacrament, what's required is some time of silence. The Blessed Sacrament is exposed by a priest or deacon and then placed on the altar and immediately incensed, usually followed by a Eucharistic hymn in Latin like "O Salutaris Hostia." There should then be a Scripture reading, some time for silent meditation, and then there may be a set of prayers like the Rosary, the Divine Mercy, or litanies which can be prayed either publicly or privately. However, the Stations of the Cross should not be done publicly, because you wouldn't be giving the Blessed Sacrament the attention It deserves. Jesus is on the altar, and instead of gazing upon Him, you'd be walking all around the church and distracting others from soaking in the rays of His presence. Again, you can pray the Stations of the Cross from your pew, and you can also do some spiritual reading, such as from the *Lives of the Saints*, something from the classics, or something more contemporary, like from Fr. Benedict Groeschel. You can mix it up with different devotions, be they reading or prayer, but some quiet meditation is highly encouraged.

Fr. Brighenti: There's a great book called the *Essence of Prayer*, written by Sr. Ruth Burrows, a cloistered Carmelite nun, which explains how prayer is God's work, and all we need to do is show up. Never underestimate the importance of the quiet time that you should be having in your Holy Hour before the Blessed Sacrament. That's the time when the Lord speaks to us, not with a little voice that we can hear, but in our interior silence.

Fr. Trigilio: If you do hear voices, you might be put away! Just kidding!

Fr. Brighenti: You're going to have to get used to switching from the outside world to the inside one. Your mind's going to be distracted by a laundry list of things suddenly popping up in your mind. You just need to bring yourself back to the center and not worry or obsess over the distractions. Sr. Ruth Burrows says in her book that prayer is happening more than just in the "brain box." It's happening in your heart. Try not to get too frustrated about practicing contemplation before Our Lord in the Blessed Sacrament. Devotions like the Rosary are great to have, as they are very scriptural and reaffirm the doctrines of our faith. *Lectio Divina* is a beautiful practice of meditating on the Scriptures, followed up with contemplation. Allow for that quiet time before the Blessed Sacrament.

Fr. Trigilio: I think it was Fr. Benedict Groeschel who put it best when he said that we sometimes need to spend quality time with our mouths shut. Some people do all the talking. Have you ever had a friend who would yak on and on? You could put the phone down, make a sandwich, come back, and they'd still be gabbing away. When you're praying, you can't do all the talking. You need to listen. You need to sit there in the presence of God without your mind racing. There should be some mental and oral prayer and then some quiet contemplative prayer.

14. Who Goes to Heaven, and What Is Pain?

Do you feel that good Christians who don't attend church will go to Heaven? If they do, then why should I go to church if we're all going to end up in the same place? My pastor thinks that most people are going to Heaven, doesn't believe in Purgatory, and says that there won't be as many people in Hell as we think. I would also like to know where pain comes from: God, the devil, or just fate? I've had eight back surgeries, and the more I pray, the worse I get. What good does prayer do? I don't want to give up, but if He won't help me, what's

the use? I'm not talking about waving a magic wand and making me
better. I would just like to be at a level of pain I can deal with or have
the strength to handle. The doctors say that nothing can be done,
and I've reached the point where I'd rather die. I just want His help.

Fr. Brighenti: First of all, I sincerely pray for you and your illness. Being pastors, Fr. Trigilio and I visit many shut-ins and
people in the hospital who we know are in severe pain as well.
This calls to mind a wonderful woman who had a debilitating
illness; she couldn't walk and was deaf and mute. She went to
Lourdes, France, on a pilgrimage, not so much for a miracle but
to have the spiritual endurance to carry her cross faithfully and
spiritually with the Lord. She received that gift. She was not
cured physically from her maladies, but she was given strength
and saw a sense of purpose in uniting her sufferings with Christ's
sufferings on the Cross, adding to the treasury of merit offered up
for the souls in Purgatory. Through her illness and through her
suffering, she became very saintly. I believe at the end of her life
she had the priest and her family with her, received the Anointing of the Sick, received the special prayer of apostolic pardon,
and her room was like a chapel with saints and devotionals surrounding her. She had great devotion to St. Joseph for a happy
death. I believe that this woman experienced her purgation here
on earth, which leads us to the second part of the question: Yes,
Purgatory exists. It is a state of being. Hell is a place and Heaven
is a place, and not only does the soul go there, but so does the
body at the rising of the dead. If your soul is in Hell, your body
will join it and suffer its pains as the soul does. If your soul is in
Heaven, your body will join it and enjoy the glories of Heaven
as your soul does. Do we know who's in Hell or not? No. But we
do know what can send us there. Think of the three children

of Fátima, how innocent they were; yet they were given a horrific vision of Hell that revealed what would come to those who continued in sin. This put them on the straight and narrow path to change their thoughts and minds.

Fr. Trigilio: Purgatory is not a punishment in the same way that Hell is punishment for our sins. The pain experienced in Hell is the eternal pain of loss and pain of sense. You're going to feel pain, and you're going to miss the presence of God. The pain of Purgatory, however, is one of cleansing—a purgation. It's like having to scrub your hands really hard to clean the dirt off of them. When we were little boys, our mothers would sometimes tell us to get back to the sink and wash our hands again. This may be discomforting, because there's some dirt deep within us that needs to be purged from our souls. God's mercy forgives our sins, but His justice demands that there be some penalty for our sins. The temporal punishment due to sin is what we call Purgatory. It's a good thing and is not to be feared. The temporary pains of Purgatory are real, but they're not as frightening as the eternal pains of Hell. The pains of Hell are brutal and terrifying, while the pains of Purgatory are necessary and temporary for our entry into Heaven. It's like the pains of childbirth that mothers are willing to endure because on the other side of that pain is the wonderful joy of a new child. On the other side of suffering through Purgatory is the joy of seeing God face to face.

Fr. Brighenti: Now, this pastor mentioned in the question clearly isn't teaching what the Church is teaching. If he is a Catholic priest, then he needs to be reported to the bishop of his diocese. Purgatory is an official doctrine of the Church, along with Heaven and Hell. It's good to pray for the dead, even if the ones you're praying for lived good lives, as they may have some attachments to sin that need to be severed. It's not that they were bad people, but they weren't necessarily perfect either.

Fr. Trigilio: I'm always edified by two particular individuals in my life. One was my brother, Michael, who had muscular dystrophy and endured horrible suffering throughout his entire life. He died at age twenty-six, but he never complained, was never bitter, and he offered up his suffering. There was then a priest in my diocese, Fr. Curtis Delarm, who was diagnosed with Lou Gehrig's disease when he was around thirty years old. In his final years, he was confined to a wheelchair and couldn't even talk anymore. He wasn't able to so much as hold the sacred host. But as long as he could, he still functioned as a priest. Every time I would see him, he'd ask me how my family and I were doing. He never despaired or sought sympathy for himself. He let his suffering transform not only himself, but everyone that he encountered. He was a priest to the very end, because his priesthood was not merely the ministerial one at the altar, but the priesthood of offering sacrifice.

Fr. Brighenti: I think of your saintly mother, too. She buried two sons and a daughter, and then her husband, and she suffered much pain. Yet despite the pain in her knees, her back, and even in her heart, every time I had the chance to see her, she never once thought about herself. She was always concerned about others, like family members who may have been falling away from the Faith. She's very inspirational through her sufferings. Now, the first part of the question needs to be addressed. Do we feel that good Christians who don't go to church will go to Heaven? I wouldn't worry so much about what other people are doing at this point. Make sure that you are going to Mass. It's important to make sure that you are growing in your relationship with the Lord by going to Mass, by hearing the Word of God proclaimed and receiving the Holy Eucharist, which will strengthen you in your sufferings and in your trials. You'll then be growing in your knowledge of the Lord, because not only do we want to be baptized in Christ, but we want to grow in knowledge and love, to know our God and the wonderful things He's done for us. Pray for those who don't go to church, as they're missing out on the holiness they can attain through God's grace at the Holy Sacrifice of the Mass.

Fr. Trigilio: A quick distinction between goodness and holiness: Goodness is based on the virtue of living a virtuous life, while holiness is the next level up and is about doing things for a more supernatural motive. "Grace does not destroy nature but perfects it," (*gratia non tolit sed perfecit naturam*) as St. Thomas Aquinas said.[20] So holiness has to have a foundation, which is first goodness and virtue, and then you can proceed to holiness. It's like when Jesus says that if someone asks you to go one mile, go two miles. If they ask for your shirt, give them your coat. Sanctity goes the extra nine yards, as opposed to simply what justice demands.

Fr. Brighenti: Also, don't underestimate the example you give by your patience, perseverance, and sufferings. By going to Mass, you may inspire those Christians who are not attending to either become Catholic and go to Mass or to become more faithful in their respective religions and go to church. Never underestimate the power of your Christian example through your sufferings. Many saints, such as Pope St. John Paul the Great in the end of his life and Mother Teresa throughout hers, are excellent examples of perseverance, patience, courage, and of being transformed by God's grace in the midst of their suffering.

---

[20] *Summa Theologica*, I, q. 1, art. 8.

Fr. Trigilio: To conclude, going to Mass is an obligation. Many times, when we were kids, there were things we had to do that we didn't want to. Maybe your parents were taking you to see your grandmother when you'd rather have been out playing ball with your friends. But there was a duty, an obligation, and there was also this love and affection for your grandmother. Maybe you weren't always in the mood to see her, but deep down inside, you knew you had to. This is the case with Mass at times. Sometimes, we may not want to go, but it is our duty, and it would be even better to go out of our love of Christ as He invites us to spend time with Him at His house.

Fr. Brighenti: Going to church is not merely fulfilling a require-ment; it is also to our spiritual health and benefit. Worshipping God as a family of faith, a community of believers, is as essential to our welfare as breathing air into our lungs or eating food to stay alive. And Mass is where we pray together and for each other. The saints in Heaven and the souls in Purgatory join us in praising God. Ask the Lord for strength and for healing.

15. Praying for Others

Why pray for other people? What good does prayer do, if any? Nothing happens whenever I pray.

Fr. Brighenti: We live in a community of believers. We have concern for each other on our pilgrimage through this life. A pilgrimage has a definite starting point and a conclusion. The starting point was being born and baptized here, and our walk of faith takes us toward Heaven. Every day, we should be cooperat-ing with the sacraments and graces that God bestows upon us. We also have each other to help us on this journey of faith. We don't walk alone, but we have our brothers and sisters in Christ.

We have to remember that the Church is broader than just the Church on earth, known as the Church Militant, as there are the souls in Purgatory which we call the Church Suffering, and there are the saints in Heaven which we call the Church Triumphant. The saints in Heaven and those of us down here on earth can help the souls in Purgatory with our prayers, and the saints in Heaven can certainly help us as well with their prayers of intercession. Is it necessary? No. Jesus is Our Only Mediator. But we follow the example St. Paul puts forth in his letters where he asks the Churches of Corinth and Galatia to pray for him as he would pray for them, and this is a precedence going even further back in Scripture. In the Old Testament, Judas Maccabeus prayed for the dead soldiers who were found with pagan amulets, and this is where we get our doctrine on the souls in Purgatory. This community of believers is to show us an expression that we're not alone on this journey of faith.

Fr. Trigilio: This also points out a wonderful reality which you underscore, Fr. Brighenti, that we are part of what the Second Vatican Council called "*Communio*," which is the concept that we're more than just an organization or an institution. We're an organic body: the Body of Christ, as St. Paul says. Just like the parts of your body are connected and meant to work together, with different organs doing different things, but all making up one whole person, so it is with the Church. If something concerns you, then it also concerns me. If you need help and you ask for prayer, you don't actually need my prayers because you could go directly to God. However, through my cooperation and participation for you, this act expresses the wonderful commonality that we share. Not only are we both fellow human beings, but we're also part of the Body of Christ, His Church. As friends and family members, it's a wonderful thing when someone says they'll pray for you, not out of necessity, but because God invites us to. When you read the Gospel, the Virgin Mary pointed out to Jesus at the Wedding of Cana (John 2:1-11) that the servants had run out of wine. It may have been a small detail that someone overlooked, but she didn't want them to be embarrassed. Jesus acquiesced to her request even though He didn't need Mary to make the matter known to Him, because He knows everything in His divine nature. Jesus allowed Mary to make her request, just as He allowed Jairus to pray for his daughter who was ill. He invites us to intercede for one another, going always to Him as the One Mediator between God and man. The Virgin Mary, the saints, you, and I all cooperate as intercessors for one another.

Fr. Brighenti: In the Sacrament of Baptism, we have this beautifully portrayed with the prayers of intercession which the whole community recites for the baby, and then we have the Litany of Saints. Why? Because the saints are still alive. Life has changed for them, but nevertheless they are still alive in Heaven, and they are special friends of God, interceding for us before His throne. In the Baptism ceremony, we continue those prayers for the baby through the intercession of the saints, to show that we are one Church, including those on earth and in Heaven.

Fr. Trigilio: Another part of the question asks if prayer changes anything and why to pray when God already knows everything and does His will. It's not so much that we change God's mind but that we open ourselves to be disposed to His will. Jesus said, "Ask and you shall receive." He didn't say what you're going to get, but if you ask or knock at the door, there will be a response. It's like Jesus' prayer in the garden: "Not My will but Yours be done."

Fr. Brighenti: When waiting for the answer to a prayer, we need to exercise patience, and we're not particularly good at practicing this virtue, especially in America where we want everything in an instant — instant technology, instant coffee, you name it. When we look into the lives of the saints, their prayers weren't always answered right away. I think specifically of St. Monica who prayed for thirty-six years for her son's conversion, and he finally converted shortly before she died. St. Monica was blessed, as she considered it a grace to see her son, St. Augustine, enter the Church. For many of us, we may not see the effects of our prayers until we die and enter Heaven. Be patient and persevere, because the Gospels tell us that "He who perseveres to the end shall have eternal life." Be consistent and don't give up, even if you don't see results. Know that you're planting the seeds, through your prayers, to open up that person's heart or soul to the Lord.

16. Prayer for Granting Forgiveness

I had a falling out with my brother four years ago. He tried to apologize, but I don't want to talk to him. Can we really forgive and forget?

Fr. Trigilio: I know exactly what you're talking about, not that I've had a serious fight with any of my siblings, but I know other families where this has happened. You'll have more disagreements and quarrels among your relatives because they know you too well, and it can be quite painful and difficult at times. This idea of "forgive and forget" is not found anywhere in Sacred Scripture. It's just something that maybe Benjamin Franklin or one of his friends had come up with as a little proverb, but it's not scriptural. We cannot actually forget, nor should we forget, because forgiveness is even more meaningful. If we forget, then there's no need for forgiveness, because we've already forgotten what happened to us. Whereas, if we don't forget, then we're able to release that grudge we may be holding. That's key here. It's not about forgetting but about letting go and accepting that you were injured or taken advantage of by someone, and then choosing to forgive that person. We can choose to give them a fresh start, which is what God does for us.

Fr. Brighenti: That is the Christian message, and I always like to meditate on humility when we are put down or become discouraged by other people. Consider Our Lord, Who was completely innocent yet hung between two thieves. He showed us the virtue of humility in its purest form, and not only that, but He also forgave all those who nailed Him to the Cross—past, present and future. How much more, then, should we be forgiving? And especially so if someone is extending the olive branch of peace. It is your duty as a Catholic and as a Christian to accept that apology and move on.

Fr. Trigilio: It's not only that we give forgiveness, but that we also receive forgiveness.

Fr. Brighenti: The Our Father prayer asks Our Lord to "Forgive us as we forgive others." Thank God that He is so much more merciful than we are, because we can be very stingy with our pardoning and forgiveness of others. We need to remind ourselves of Our Lord and His perfect example of complete mercy and forgiveness.

17. Prayer in Exchange for Abstaining from Meat on Fridays

If one does not abstain from eating meat on Fridays, excepting solemnities, can attending Mass, visiting the Blessed Sacrament, or attending night prayer on Friday substitute for the abstinence of meat? I occasionally forget and will eat meat on Fridays but still attend Mass.

Fr. Trigilio: I'm glad you asked this question, because we want to point out to our audience that the Church tweaked, if you want to use that terminology, the laws of fasting and abstinence after the Second Vatican Council. We did not abolish the practice of fasting, and particularly abstinence from meat on all Fridays, as it still was in the Code of Canon Law in 1983. Only the Fridays from Ash Wednesday to Good Friday require we not eat meat if you're over the age of fourteen, while fasting has an age limit from eighteen to fifty-nine years old. Now, abstaining from meat is still a penitential practice which can be followed outside of Lent, but the American bishops had asked for dispensation from abstinence on Fridays outside of Lent, as it was becoming burdensome for the people at times to abstain from meat year-round. So, you are allowed to substitute abstinence with another act of penance, piety, or one of the corporal or spiritual works of mercy outside of Lent. During Lent, you can be dispensed on a one-time basis if you go to your pastor with a valid excuse, such as the need to attend a wedding reception where the only two choices are steak or chicken, and there is no alternative. In this case, a pastor is authorized to dispense his parishioners, and a bishop can dispense the whole diocese.

Fr. Brighenti: Sometimes the bishop of the diocese will authorize the removal of abstaining from meat on St. Patrick's Day if it falls on a Friday, even though it's not a solemnity.

Fr. Trigilio: That's right, because in my diocese and others, there are a large contingent of Irish Catholics. St. Joseph's Day and the Feast of the Annunciation are solemnities and automatically dispense you from abstaining from meat as long as they don't fall on a day during Holy Week. If you're ever in doubt, just ask your parish priest or call the diocese. They're always happy to answer your questions about this and other related questions.

Fr. Brighenti: I know a lot of people who decide to perform an act of penance on Fridays outside of Lent or abstain from things they're addicted to, such as television or the internet, which they'll then replace with Bible reading, devotions to saints, and so on. This act of fasting on our own is one of piety that we have unfortunately lost in our modern society. Fish has become quite expensive today to afford for every Friday, so I think this was also a reason for the slight change in abstinence requirements following the Second Vatican Council.

Fr. Trigilio: Today, a good number of people are vegetarians or vegans, so since it's no longer a penance for them to abstain from meat, they should think of something else they can offer up as a sacrifice.

Fr. Brighenti: The bottom line is that you must abstain from meat on Fridays during Lent if you are fourteen years old and older, yet younger than sixty years of age.

About the Authors

Fr. Kenneth Brighenti, Ph.D., was ordained in 1988 for the Diocese of Metuchen, New Jersey. He is the pastor of St. Mary Magdalen di Pazzi Church in Flemington and has served as vice rector of Mount St. Mary's Seminary and as a chaplain in the U.S. Naval Reserve. He has been the co-host of EWTN's *Council of Faith: Post Conciliar Encyclicals, Crash Course in Catholicism, Crash Course on the Saints, Crash Course on Pope John Paul II*, and *Web of Faith 2.0*. He is the co-author of *Catholicism for Dummies, Saints for Dummies, Women in the Bible for Dummies, John Paul II for Dummies, Catholic Mass for Dummies, The Everything Bible Book, The Catholicism Answer Book: The 300 Most Frequently Asked Questions*, and *101 Things Everyone Should Know about the Bible: Essential Teachings and Principles from the Old and New Testament*. Fr. Brighenti is a Knight of Grace in the Sacred Military Constantinian Order of Saint George.

Fr. John Trigilio Jr., Ph.D., Th.D., was ordained in 1988 for the Diocese of Harrisburg, Pennsylvania. He is the director of pastoral formation at Mount St. Mary's Seminary and has been the co-host of a number of EWTN television programs: *Web of Faith, Council of Faith: Vatican II Documents, Council of Faith: Post Conciliar*

Web of Faith

Documents, Council of Faith: Post Conciliar Encyclicals, Crash Course in Catholicism, Crash Course on the Saints, Crash Course on Pope John Paul II, and *Web of Faith 2.0.* He is also a guest host on Catholic Answers Radio and on EWTN Radio's *Open Line Monday.* He is also the co-author of *Catholicism for Dummies, Saints for Dummies, Women in the Bible for Dummies, John Paul II for Dummies, Catholic Mass for Dummies, The Everything Bible Book, The Catholicism Answer Book: The 300 Most Frequently Asked Questions,* and *101 Things Everyone Should Know About the Bible: Essential Teachings and Principles from the Old And New Testament.* Fr. Trigilio is a Knight of Grace in the Sacred Military Constantinian Order of Saint George.